A World Made Safe
for Differences

American Intellectual Culture

Series Editors: Jean Bethke Elshtain, University of Chicago,
Ted V. McAllister, Pepperdine University,
Wilfred M. McClay, University of Tennessee at Chattanooga

The books in the American Intellectual Culture series examine the place, identity, and public role of intellectuals and cultural elites in the United States, past, present, and future. Written by prominent historians, philosophers, and political theorists, these books will examine the influence of intellectuals on American political, social, and cultural life, paying particular attention to the characteristic forms—and evolving possibilities—of democratic intellect. The books will place special, but not exclusive, emphasis on the relationship between intellectuals and American public life. Because the books are intended to shape and contribute to scholarly and public debates about their respective topics, they will be concise, accessible, and provocative.

A World Made Safe for Differences

Cold War Intellectuals and the Politics of Identity

Christopher Shannon

ROWMAN & LITTLEFIELD PUBLISHERS, INC.
Lanham • Boulder • New York • Oxford

ROWMAN & LITTLEFIELD PUBLISHERS, INC.

Published in the United States of America
by Rowman & Littlefield Publishers, Inc.
4720 Boston Way, Lanham, Maryland 20706
www.rowmanlittlefield.com

12 Hid's Copse Road
Cumnor Hill, Oxford OX2 9JJ, England

British Library Cataloguing in Publication Information Available

Library of Congress Cataloging-in-Publication Data
Shannon, Christopher, 1962–
    A world made safe for differences : cold war intellectuals and the politics of identity /
Christopher Shannon.
        p. cm. — (American intellectual culture)
    ISBN 0-8476-9057-1 (alk. paper)
    1. Toleration. 2. Liberalism. 3. Individualism 4. Identity (Psychology)—Political
aspects. 5. Cold War. I. Title. II. Series.
    HM1271 .S45 2001
    303.3'85—dc21   00-040287

Printed in the United States of America

∞™ The paper used in this publication meets the minimum requirements of American
National Standard for Information Sciences—Permanence of Paper for Printed Library
Materials, ANSI/NISO Z.39.48-1992.

For Karen

Contents

Acknowledgments

This book began as a course I designed for the junior seminar in the American Studies Program at Yale University in the spring of 1991. I would like to thank Jean-Christophe Agnew for the opportunity to teach this course, for his exemplary model of intellectual rigor, and for his continued support over the years. From Yale, I would also like to acknowledge my deep gratitude to James Fisher for years of encouragement, support, and friendship—as well as his exhaustive knowledge of the cultural politics of U.S. intervention in Southeast Asia. The entire book has benefited from my engagement with his lively and wide-ranging intellect. The first chapter in particular benefited from my participation in a conference, Asia and the Liberal Imagination, that Jim organized at St. Louis University in the spring of 1999. From that conference, I would also like to thank Jonathan Nachel for his insights into the escapades of the original Ragtime Kid, Col. Edward Lansdale. Part of this first chapter appeared in the *American Quarterly* as "A World Made Safe for Differences: Ruth Benedict's *The Chrysanthemum and the Sword*." At *AQ* I would like to thank Lucy Maddox for seeing the article through a difficult editorial process and especially David Hollinger, without whose support the article might never have been published at all. Whatever my disagreements with Professor Hollinger, I am thankful that in the case of this article he proved to be a model of liberal tolerance.

The article would never have become a book without the intervention of Bill McClay. Despite the best efforts of the profession to ignore my first book, Bill saw the book as a reason to sign me on to this series, and he followed through with support at every step of the publication process. The conclusion in particular benefited from his critical comments on a draft of the manuscript and from a conference, Refurnishing the Public Square, that Bill hosted with Michael Lacey of the Woodrow Wilson Center for International Scholars. At Rowman &

Littlefield, I would also like to thank Ted McAllister. An especially thorough reader, Ted's critical yet sympathetic comments have saved me from many (but not all) of the worst instances of my tendency toward sweeping, undocumented assertions. Stephen Wrinn guided me through the more technical aspects of the publication process and proved a gracious host on several meetings in Washington. Finally, I would like to thank Jean Elshtain for the continued support she has shown me since she first responded favorably to a request from an unknown graduate student to write a dust jacket blurb for a first book.

For completion of the manuscript, I owe my greatest debt to James Turner and the staff and fellows of the Erasmus Institute at the University of Notre Dame. An exciting and genuinely new development in academic life, the Erasmus Institute supports the work of scholars interested in bringing the insights of the Abramic faith traditions to bear on topics of inquiry normally the province of secular scholarship. For a fruitful year that I spent writing and discussing many of the issues that found their way into this book, I would like to thank the staff of Erasmus—Jeanne Heffernan, Terri O'Reilly, and Robert Sullivan—and the fellows: Clarke E. Cochran, Benjamin A. Ehlers, John E. Hare, Jeffrey Hensley, Mark C. Murphy, Daniel Philpott, Marianne Sawicki, Stephen Schloesser, S.J., Alan J. Torrance, and John von Heyking. At Notre Dame, I would also like to thank R. Scott Appleby, Barbara Lockwood, and James P. McCartin of the Cushwa Center for the Study of American Catholicism. I could not have asked for a better group of colleagues to work with during the year I completed my final revisions on the manuscript.

I would also like to acknowledge the general support of the following friends and colleagues: Una Cadegan, Donald Critchlow, Grace Goodell, Michael Lacey, Elizabeth Lasch-Quinn, Eugene B. McCarraher, David J. O'Brien, Ray Quinn, Glenn Wallach, Mark Weiner, and Daniel Wickberg.

Finally, I would like to thank Karen Ferne Kahler Shannon, for sharing her love and faith through difficult and uncertain times. She deserves better than this book.

Introduction

Liberals have always prided themselves on their commitment to tolerance. At no time was this value more central to American liberalism than during the cold war era. The racial and totalitarian ideologies that seemed to precipitate World War II brought forth a postwar vision of what the anthropologist Ruth Benedict called "a world made safe for differences," in which cultural freedom would serve as the basis for world peace.[1] Throughout the cold war era, liberal policy makers, no less than their critics, decried the gap between the theory and the practice of tolerance, but few critically analyzed the idea of cultural tolerance itself; historical treatments of tolerance have suffered from the same deficiency. In this study, I wish to shift this debate from the social to the intellectual level through a close reading of a few key texts in the development of the postwar ideology of tolerance.

The current vogue of multiculturalism has revived "tolerance" and "pluralism" as fighting faiths in almost complete ignorance of the cold war history of these terms. Popular and academic accounts alike present the celebration of diversity as a heroic achievement of the 1960s, against which the 1950s appear as a Victorian dark age of social conformity and sexual repression. In this study I will argue that the shift from the 1950s to the 1960s is best understood not as an ideological revolution but as a generational rebellion, a struggle for control of a common cultural inheritance. Post-1960s radicalism continues to perpetuate the stale liberal dichotomy of tolerance/intolerance that has proven incapable of allowing for social relations that transcend individual choice. The close link between multiculturalism and contemporary identity politics reflects a persistent link between tolerance and some self-evidently neutral conception of "freedom" that has served to naturalize the social relations of modern Western individualism.

Poststructuralist theoretical fashions have failed to advance the analysis of tolerance much beyond the neo-Marxist critique offered by Herbert Marcuse some forty years ago. Marcuse developed his social theory initially as an attempt to understand the rise of fascism by supplementing classical Marxist economic analysis with psychological concepts drawn from Freudian psychoanalysis. Marcuse and his colleagues at the Institute for Social Research in Frankfurt "explained" fascism only to have the logic of historical materialism once again confounded, this time by the affluence of postwar Western society, particularly that of the United States. Through a series of books written during the 1950s and 1960s, Marcuse struggled to explain the failure of workers to develop revolutionary consciousness. Faced with the absence of the external, coercive restrictions of the industrial age, Marcuse relocated social oppression in the very freedom and tolerance promoted by the "open" society. Marcuse characterized the affluent society of postwar America as a regime of "repressive tolerance" that "encourages nonconformity and letting-go in ways which leave the real engines of repression in the society entirely intact." Marcuse and his followers among the student New Left placed much of the blame for the spread of this regime on social therapists who preached self-fulfillment via "adjustment" to the dominant cultural norms. This critique presented social engineering as the representative mode of domination in "a society of total administration," which pacifies political dissent through a therapeutic regime of bureaucratic social control.[2] In retrospect, this critique seems as naive as the official tolerance it directed itself against. Even a cursory reading of Marcuse's work reveals him to be deeply indebted to the classical liberal definition of freedom as autonomy. Contemporary critical theorists uncover ever deeper, ever darker structures of repression, only to assert ever more radical formulations of a fundamentally bourgeois understanding of human liberation.[3]

The psychological language of "identity" set the terms for the debate over the nature of autonomy in cold war America. Erik H. Erikson's *Childhood and Society* (1950) marks the entry of the concept of identity into the mainstream of American intellectual discourse. In subsequent publications, Erikson would acknowledge the lack of technical precision in his own use of the term, but "identity" quickly took on a life of its own apart from the discourse of professional psychologists.[4] The concept of identity provided the language for a broader discourse on the self. To have an identity was to be a full, complete, mature person. Identity, or ego integrity, signaled the completion of the developmental pattern outlined by Erikson in *Childhood and Society:*

It is the ego's accrued assurance of its proclivity for order and meaning. It is a postnarcissistic love of the human ego . . . as an experience which conveys some world order and spiritual sense, no matter how dearly paid for. It is the acceptance of one's one and only life cycle as something that had to be and that, by necessity, permitted of no substitutions. . . . It is a comradeship with the ordering ways of distant times and different pursuits, as expressed in the simple products and sayings of such times and pursuits. Although aware of the relativity of all the various life styles which have given meaning to human striving, the possessor of integrity is ready to defend the dignity of his own life style against all physical and economic threats. For he knows that an individual life is the accidental coincidence of but one life cycle with but one segment of history; and that for him all human integrity stands or falls with the one style of integrity of which he partakes. The style of integrity developed by his culture or civilization becomes the "patrimony of his soul," the seal of his moral paternity of himself. . . . In such final consolidation, death loses its sting.[5]

A look back at Erikson's formulation of mature ego integrity suggests just how little has changed in American cultural discourse since World War II. All the tropes of multiculturalism—the dignity of all cultures, the legitimacy of a special loyalty to one's own culture, and the existential necessity of self-authorship—appear here in a text that provided the postwar "liberal" consensus with its psychological orthodoxy.

This conception of identity provided a model of selfhood appropriate to the midcentury triumph of the cultural revision of classical liberalism. In the first half of the twentieth century, the rise of the private corporation and the regulatory state discredited the social ideals of free-market individualism. Intellectuals found in the anthropological concept of culture as a whole way of life a language appropriate to the new economic and political realities. The anthropology of Franz Boas, popularized by Margaret Mead and Ruth Benedict, proved particularly appealing to humanist intellectuals. The Boasian stress on the unity of each culture fit the increasing economic and political integration of American society, while the Boasian understanding of this unity as a pattern of values assured intellectuals of the persistence of a moral order despite the restructuring of American society by large-scale, impersonal, morally neutral bureaucracies.

As depression and world war gave way to prosperity and peace, culture as liberating unity gave way to culture as repressive conformity. Erikson no less than Marcuse recognized the dangers of psychotherapy as a tool for manipulative social engineering; however, neither the liberal Erikson nor the radical Marcuse questioned the central role of a properly democratic social science in the construction of a progressive social order geared toward individual liberation.[6] The problem of "manipulative" social science has obscured the deeper problem of "democratic" social science.[7] The easy equation of culture and conformity suggests an unresolved tension within the culture concept itself. Initially used to affirm diversity among cultures, the culture concept quickly became a tool to promote diversity within each culture. Ironically, culture promoted individualism.

The general conflation of culture and individualism followed from reflection on the distinctly individualistic nature of American culture. In his chapter "Reflections on the American Identity," Erikson comments:

> The process of American identity formation seems to support an individual's ego as long as he can preserve a certain element of deliberate tentativeness of autonomous choice. The individual must be able to convince himself that the next step is up to him and that no matter where he is staying or going he always has the choice of leaving or turning in the opposite direction if he chooses to do so.[8]

Erikson explains this particular style of ego integrity in terms of America's frontier history as an unsettled people, constantly on the move. Subjected "to more extreme contrasts and abrupt changes during a lifetime . . . than is normally the case with other great nations," America made rootlessness and transience into a whole way of life.

American ego integrity reflects the pervasive instability of place, community, and family:

> Thus, the functioning American, as the heir of a history of extreme contrasts and abrupt changes, bases his final ego identity on some tentative combination of dynamic polarities such as migratory and sedentary, individualistic and standardized, competitive and co-operative, pious and freethinking, responsible and cynical, etc.[9]

Against the harmony of ego integrity in general, Erikson sees in American identity only tension and conflict. The healthy American does not achieve a stable state of integrity as much as he participates in a constant process of reintegration driven by the dynamic tension of various cultural polarities.

These tropes appear throughout cold war social thought alternately as uniquely American or more broadly modern. Erikson's contrast between the settled, traditional societies of the old world and the rootless frontier society of the new thus also appears as a historical narrative of the development of psychoanalytic theory since Freud. According to Erikson, "the patient of early psychoanalysis suffered most under inhibitions which prevented him from being what or who he thought he knew he was," whereas "the patient of today suffers most under the problem of what he should believe in and who he should—or, indeed, might—be or become." Freud's patients suffered from "fears" that focused on "isolated and recognizable dangers," whereas the contemporary patient suffers from "anxieties" or "diffuse states of tension." The modern world, like America, suffers the psychological consequences of unsettled social conditions:

> Industrial revolution, world-wide communication, standardization, centralization, and mechanization threaten the identities which man has inherited from primitive,

agrarian, feudal, and patrician cultures. What inner equilibrium these cultures had to offer is now endangered on a gigantic scale. As the fear of loss of identity dominates much of our irrational motivation, it calls upon the whole arsenal of anxiety which is left in each individual from the mere fact of his childhood. In this emergency masses of people become ready to seek salvation in pseudo identities.[10]

Writing in the wake of fascism, Erikson here rejects the return to tradition as a false and potentially deadly retreat to "pseudo identities." To this universally modern problem, he proposes a distinctly American solution—the creation of "a new manner of man, one whose vision keeps up with his power of locomotion, and his action with his boundless thinking." Against the dogma and prejudice of tradition, Erikson offers a modern ethic of "judiciousness," which "in its widest sense is a frame of mind which is tolerant of differences, cautious and methodical in evaluation, just in judgment, circumspect in action, and—in spite of all this apparent relativism—capable of faith and indignation." The "clinical way of work" for the modern therapist lies in cultivating "a judicious way of life" among his patients.[11] By fostering a fluid, open psyche appropriate to the ceaseless flux of modernity, the therapist transforms diffuse anxiety into creative tension. Narratively, the world becomes America.

This historical narrative of the shift from tradition to modernity, from prejudice to tolerance, proved to be the most powerful explanatory framework of postwar intellectual life. It shaped the dominant understanding of America's relation to the foreign cultures of the emerging Third World, as well as to the emerging domestic subcultures of youth, race, ethnicity, gender, and sexuality. It provided the language for the integrationist discourse of the 1950s, as well as the separatist discourse of the 1960s. Viewed in the context of this overarching narrative, the move from integration to separatism appears less a cultural revolution than a shift in emphasis within a common search for a privileged point of tension between integration and separatism. Continuing racial strife and the escalating war in Vietnam helped to shift the locus of creative tension from the master opposition of tradition and modernity to the micro fault lines of culture/counterculture, white/black, Anglo/ethnic, male/female, heterosexual/homosexual. Integrationists looked suspiciously on traditional indignation and separatists looked suspiciously on modern relativism, but the most sophisticated thinkers on both sides of this debate strove for Erikson's ideal of a relativism capable of indignation.

In my first book, *Conspicuous Criticism,* I showed that during the first half of the twentieth century this humanist irony, particularly as embodied in the rise of the culture concept, masked a deeper consensus on the instrumentalization of nature and society in the service of human liberation.[12] In this study, I show how in the second half of the twentieth century this same instrumentality came to structure the supposedly oppositional discourses of the counterculture, race, gender, ethnicity, and sexuality.

Throughout this period, and to the present time, this consensus on instrumental-ism has been obscured by the humanist rhetoric of participation. Here again, Erikson's work is representative of a broader, more pervasive intellectual eva-sion. Over a decade before Marcuse's "repressive tolerance" became a mantra for New Left radicals, Erikson wrote of the "humanistic crisis" of psychology. He attacked the tendency of the human sciences to treat "human data . . . as if the human being were an animal, or a machine, or a statistical item" and warned of the increasing role of psychology as "the manipulator of man's will." The "basic inequality" in the doctor–patient relation made psychology especially susceptible to such exploitation, but the same power relations threatened the other social sciences as well. Like his counterparts in other disciplines, Erikson framed the alternatives to manipulation in terms of tradition and modernity: boldly rejecting "the reassurances which once emanated from a continuity of tra-dition," he called on his fellow humanists to commit themselves to developing "the new techniques of discussion" most appropriate to the exercise of authority in modern democratic society.

Against the iron cage of positivism, humanism offers only a padded cell. For the democratization of his own discipline, Erikson proposed the "moral idea" of psychoanalysis as a "judicious partnership." Erikson conceived of the doctor–pa-tient relation as a "human relationship in which the observer who has learned to observe himself teaches the observed to become self-observant." Despite the dan-gers, "only in the clinical situation does the full motivational struggle of a human being become part of an interpersonal situation in which observation and self-ob-servation become contemporaneous expressions of a mutuality of motivation, of a division of labor, of a common research." With both doctor and patient "subject to historical change," clinical knowledge "must ever again yield to interpersonal experiment: fresh impressions must ever again be regrouped into their common denominators in configurations; and the configuration, finally, must be abstracted into suggestive conceptual models." Self-observation requires self-alienation—a willingness to open oneself to constant experimental reconfiguration. Against the manipulation of the patient by the doctor, Erikson merely proposes the active par-ticipation of the patient in his own manipulation. Beyond the therapeutic situation proper, Erikson looks to "the systematic cultivation of new forms of group dis-cussion" in the broader society.[13] Here humanism proves ironically to be more ag-gressively expansive than any narrow positivism: Sensitivity to the cultural con-text of self-observation requires the opening of the world to the same process of constant reexamination.

Historians dismiss Max Weber's thesis on "the Protestant ethic and the spirit of capitalism" as a hopelessly simplistic account of the origins of modernity, yet the central tropes of that thesis—the instrumentalization of nature and the internalization of authority—continue to extend their power into ever more intimate aspects of human life. This power has exercised itself not by constructing stable identities and silencing alternative voices but by deconstructing all established identities and inciting the creation of ever more alien norms. Civil rights activists endured violent resistance by whites only to be dismissed as Uncle Toms by a new generation of black power activists. Domestic writers of the baby boom era endorsed the modern revolt against Victorianism only to have their vision of sexual liberation attacked by feminists as a new form of repression. Perhaps most disturbing of all, procreative sex came to be seen as unnatural compared with the psychological and emotional creativity made possible by artificial birth control. These and other revisions proceed from no logic other than change itself. Erikson's utopian vision of progress as "a judicious mixture of eternally natural and progressively technical methods," a vision that still guides most "progressive" social thinking, obscures the steady rise to mastery of the technical over the natural. The "psychoanalytic situation" reflected in contemporary identity politics is not simply "a Western and modern contribution to man's age-old attempts at systematic introspection."[14] In the degree to which it is modern and Western, it stands on one side of a historical rupture that has seen the triumph of an instrumental worldview incapable of imagining nature and society as anything other than a resource for human development.

I write from a Roman Catholic traditionalism rooted in the other side of this historical divide. The traditional Catholic insistence on the priority of authority to freedom and the community to the individual stands outside the modernist consensus for which Erikson spoke, and as such it provides a critical lens through which to evaluate the internal contradictions of this consensus. The Catholic philosophical refusal to segregate normative thinking into the discrete category of "morality" provides the starting point for my deconstruction of the neutrality of modern pluralism. Some fifty years after secular intellectuals declared their final victory over medieval, "essentialist" thinking, the intellectual regime of historical and cultural relativism has proven itself the guardian of an essence distinctly modern in its refusal to acknowledge itself as such.[15] At best, the instrumental reason at the heart of modern relativism must be seen as merely one among the many "warring gods" that make up modern pluralist societies; at worst, it must be recognized as an insidiously jealous god that has come to dominate public political and intellectual discourse, all the while insisting that competing value systems remain segregated in the private sphere of personal choice. It is my hope that recognition of the inescapably substantive dimension of even so procedural a norm as instrumental reason will open up a space in public discourse for noninstrumental traditions such as Catholicism to defend themselves against the imperialism of the dominant secular consensus.

A philosophical lens through which to view postwar social thought, the contrast between Catholic traditionalism and modern secularism is also firmly rooted
historically in intellectual debates specific to mid-century American intellectual
life. On the eve of World War II, Roman Catholicism stood poised to secure a
place within mainstream American intellectual discourse. A significant number of
non-Catholic thinkers had begun to consider the Catholic natural law tradition as
an antidote to the moral nihilism of scientific naturalism and the totalitarian
state.[16] At the same time, the rise of fascist regimes in the Catholic countries of
Italy and Spain revived long-standing American Protestant concerns over
Catholic "authoritarianism." Roman Catholicism as a social and intellectual tradition was at the heart of a fierce debate over the relation of science and religion
to democracy. Following the outbreak of World War II, concerned intellectuals
organized a conference called Science, Philosophy, and Religion in Their Relation to the Democratic Way of Life, an annual event that continued well into the
1950s. In 1943, John Dewey and a group of like-minded intellectuals broke away
to organize a more narrowly secular conference, Scientific Spirit and Democratic
Faith.[17] From the clash of worldviews, a rough consensus formed around the existential "neo-orthodoxy" of the Protestant theologian Reinhold Niebuhr. Firmly
within the tradition of American civil religion, Niebuhr's ruminations on original
sin proved doctrinally vague enough to satisfy believers and atheists alike. Also
within this tradition, Niebuhr's neo-orthodoxy reinforced the secular-Protestant
equation of Roman Catholicism and authoritarianism.

The anti-Catholic animus of this consensus received its most revealing expression in the writings of Dewey's bulldog, Sidney Hook. In *Reason, Social Myths,
and Democracy*, his 1940 critique of fascist and communist mystification, Hook
declared the Catholic Church "the oldest and greatest totalitarian movement in
history." Throughout his wartime polemics, Hook consistently singled out the
Catholic Church as the most dangerous element of the general religious revival
he dubbed "the new failure of nerve." In his lead essay in a *Partisan Review* sym-
posium on this revival, Hook warns of the "increasing . . . power and influence"
of the Catholic Church in otherwise democratic countries. Once again, he charges
that the Church "demands as great a control over social and political life as any
totalitarian party." Hook sees "a sting of death to the free spirit in every measure
the Church proposes to take to safeguard its dogmas." More specifically, Catholicism "is in the van of attack against the best liberal traditions of American culture
and education." The Catholic refusal to separate faith and learning, as well as its
insistence on a separate educational system, portends a vast authoritarian attempt
to capture education. Should this Catholic conspiracy succeed, "education would
have to be purged of all freethinkers," and the "social usefulness of ideas to those
who possessed power . . . would become the criteria of accepted truth." Lest any

Protestants be seduced by the Catholic call for a more ecumenically "Christian" society, Hook points to the new "Counter-Reformation whose secular form already prevails in totalitarian Europe."[18]

Hook's attack on Catholicism was part of a broader effort to establish science as the common philosophy of a thoroughly secularized public sphere. In this effort he extended his critique to those secular, existential philosophies that asserted the truth claims of private experience against those of science. In "The New Failure of Nerve," Hook contrasts this subjectivism with objective science: "The relative validity of different scientific judgments is established by methods of public verification open to all who submit themselves to its discipline, whereas the relative validity of feelings is decided by another private feeling." Science is "open," whereas religion and other nonscientific philosophies are "closed." Science "does not forbid but explores and tests." As it does not forbid, it must not be forbidden. Against those who claim "that modern ills are the consequence of our attempt to live by scientific theory and practice," Hook insists that "the chief causes of our maladjustments are to be found precisely in these areas of social life *in which the rationale of scientific method has not been employed.*"

After ten years of the New Deal, Hook could still maintain that no Western state has even "attempted to meet scientifically the challenge of poverty," that true science has been consistently restrained by "class interests and privileges," "outworn traditions," and "opportunist [sic] compromises." Against this present state of affairs, Hook looks forward to a postwar vision of "a democratic, freedom-and-welfare-planning economy" guided by the scientific method of "rational experiment and analysis." Even the best thought of the religious revival, Reinhold Niebuhr's neo-orthodoxy, has little to contribute to this democratic vision. Science too acknowledges "that man is a limited creature." Unlike theology, it seeks to understand the causes of these limitations, "so that by reducing the margins of ignorance and increasing their scientific knowledge, they may be less limited." Finally, science is "self-corrective" and undercuts "the dogmatism, absolutism and fanaticism" of theology.[19]

Few stated the case as sharply, and most were more open to Niebuhr's neo-orthodoxy. Still, Hook's polemic expressed the core beliefs of his intellectual generation. His interpretation of the "failure of nerve" affirmed the secular prejudices that had gained ascendancy in intellectual circles through the first half of the twentieth century and would shape public life in the second. The victory over Hitler and the return of prosperity confirmed the basic goodness and rightness of the "American way of life." Popular celebrations of Americanism continued to present America as in some vague sense a Christian nation—particularly when contrasted with the "godless" Soviet Union—but secular modernism emerged triumphant in intellectual life.

In the early years of the Cold War, anti-Catholicism continued to play a high-profile role in the consolidation of the "democratic" consensus among intellectuals. Paul Blanshard's best-selling 1949 book, *American Freedom and Catholic Power,* declared the Catholic Church to be an even greater threat to democracy than the Soviet Union. A Book-of-the-Month Club selection, Blanshard's book received universal praise from mainstream liberal intellectuals such as Dewey, Niebuhr, and Albert Einstein. Sidney Hook dissented only in his estimation of the relative practical danger of the two totalitarian ideologies: communism was treason, whereas Catholicism was merely heresy, and freedom-and-welfare planning democracies must tolerate heresy, however noxious.[20] As the 1950s wore on, the Catholic support for the military cold war against communism and the liberalizing developments within the Catholic Church itself made these polemics increasingly irrelevant. Catholic intellectuals became less defensive and more apologetic; Catholic universities gradually abandoned the old Thomistic synthesis for modern secular models of learning. In 1960, John F. Kennedy became the first Roman Catholic president of the United States, in part because of his insistence on the strict separation between his "private" religious faith and his "public" political life.

Most contemporary historians take the secularization of postwar intellectual life for granted. As a historical process, secularization seems to require not explanation but merely acknowledgment as the natural unfolding of the triumph of reason over superstition. David Hollinger, the leading historian of postwar secularization, remains very much a child of Hook on the issue of religion and intellectual life. Looking back on the failure-of-nerve debate, Hollinger insists that "the Protestant, Jewish, and agnostic intellectuals who rallied to the banner of science and democracy had strong reason for believing that Roman Catholic priests and their fellow-traveling intellectuals were a genuine and formidable enemy in a struggle over the future of American culture."[21] Essentially a court history, Hollinger's account has met with few substantial objections from secular intellectuals.

Within this secular consensus, historians have located the central conflict in postwar intellectual life in the shifting fortunes of liberalism and radicalism. Historians who study the 1950s have sought to understand the deradicalization and the triumph of liberalism, while those who study the 1960s have sought to understand the revival of radicalism and its legacy. The most perceptive recent account of these fluctuations remains Howard Brick's study of Daniel Bell. Brick makes clear, as few others have, the importance of Max Weber's thought, and modernization theory in general, to postwar intellectual life.[22] Still, Brick treats Bell's turn away from socialist notions of class struggle to liberal ideas of bureaucratic managerialism as prelude to the revival of socialism in the 1960s: the

Vietnam War, race riots, and the failure of the War on Poverty show the inadequacy of the liberal welfare state to deliver the goods once rightly felt to be attainable only through radical class struggle. The debate over the relative merits of bureaucracy and class struggle continues with a conspicuous silence as to the shared ends of these distinctly modern political means: both liberals and radicals understand the freedom-and-welfare-planning society in terms of the liberation of the individual through the rational control of nature. I take this consensus on instrumental reason to be the central problem of postwar intellectual history.

Ultimately Catholic in its orientation, the critique of modern secularism I advance in this book nonetheless has its roots as well in the secular intellectual history of midcentury America. For one brief moment at the end of World War II, the polemical juggernaut of scientific progress came to a screeching halt. Reports from the liberated Nazi death camps shook the faith of even the most thoroughgoing secular modernists. The shock of a rationalized, bureaucratic, mass production of death called into question the dominant interpretation of fascism as regression to primitive or Catholic barbarism. Following reports from the death camp at Maidanek, no less a modernist than Dwight Macdonald conceded:

> The Nazis learned much from mass production, from modern business organization. It all reads like a sinister parody of Victorian illusions about scientific method and the desirability in itself of man's learning to control his environment. The environment was controlled at Maidanek. It was the human beings who ran amok.[23]

The Holocaust led to a fundamental questioning of the left-liberal narrative of modern progress. In their *Dialectic of Enlightenment*, Max Horkheimer and Theodor Adorno declared that "enlightenment is as totalitarian as any system." No mere regression to past barbarism, "the fallen nature of modern man cannot be separated from social progress." The modern "awakening of the self" has led to "the submission of everything natural to the autocratic subject."[24] The liberation of man through the domination of nature has led to the domination of man as inescapably part of nature. Modern universal reason has merely rationalized the means for modern universal domination.

This moment of modernist self-doubt proved short-lived. The spirit of liberal triumphalism that followed the victory in World War II soon led intellectuals to mute the distinctly modern elements of fascism and communism in favor of a simplistic narrative of totalitarianism as barbaric regression. The violence of the Vietnam War proved unable to shake this modernist consensus: radicals simply redirected the critique of totalitarianism toward the liberal state itself, while contrite liberals could do no more than see the war as a betrayal of "true" liberalism.

It is my hope that the following account of postwar social thought might revive a constructive self-doubt among modernist intellectuals. The postwar academy that opened itself up to ethnic minorities also opened itself up to the development of technologies of mass destruction. Liberal cosmopolitanism cannot be understood apart from cold war internationalism; it is in this sense that I take thinkers as diverse as Ralph Ellison, Nathan Glazer, Betty Friedan, and Alfred Kinsey to be cold war intellectuals. The modernist assault on traditional ethnic and religious subcultures on the domestic front appears relatively benign in comparison to the carpet bombing of Vietnamese peasants only because the most violent phase of this offensive has receded into the euphemisms of "immigration" history; the wonder is how even so attenuated a set of traditions as survived among Americans in the mid–twentieth century could have inspired such fear and loathing among enlightened, tolerant intellectuals.

Modernity has no monopoly on violence, only on the denial of violence. This denial of violence stems from a more basic denial of the ontological integrity of the objects of its violence—first the sacred, then nature, and eventually all other sources of authority outside the instrumental consciousness of the modern subject. In rejecting the possibility of an essential, normative orientation in the natural world, modern secular thought has undermined the rational basis for those positive values—particularly the sanctity of the self and inviolability of individual rights—to which it still gives its emotive assent. The self-deconstruction of secular reason follows most immediately from the failure of secular thinkers to engage the substantive account of nature put forth most insistently, if not always most convincingly, by the Catholic natural law tradition.

The argument I present in this book is less an explicit defense of this tradition than an analysis of the self-referential nihilism of its dominant secular alternative. The natural law tradition serves as a critical foil to the instrumental individualism of "identity" primarily by virtue of its insistence on the integrity of an objective normative order not subject to the arbitrary desires of the will to power. In my conclusion, however, I will return to the natural law debate of the 1940s to sketch an outline of a road not taken—an alternative, distinctly Catholic social vision available to, but ultimately rejected by, midcentury intellectuals. The merits of this social vision are as contested today as they were in the 1940s; in my conclusion, I wish primarily to establish Catholic traditionalism as a genuinely *alternative* social vision, against which the identities of culture, race, ethnicity, gender, and sexuality differ only as competing interest groups within a broader cultural consensus on individualism. These individualisms have flourished through the coercive power of the state and the capitalist corporation; Catholic communalism cannot flourish without protection from this violence.

Finally, a note on the scope and structure of what follows. This book is not a general history of social thought during the cold war era. In many ways an antihistory, it argues against change and provides little of the context generally expected of a properly historical work. Most of the chapters focus on two texts, one each from the cultural eras commonly identified as "the fifties" and "the sixties." I do not take these texts as representative of the general social thought of their times, but as representative of the problem of formulating difference within the various discourses of culture, race, ethnicity, gender, and sexuality. In *Conspicuous Criticism*, I tried to show how a conventionally contextualist approach would only reproduce the very objective detachment that I attack in my critique of the culture concept. In this book, I again argue primarily through close readings of a few texts. These readings are historical in that they attempt to make sense of a recognizably historical phenomenon, the seemingly revolutionary cultural upheaval of postwar America. My hope is that the readings may prove illuminating even to those historians who do not accept my methodological biases and assumptions.

A World Made Safe
for Differences

1

Integrating the World

The Pacific war bequeathed a racist rhetoric at odds with the ideal of tolerance so central to the ideological battle against European fascism. As the United States sought to enlist the support of the emerging nations of Asia, Africa, and Latin America in the cold war against the Soviet Union, American intellectuals made a special effort to extend official tolerance to the peoples and cultures of the non-Western world. Affirming the universality of Western democracy, intellectuals nonetheless repudiated the nineteenth-century legacy of Western imperialism. The anthropological concept of culture provided intellectuals with a language to mediate between a lingering Enlightenment universalism and a new respect for national self-determination.

This anthropological consensus transcends the political divide between cold war liberalism of the 1950s and the antiwar radicalism of the 1960s. At the dawn of the cold war, Ruth Benedict wrote *The Chrysanthemum and the Sword* (1946) to argue for intercultural understanding as the key to success in the postwar reconstruction of Japan; at the end of the heroic phase of cold war internationalism, Frances Fitzgerald wrote *Fire in the Lake* (1972) to argue for the lack of intercultural understanding as the key to the failure of U.S. policy in Vietnam. In both of these works, the attack on conventional cultural imperialism fosters a subtler imperialism of "culture" as a social-scientific mode of perceiving all particular cultures. Throughout the cold war era, both defenders and critics of U.S. foreign policy demanded that non-Western peoples learn to view their cultures with a certain anthropological detachment, to see their received values as relative and therefore open to revision in the service of consciously chosen ends. Within this consensus, the battle between capitalism and communism appears epiphenomenal to a deeper process of modernization, conceived not merely as

1

economic development but as the subordination of all cultures to the demands of individual liberation.

The conception of tolerance that informs this foreign policy discourse grew out of an understanding of cultural relativism developed by Franz Boas. The leading anthropologist of the early twentieth century, Boas rejected the evolutionary framework of Victorian anthropology, which viewed the whole "way of life" of human culture as a single, developing entity to be divided into various stages ranging from the savage to the civilized. Boas argued that culture must be seen as a plurality of integrated wholes, each organized according to a distinct and unique pattern of values. He insisted on the relativity of values among cultures but nonetheless affirmed the absolute value of "culture" as a way of understanding social organization. In this, Boas explicitly rejected racial explanations for the differences among peoples. Culture, not race, determined behavior, and culture was not innate or biological but was a pattern of values learned in daily life. The learned quality of culture gave it a malleability that notions of race seemed to lack, and Boas hoped that an awareness of the diversity and flexibility of cultures would inspire a general tolerance for cultural differences.[1]

A student of Boas, Ruth Benedict embraced not only his anthropological theories but also his commitment to liberal reform. No single work did more to popularize Boas's humanist agenda than Benedict's *Patterns of Culture*, published in 1934. Benedict's book presented an account of three different "primitive" cultures as a way of reflecting on the relativity of all cultures, particularly American culture. Benedict insisted that values differ not only among cultures but also within cultures over time. In light of the Great Depression, she urged Americans to reconsider the permanence of some of their own cultural values, such as the association of economic competition and limited government with moral virtue. In support of the New Deal, Benedict argued that traditional American values of liberty and equality could be preserved only if Americans gave up their equally traditional hostility to cooperative planning and government regulation of the economy.[2]

In the late 1930s, the national focus shifted from depression to war. As American involvement in World War II appeared inevitable, Benedict attempted to translate her understanding of culture into practical programs that would aid the war effort. The New Deal flirtation with "planning" had created a hospitable environment for experts and academics in government, and Benedict was one of the hundreds of social scientists who offered their services to Washington for the coming war. Along with her fellow Boas student Margaret Mead, Benedict formed the Committee for National Morale in 1939 to examine ways in which to apply psychology and anthropology to the problem of building morale during the war. In 1941, she joined the war effort in a more official capacity as a member of the Committee on Food Habits, a joint venture of the Department of Agriculture and the National Research Council designed to improve the food habits and nutrition of an American population mobilizing for total war.[3] War, like culture, came to be seen as a whole way of life.

For all of her attention to American culture, Benedict's most significant wartime work came in the more conventionally anthropological role of interpreting non-Western cultures for Westerners. In June 1943, Benedict replaced her friend (and Japan expert) Geoffrey Gorer as head analyst at the overseas intelligence division of the Office of War Information (OWI). Benedict's job was to prepare cultural profiles of various countries as requested by either an operational division of the OWI or the Bureau of Overseas Intelligence. Restricted from conventional fieldwork by the war, Benedict prepared her reports by examining available studies of the country and interviewing first- and second-generation immigrants living in America. Through 1943 and early 1944, Benedict prepared brief reports on Thailand, Romania, and the Netherlands; each report contained suggestions for "psychological warfare" based on the pattern of culture particular to each country. In June 1944, the psychologist Alexander Leighton, a friend of Benedict's from New York and head of the foreign morale division of the OWI, assigned Benedict to conduct a study of Japan despite her lack of any particular expertise in Japanese language or culture. Benedict revised and expanded her OWI report after the war and published it in 1946 as *The Chrysanthemum and the Sword*.[4] A kind of cultural guidebook for American officials overseeing the reconstruction of Japan, Benedict's book argues for a greater understanding and tolerance of all cultures as the key to preserving world peace.

Although the sincerity of Benedict's plea for tolerance is unassailable, the circumstances of the writing of *The Chrysanthemum and the Sword* do bring into special relief issues of power that have plagued anthropology since its birth as a distinct intellectual discipline. Benedict's contribution to the psychological warfare efforts of the OWI recalls nothing if not the role of anthropology in helping European colonial administrators subdue indigenous peoples during the nineteenth century. Mead, Benedict, and other proponents of "humanistic science" were well aware of anthropology's imperial past but believed that a self-critical anthropology, directed toward the true "dignity of man," could serve as the basis for a truly democratic form of social engineering that would foster mutual respect among all the nations of the world.[5] This ideal of a self-critical anthropology decentered the West in relation to the East only to center the detached perspective of anthropology itself in relation to both West and East. Within Benedict's Boasian framework of cultural relativism, the old anthropological opposition of civilization to savagery gives way to a more abstract dichotomy of the anthropological and the nonanthropological, with anthropology as a neutral, placeless principle of rationality distinct from all particular cultures.

In Benedict's work, anthropological detachment, like "civilization" before it, serves as a universal standard by which to judge all the peoples of the world. Consequently, Benedict locates her savage "other" in nonanthropological attitudes toward culture. In *The Chrysanthemum and the Sword*, Benedict identifies many of the traits conventionally associated with the savage—the lack of self-consciousness, neurosis, immaturity—with the modern West itself, particularly with America.[6] Lacking a proper understanding of the anthropological notion of culture, Americans "still have the vaguest and most biased notions, not only of what makes Japan a nation of Japanese, but of what makes the United States a nation of Americans."[7] Such ignorance fosters fear and insecurity. Americans become "so defensive about their own way of life that it appears to them to be by definition the sole solution in the world," and they "demand that other nations adopt their own particular solutions" (*CAS*, 15–16). This "neurotic" attempt to repress others leads Americans to repress themselves (*CAS*, 15). By demanding cultural uniformity, Americans "cut themselves off from a pleasant and enriching experience" and deny themselves "the added love of their own culture which comes from a knowledge of other ways of life" (*CAS*, 16). This childish, neurotic fear of difference threatens to leave America culturally isolated and stagnant, as America's inability to appreciate other cultures ultimately issues in a self-destructive inability to appreciate its own.

Even as Benedict rejects the single standard of American culture, she constructs a single standard of a certain attitude toward all cultures:

> It sometimes seems as if the tender-minded could not base a doctrine of goodwill upon anything less than a world of peoples each of which is a print from the same negative. But to demand such uniformity as a condition of respecting another nation is as neurotic as to demand it of one's wife or one's children.
>
> The tough-minded are content that differences should exist. They respect differences. Their goal is a world made safe for differences, where the United States may be American to the hilt without threatening the peace of the world, and France may be France, and Japan may be Japan on the same conditions. To forbid the ripening of any of these attitudes toward life by outside interference seems wanton to any student who is not himself convinced that differences need be a Damocles' sword hanging over the world. Nor need he fear that by taking such a position he is helping to freeze the world into the status quo. Encouraging cultural differences would not mean a static world. (*CAS*, 14–15)

Benedict's concept of "ripening" implies not only a temporal narrative of maturation but also a spatial narrative of detachment. The peace of the world depends on replacing the neurotic, "insider" perspective of nationalism with the rational, "outsider" perspective of anthropology. According to Benedict, all nations, including America, exist within particular cultures; they take their cultural values "for granted" as if those values were "the god-given arrangement of the land-scape," and thus they cannot properly evaluate either their own culture or another nation's culture. In contrast, the discipline of anthropology operates outside of all particular cultures and thus may examine them objectively.

Benedict conceptualizes this neutral, scientific detachment through metaphors of vision. Culture functions as the "lenses through which any nation looks at life." As the "oculist" of culture, the anthropologist is "able to write out the formula for any lenses we bring him." Benedict even predicts that "someday, no doubt we shall recognize that it is the job of the social scientist to do this for the nations of the contemporary world" (*CAS*, 14). Benedict clearly offers *The Chrysanthemum and the Sword* as a model for this kind of anthropological mediation, although her choice of metaphor is more appropriate than she may have intended. Oculists not only describe formulas but also prescribe them. In writing prescriptions, an oculist analyzes the deviations of individual vision so as to correct that vision. Understanding of and sympathy for the variety of deviations in vision in no way prevents the oculist from correcting vision with proper prescriptions. Benedict follows something of the same procedure in *The Chrysanthemum and the Sword*. The description of difference serves as prelude to the prescription of uniformity.

To be fair, most of the book remains true to the ideal of detached description that Benedict wishes to evoke with her metaphor of the oculist. Roughly half of the chapters devote themselves simply to mapping out some particular aspect of "the great network of mutual indebtedness" that Benedict presents as the pattern of Japanese culture (*CAS*, 98). Separate chapters deal with such topics as the debt owed to parents, the debt owed to one's own reputation, and the conflicts between equally valid obligations. The intricacy of the networks Benedict describes threat-ens to play into contemporary stereotypes concerning the rigidity of Japanese cul-ture, yet Benedict insists throughout that submission to these obligations stems from the cultural value of common loyalty, not arbitrary authority. Benedict sees in the obligation network of Japanese culture a flexibility absent from both the authoritarianism of America's other major wartime enemy, Nazi Germany, and the caste hierarchies of other non-Western societies, such as that of India. To counter the image of the Japanese as machinelike automatons, Benedict includes a chapter entitled "The Circle of Human Feelings." (In this chapter, she informs her readers that "the Japanese do not condemn self-gratification. They are not Pu-ritans.") She concludes her study with an account of the intimate relations be-tween parents and children as seen through Japanese child-rearing practices (*CAS*, 177).

Still, the concern to refute stereotypes does not lead Benedict to gloss over the substantive differences between Japan and America. She begins her account of Japanese culture proper with a chapter entitled "The Japanese in the War," and her initial analysis reveals a culture completely at odds with American values. According to Benedict, the "very premises which Japan used to justify her war were the opposite of America's" (*CAS*, 20). Japan fought because it saw "anarchy in the world as long as every nation had absolute sovereignty" and felt "it was necessary for her to fight to establish a hierarchy—under Japan, of course." America, however, fought because Japan "had sinned against an international code of 'live and let live' or at least of 'open doors' for free enterprise" (*CAS*, 21). From this initial opposition of hierarchy to equality flow a series of sharp contrasts. The Japanese rely on "a way of life that is planned and charted beforehand," whereas Americans expect "a constantly challenging world" (*CAS*, 28). Unlike Americans, the Japanese value fixed social stations over social mobility, the spiritual over the material, honor over profit, and the external sanctions of shame over the internal sanctions of guilt (*CAS*, 23, 146–47, 223). Through these oppositions, Benedict creates a picture of the Japanese as a people bound together by a complicated network of ordered, hierarchical, personal obligations, which contrasts sharply with the easygoing individualism of American culture.

This contrast between America and Japan is as predictable as it is extreme. Oppositions such as hierarchy versus equality and shame versus guilt have structured America's conception of itself in relation to not only non-Western cultures but Europe as well.[8] The differences that Benedict observes are variations on the differences between the Old World and the New offered by commentators at least as far back as Michel-Guillaume-Jean de Crèvecoeur. Before these oppositions served as a cultural narrative contrasting East and West, they served as a historical narrative of the passage from the medieval to the modern; indeed, much of the hostile criticism of Japan on the part of Western observers can be seen as an extension of the self-critique that drove the modern West to throw off its own primitive, childish, neurotic feudal past. Commentators ranging from the filmmaker Frank Capra to General Douglas MacArthur spoke of the negative aspects of Japanese culture as residues of "feudalistic forms of oppression"; the anthropologist Geoffrey Gorer specifically compared Japanese attachment to the emperor with the attachment of medieval Catholics to the pope.[9] In general, the degree of hostility expressed in wartime accounts of Japanese culture depended on the relative weight given to its premodern dimensions, as opposed to its more palatable modern aspects, such as its enthusiastic embrace of Western science and technology. This hostility often slid into racism when premodern traits came to be seen as rooted in the biological makeup of the Japanese people, but the demonizing of these traits themselves predates and transcends racial categories.

Benedict avoids the racist excesses of other American commentators by taking a historical approach to the seeming inconsistencies of Japanese culture. Through her use of history, Benedict replaces the demonized "other" with a relatively domesticated "self." That is, Benedict presents the Japanese as essentially historical beings who share with Americans a basic, fundamental human character trait: the ability to adapt to change. In her sympathetic account of Japanese modernization under the Meiji reform of the late nineteenth century, Benedict interprets Japan's acceptance of modern science and technology not as a capitulation to Western values but as an adaptation of enduring Japanese cultural patterns to changing circumstances. She praises the "energetic and resourceful statesmen who ran the Meiji government" for rejecting "all ideas of ending hierarchy in Japan"; Meiji reformers "did not unseat hierarchical habits" but simply "gave them a new locus" in economic, scientific, and technological development (*CAS,* 79–80). Benedict's account ultimately endorses neither hierarchy nor technology so much as the general cultural process of hybridizing often contradictory values. Japan's participation in this process serves as evidence of its basic humanity against its racist detractors.

In Benedict's account, even Japan's flaws appear as common human flaws. Despite the admirable cultural "ripening" of the Meiji period, "Japan's nemesis came when she tried to export her formula." In launching a campaign of aggressive foreign expansion, Japan "did not recognize that the system of Japanese morality which had fitted them to 'accept their proper station' was something they could not count on elsewhere" (*CAS,* 96). Thus, the Japanese have demonstrated both the common human capacity to adapt to change within their own culture and an all-too-common human unwillingness to accept the differences among cultures. The Japanese made the mistake of committing themselves to specific values rather than to the general process of organizing values into specific patterns, and this is the very mistake that Americans are in danger of making as they assume a leadership role in world affairs. Thus, in virtue and in vice, Japan serves as a mirror for America: a model of what Americans are as cultural beings and an example of what Americans might become if they refuse to accept their status as cultural beings.

Held to the same standard of cultural consciousness, Japan and America nonetheless stand in different proximity to this standard. America's potential intolerance on the international scene contrasts with the easygoing, live-and-let-live attitude within America itself. America's cultural ripening simply requires Americans to extend their tolerance of individual differences within America to the individual nations of the world. Japan's proven intolerance, however, stems from its cultural values and its inability to accept individual differences within its own culture. According to Benedict, the reverence for hierarchical social ties that sustained the Japanese through the transformations of the Meiji period carried within itself the seeds of imperial aggression:

> Social pressures in Japan, no matter how voluntarily embraced, ask too much of the individual. They require him to conceal his emotions, to give up his desires, and to

stand as the exposed representative of a family, an organization, or a nation. The Japanese have shown that they can take all the self-discipline such a course requires. But the weight upon them is extremely heavy. They have to repress too much for their own good. Fearing to venture upon a life which is less costly to their psyches, they have been led by militarists upon a course where the costs pile up interminably. Having paid so high a price they become self-righteous and have been contemptuous of people with a less demanding ethic. (*CAS*, 315)

Benedict's analysis of Japanese intolerance parallels the psychological profile of American intolerance with which she opens her study. For both Japan and America, intolerance stems from a repression rooted in group allegiances and the fear of new experiences; however, whereas Benedict traces America's intolerance to a kind of free-floating cultural chauvinism, she traces Japan's to a concrete cultural pattern geared toward repressing the individual. Japanese and Americans will have to give up their chauvinistic ties to their respective nations, but the Japanese will also have to give up their irrational ties to "family" and "organization," which have proven incompatible with world peace.

The achievement of an anthropological detachment from one's culture thus issues in an affirmation of the very American value of individual freedom. For Benedict, the American victory in World War II will be complete only if America can ensure this individual liberation for the people of Japan. As Commodore Perry's gunboats opened Japan to modern science and technology, so the administrators of America's postwar occupation must open Japanese culture to the modern Western value of individual freedom. The "new goals" that Benedict suggests for this cultural reorientation include

accepting the authority of elected persons and ignoring "proper station" as it is set up in their hierarchical system . . . adopting the free and easy human contacts to which we are accustomed in the United States, the imperative demand to be independent, the passion each individual has to choose his own mate, his own job, the house he will live in and the obligations he will assume. (*CAS*, 314)

That a middle-class American intellectual takes these goals for granted should come as no surprise, but it is not clear what would be left distinct to Japanese culture after the achievement of these "new goals." The liberation of the individual—and thus the peace of the world—would seem to require the full-scale acceptance of modern American social relations on the part of the Japanese.

With this vision of cultural ripening, the trajectory of Benedict's encounter with difference becomes clear. For Benedict, Japan's values are incommensurable with America's, yet the Japanese share in the common human practice of organizing values into coherent patterns; respect for the Japanese must be rooted not in respect for their values per se but in respect for their ability to organize and reorganize values into coherent patterns. Having abstracted a general cultural process from particular values, Benedict figures cultural freedom not so much as the freedom of different values to flourish, but as the freedom of different peoples to exercise active and creative roles in the shaping and reshaping of their culture. Thus, Benedict insists that "the United States cannot . . . create by fiat a free, democratic Japan"; America may set the goal of democratic freedom, but the Japanese "cannot be legislated into accepting" that goal (*CAS,* 314).

Against those who think the Japanese incapable of becoming democratic, Benedict points to encouraging "changes in this direction" that the Japanese themselves have made since the war:

> Their public men have said since VJ-Day that Japan must encourage its men and women to live their own lives and to trust their own consciences. They do not say so, of course, but any Japanese understands that they are questioning the role of "shame" (haiji) in Japan, and that they hope for a new growth of freedom among their countrymen. (*CAS,* 315)

For Benedict, the Japanese have proven themselves capable of taking their culture into their own hands and uplifting themselves to the internal authority of conscience required of a responsible democratic citizenry. The Japanese have earned a certain autonomy from America by exercising a certain autonomy from themselves, that is, from their culture. Outside interference by America would only inhibit the growth of this democratic autonomy.

The very sincerity of Benedict's demand for Japanese self-determination suggests the need for a fundamental rethinking of the power relations of anthropology as a mode of intercultural mediation. The imperial vision of *The Chrysanthemum and the Sword* lies not in making Japan a cultural colony but in making Japan a cultural equal. Benedict asks of Japan simply what she asks of America: that it open itself to the "pleasant and enriching experience" of another culture (in this case, America itself) and that it come to "know the added love of [its] own culture which comes from a knowledge of other ways of life" (*CAS,* 16). For Benedict, cultural autonomy requires a certain autonomy from culture. Japan and America must learn to detach themselves, each from its own culture, to appreciate different cultures yet somehow remain engaged with their own culture and appreciate it as well.

Benedict herself serves as a model of this detached-yet-engaged autonomy for Americans. True to her commitment to self-determination, she offers Japan indigenous Japanese models for such autonomy. Benedict's anthropological account of Japan finds its Japanese equivalent in the autobiographical accounts of two Japanese women confronting American culture. Like Benedict's anthropology, these autobiographies figure the contrast between Japan and

America as a conflict between tradition and modernity. In *My Narrow Isle*, Sumie Seo Mishima tells of the conflict between her desire to study in America and what Benedict describes as "her conservative family's unwillingness to accept the *on* [the incurred obligation] of an American fellowship" (*CAS*, 225–26). Mishima ends up going to Wellesley despite her parents' objections, yet she feels out of place:

> The teachers and the girls, she says, were wonderfully kind, but that made it, so she felt, all the more difficult. "My pride in perfect manneredness, a universal character- istic of the Japanese, was bitterly wounded. I was angry at myself for not knowing how to behave properly here and also at the surroundings which seemed to mock my past training. Except for this vague but deep-rooted feeling of anger there was no emotion left in me." She felt herself "a being fallen from some other planet with senses and feelings that have no use in this environment where I was completely blind, socially speaking." It was two or three years before she relaxed and began to accept the kindness offered her. Americans, she decided, lived with what she calls "refined familiarity." But "familiarity had been killed in me as sauciness when I was three." (*CAS*, 226)

A microcosm of Benedict's argument as a whole, Mishima's story begins with the contrast between tradition and modernity only to end with the passage from tra- dition to modernity. On the personal as well as the geopolitical level, peace de- pends on the acceptance of the easygoing relations of American individualism.

Mishima functions as a synecdoche for Japan. Benedict places Mishima's story at the end of a chapter on Japanese social obligations entitled "The Dilemma of Virtue" and insists that it embodies "in its most acute form the Japanese dilemma of virtue" (*CAS*, 227). Such a reading of Mishima's story, however, works against Benedict's own interpretation of Japanese culture. Throughout the chapter, Bene- dict describes the Japanese dilemma of virtue in terms of the conflict between competing and equally valid obligations within a single culture, while she pres- ents Mishima experiencing a qualitatively different conflict between a way of life in which formalities and obligations are important and one in which they are not.

In making Mishima a representative figure, Benedict translates this conflict be- tween cultures into an inevitable historical progression within Japanese culture: "Once Japanese have accepted, to however small a degree, the less codified rules that govern behavior in the United States they find it difficult to imagine their being able to experience again the restrictions of their old life in Japan" (*CAS*, 227). Benedict concedes that some Japanese experience this change as loss; how- ever, as gain or loss, she fails to show how this experience offers any "added love" for Japanese culture itself. A culture would already have to place a premium on new and enriching experiences in order to benefit from an encounter with American culture, and clearly Japanese culture does not. By the single (and very

American) standard of individual autonomy, Japanese culture comes off as something second rate.

Obviously Mishima's experience is not representative in any empirical sense. Most Japanese do not go to Wellesley and do not write autobiographies. What Mishima does represent is the experience of marginality with respect to one's own culture that Benedict deems necessary to living in a world made safe for differences. In such a world, marginality must be central; it must be the representative experience of individuals within cultures. These individuals may not actually become anthropologists or write autobiographies, but, ideally, they would achieve a certain kind of anthropological and autobiographical consciousness, an ability to detach themselves enough from their own culture so as to examine their relation to that culture in some kind of objective manner. Within this universal form of marginality, difference lies in the specific content of marginality, the variety of loci for marginality. The individuals of the world must all become marginal figures, but they will always be marginal to different cultures in different places at different times.

Benedict closes her account of Japanese culture by offering an example of how difference might persist despite the uniformity of marginality. Once again, she turns to the story of a Japanese woman confronting Western freedom—Etsu Inagaki Sugimoto's account of her experiences in a mission school in Tokyo, *A Daughter of the Samurai*. Sugimoto's epiphanic encounter with Western freedom comes when her teachers give each girl at the school a plot of ground on which to plant anything they want. Benedict quotes Sugimoto:

> This plant-as-you-please garden gave me a wholly new feeling of personal right. . . . The very fact that such happiness could exist in the human heart was a surprise to me. . . . I, with no violation of tradition, no stain on the family name, no shock to parent, teacher or townspeople, no harm to anything was free to act. (*CAS,* 294)

After this experience, Sugimoto cannot look at her own culture in the same way again. She now realizes that although at her "home there was one part of the garden that was supposed to be wild . . . someone was always busy trimming the pines or cutting the hedge" (*CAS,* 294). According to Benedict, Sugimoto's realization of the "simulated wildness" and "simulated freedom of will" of Japanese culture initiated a "transition to a greater psychic freedom" through which she discovered the "pure joy in being natural" (*CAS,* 295). Like Mishima's experiences at Wellesley, Sugimoto's detachment from tradition, family, teacher, and townspeople serves as a model of "natural" social relations for postwar Japan. A "self-respecting Japan" will be a Japan that respects the self or, more precisely, the individual (*CAS,* 150). To be a responsible member of the family of nations, Japan must "set up a way of life which does not demand the old requirements of individual restraint" and move toward "dispensation which honors individual freedom" (*CAS*, 295–96).

Just when Benedict seems to have completely dismissed Japanese culture, she pulls back. Insisting on respect for the individual within Japanese culture, Benedict also insists on the individuality of Japanese culture within the global family of nations. Adopting a universal formal relation between the individual and culture, Japan must nonetheless cultivate a particular cultural content consistent with its own cultural traditions. Benedict insists not only that Japan must work toward greater self-respect and greater psychic freedom but also that Japan "will have to rebuild her self-respect on her own basis, not ours" and "purify it in her own way" (*CAS*, 150). She even suggests that "certain old traditional virtues . . . can help to keep [Japan] on an even keel" as it purifies its culture (*CAS*, 295–96). Condemned as constraint, culture may be recovered as resource.

Benedict takes Sugimoto's story as an occasion for reflecting on the possibility of purifying two central symbols of Japanese culture: the chrysanthemum and the sword. Both symbols embody the contradictions of Japanese culture, and these contradictions need to be resolved in order for Japanese culture to ripen. Chrysanthemums, for all of their beauty, "are grown in pots and arranged . . . with each perfect petal separately disposed by the grower's hand and often held in place in a tiny invisible wire rack inserted in the living flower" (*CAS*, 295). Purification demands that the Japanese "put aside the wire rack" and accept that "chrysanthemums can be beautiful without wire racks and such drastic pruning" (*CAS*, 295–96). Conversely, the cult of the sword, which fostered international aggression, contains within it "a simile of ideal and self-responsible man" (*CAS*, 296). The sword stands not only for the warrior code but also for a more general code of personal conduct, and the Japanese "have an abiding strength in their concern with keeping an inner sword free from the rust which always threatens it" (*CAS*, 296). Viewed in this nonaggressive sense, the sword "is a symbol [the Japanese] can keep in a freer and more peaceful world" (*CAS*, 296). Purified of their repressive connotations, these symbols can serve as a particular language through which the Japanese may participate in a single, universal conception of freedom to be shared by the nations of the world.

The fate of the chrysanthemum and the sword reveals the necessity that serves as the basis for Benedict's vision of cultural freedom in the postwar world. The idea of a world made safe for differences allows for the retention of indigenous cultural symbols, provided they be abstracted from the often restrictive, normative contexts that originally gave them meaning, and then instrumentalized in the service of the greater psychic freedom of the individual. Naturalized as a neutral, universal principle of order, Benedict's prescription for cultural freedom nonetheless demands that the Japanese learn to internalize both aesthetic and ascetic authority in a manner suspiciously like that of the cold war liberal elite emerging in postwar America. The chrysanthemum and the sword stand for the "soft" and the "hard" sides of the personal ethic that would come to define establishment liberal intellectuals during the cold war: on the one hand, an aesthetic of cultural cosmopolitanism open to the beauty of all cultures while being bound to none; on the other, an ascetic code of "responsibility" able to transcend the easy answers of both the left and the right and adopt a "realistic" attitude toward questions of foreign and domestic policy.[10]

An attempt to democratize this ethic, *The Chrysanthemum and the Sword* argues that the peace of the world depends not on a liberal intellectual elite controlling world events but on the peoples of the world controlling themselves in accord with the values of that elite. The achievement of this self-control depends on the peoples of the world being able to achieve a certain anthropological detachment from their own culture and to see their culture as a means to the end of individual growth. Benedict's conception of a world made safe for differences ultimately reduces to a vision of a world made safe for the personal ethic of the cosmopolitan, responsible, liberal intellectual.

This ethic found its most influential evangelist in the ubiquitous Arthur Schlesinger Jr. A Harvard-trained academic, Schlesinger served as the unofficial court historian of the Democratic party for the period of liberal dominance from the end of World War II to the withdrawal from Vietnam. His 1946 Pulitzer Prize–winning *The Age of Jackson* provided liberals with a genealogy of radical democracy stretching from Andrew Jackson to Franklin Roosevelt; his 1965 *A Thousand Days* did more than any other single book to canonize John F. Kennedy as the patron saint of activist liberal intellectuals. In 1947, Schlesinger helped to found Americans for Democratic Action (ADA), a liberal activist group that sought to combine a progressive domestic social agenda with a tough, but "rational," anticommunist foreign policy. Synthesizing idealism and realism into a coherent anticommunist strategy, ADA liberals such as Schlesinger saw the promotion of racial justice and economic equality at home as a necessary complement to the deployment of troops abroad. The immediate need to secure Europe against the Soviet Union focused liberal energies on "hard" military strategies, such as the formation of the North Atlantic Treaty Organization (NATO); indeed, the ADA had been formed largely to combat what its members thought to be the dangerously conciliatory attitude toward the Soviet Union promoted by Henry Wallace and his Progressive Citizens of America party. The "loss" of China in 1949 raised the problem of communism in the developing world, and it directed liberal attention back to the "soft" issues of intercultural mediation raised by Benedict in *The Chrysanthemum and the Sword*.

In his influential polemic *The Vital Center* (1949), Schlesinger introduces an explicitly existential dimension to the cultural interpretation of U.S. policy goals in Asia. Schlesinger sees both Asian peasants and urban Americans trapped in an "Age of Anxiety" brought on not by impending nuclear war but by that old standby of social science, the dislocations of modernity. Both Asia and America suffer the loss of those organic social ties that had sustained traditional societies for centuries. Both Asia and America face the threat of what Schlesinger calls "millennial nostalgia": in America, this manifests itself in a conservatism that looks back to the utopian past of the nineteenth century, while in Asia it appears in the guise of a radicalism that looks ahead to the utopian future of communist revolution. Schlesinger sees both extremes as irrational and authoritarian; indeed, he tends to view any political position outside of his brand of liberalism as symptomatic of deep psychological disorder (at one point he refers to the National Association of Manufacturers as "the characteristic expression of the capitalist libido"). The rational liberal response to modern dislocation is, once again, a "genuine cultural pluralism," a reconstruction of the kind of communal life and "group activity" that can soothe the anxieties that lead people at home and abroad to illiberal extremism.[11]

A good New Deal liberal, Schlesinger conceives of communal revival in concrete policy terms as a "campaign against social anxiety." This campaign entails nothing less than the development of "an organizational framework . . . within which self-realization on a large scale is possible." Looking at America, Schlesinger conceives of this organization through a kind of Freudian interpretation of Tocqueville: "By the revitalization of voluntary associations, we can siphon off emotions which might otherwise be driven to the solutions of despair." Asia, lacking America's democratic traditions and only recently emerging from feudal oppression, requires a more comprehensive strategy to achieve psychic security:

> Support for nationalist governments is . . . necessary; but it will not be enough if all we do, as we did in China, is to back a native despot instead of a foreign one. We must encourage the native governments to evolve in a democratic direction; we must strengthen them internationally—for example, by welcoming the development of a South Asia regional system; and we must collaborate with such a federation in working out affirmative programs to meet the problems causing the surge of revolution. . . . American funds can buy out landlords; American methods of scientific farming and of land rehabilitation can increase production; American study of village sociology could help us to understand how we may most effectively release the energies so long pent up in the villages of Asia.[12]

Benedict's world made safe for differences thus realizes itself through social and economic modernization. The outbreak of the Korean War in 1950 delayed the first serious attempts to implement this peaceful development policy, but liberal anticommunists would continually invoke versions of this strategy throughout the cold war era. By the mid-1950s, Vietnam emerged as the ideal laboratory for this liberal, developmental anticommunism.

The decision to focus on Vietnam was, as the Marxists say, overdetermined. With the stalemate in Korea, Southeast Asia appeared to be the most promising direction for communist military expansion; conversely, the region's proximity to China enhanced its strategic value as an intelligence listening post for the "free" world. Economically, U.S. policy makers saw the region as key to the economic recovery of Europe and Japan. British Malaysia, for example, produced the rubber and tin that were the United Kingdom's only marketable resource in trade with the United States. The entire region, moreover, represented a potential consumer market for Japanese goods, and U.S. policy makers saw the reestablishment of Japan's prewar economic dominance of the region as a key to fighting the spread of communism. Vietnam, or French Indochina, became the particular focus of U.S. attention in large part because of the strength of its communist insurgency. The war against Ho Chi Minh's communist revolutionaries proved a tremendous military and economic drain on France at a time when the United States was looking for French support for its NATO strategy in Europe. The United States saw the rearmament of Germany as essential to establishing a defense zone against Soviet westward expansion. Remembering its humiliation at the hands of the Nazis, France refused to support this policy while its own military commitments in Indochina left it exposed to potential aggression from a newly militarized Germany. The defeat at Dien Bien Phu in 1954 signaled the end of French colonial rule in Vietnam, but France refused to support NATO efforts in Europe as long as they were to be saddled with responsibility for the postcolonial "transition to democracy." As leader of the free world—and in exchange for support for German rearmament—the United States agreed to take responsibility for "nation building" in Vietnam.[13]

The scale of U.S. military involvement in Vietnam during the 1960s has obscured the depth of its commitment to the cultural/developmental side of the liberal anticommunist strategy outlined in *The Vital Center*. The "village sociology" dimension of Schlesinger's vision had its most enthusiastic and influential advocate in Colonel Edward G. Lansdale. An OSS officer during World War II, Lansdale naturally gravitated toward intelligence work in the newly formed Central Intelligence Agency. Lansdale gained fame in intelligence circles for the innovative techniques of psychological warfare he deployed while fighting communist insurgents in the Philippines. At the height of his influence in the late 1950s and early 1960s, Lansdale was thought of as "our man in Asia" by CIA director Allen Dulles and praised as "America's James Bond" by John F.

Kennedy. Throughout his career, Lansdale insisted that successful counterin-
surgency in the non-Western world required a sophisticated, and sympathetic,
understanding of native cultures. Sophistication alone could prove quite grue-
some. On one occasion in the Philippines, Lansdale planted the blood-drained
corpse of a captured communist insurgent in a communist-controlled area of the
countryside to play on traditional local fears concerning vampires. The tactic
worked, as peasants fled the region en masse, depriving the communists of a
potential base of popular support. Lansdale nonetheless appears to have har-
bored a genuine love for Asian cultures, particularly that of the Vietnamese.
Long after the United States had abandoned culture for war, Lansdale continued to compile tapes of Vietnamese folk songs and play them for skeptical government officials. Like Benedict on Japan, Lansdale insisted on the unique
beauty of Vietnamese culture yet believed that it was perfectly compatible with
Jeffersonian democracy and can-do American pragmatism.[14]

Lansdale provided the inspiration for one of the most popular fictions of the
cold war era, William Lederer and Eugene Burdick's *The Ugly American*
(1958). A series of vignettes concerning the work of U.S. diplomats and ad-
visers in the fictional Southeast Asian country "Sarkhan," the novel employs
accessible, *Saturday Evening Post*–style storytelling to argue for intercultural
understanding and native self-determination as the most effective strategies for
fighting communism in Asia. A Book-of-the-Month Club selection, the novel
spent seventy-eight weeks on the best-seller list, clearly striking a powerful
chord with the American reading public. Much of the book's initial notoriety
stemmed less from its cautiously optimistic projections on future U.S. policy
than from its scathing indictment of current U.S. practice. *Time* hailed the
novel's portrayal of the imperial arrogance of the U.S. diplomatic corps as "a
slashing, over-simplified . . . yet not-to-be-ignored attack on the men and
women who have taken up the white man's burden for the U.S. in Southeast
Asia." Senator John Kennedy presented every member of the Senate with a
copy of the book, and President Eisenhower appointed a committee to investi-
gate Lederer and Burdick's accusations.

Like Lansdale at his most liberal, Lederer and Burdick present culture as both
problem and solution. The authors frame the novel with two diplomats, and two
different views of diplomacy. The novel opens with a portrait of the "Honorable
Louis Sears, American ambassador to Sarkhan," who looks on Asians as "strange
little monkeys." It concludes with the reflections of Sears's successor, Ambassador Gilbert MacWhite, who, despite his conscientious consultation of anthropologists, sociologists, and political scientists, must concede his failure to grasp
"the Asian personality." MacWhite remains convinced, however, that a proper
understanding of the Asian personality does in fact hold the key to the success of

U.S. efforts in the region. In classic ADA liberal fashion, MacWhite argues that this cultural sensitivity is "tough" and "hard," not "romantic" or "sentimental." From his own practical experience, MacWhite concludes, "To the extent that our foreign policy is humane and reasonable, it will be successful. The extent that it is imperialistic and grandiose, it will fail." A "tiny handful of effective men," including a Catholic priest, an engineer, and an Air Force colonel (Edwin B. Hillandale, directly modeled on Lansdale), have convinced MacWhite that the United States must proceed through small-scale, cooperative ventures that address specific local needs and enlist the active participation of the native population.[15] The vignettes that compose the novel offer exemplary tales of such democratic, culturally sensitive intervention.

The story of the engineer Homer Atkins, the ugly American of the book's title, provides the best representation of Lederer and Burdick's practical idealism. Homer and his wife, Emma, have volunteered to help the natives of Sarkhan fight communism. The couple live in a simple cottage outside the main city, Haidho. Upon arrival, Emma sets out to learn the native language while Homer addresses the practical problem of irrigation in the region's terraced rice paddies. Homer is "ugly" not only in his rough looks but in his willingness to get his hands dirty working with the people at the grassroots level. Still, even as he constructs a simple water pump entirely from locally available materials, Emma warns him against imposing an intrusive foreign technology: "You have to let them use the machine themselves and in their own way. If you try to jam it down their throats, they'll never use it" (*UA*, 218). Following Emma's advice, Homer approaches the villagers with an offer of half-interest in the pump patent for anyone who can make the pump practical. Jeepo, the local mechanic, the "ugly Sarkhanese," suggests a treadmill that will maintain the pump's bicycle-powered drive mechanism without sacrificing a scarce and necessary means of transportation through the permanent attachment to the pump apparatus required by Homer's original design. The story concludes with Homer publicly acknowledging Jeepo's contribution and agreeing to split all profits from the pump with him.

The chapter following the parable of the pump features Emma in a more explicitly confrontational encounter between technology and tradition. Emma, "a simple and straightforward person," and certainly "not a busybody," happens to notice that the old people of the village all have bent backs. Upon closer observation, she links this condition to the short-handled brooms that force people to stoop over when sweeping. The villagers scoff at Emma's explanation, insisting, "It's just that old people become bent. . . . That's the natural thing which happens to older people," and "brooms are not meant to have long handles. . . . It has never been that way." Following her own advice to Homer, Emma refuses to attempt to impose technological improvements on the villagers. Constructing a long-handled broom from reed stalks growing just outside the village, Emma leads by example, "and everyone watching was aware of the greater efficiency of being able to sweep while standing up" (*UA*, 233–36). The villagers soon begin to construct their own long-handled brooms.

The story concludes four years later, with Homer and Emma back in America, reading a letter sent to them by the head of the village. The letter thanks Emma, "wife of the engineer," for unbending the backs of the people through the "lucky accident" of the long-handled broom. The villagers have constructed a small shrine in Emma's memory: "It is a simple affair; at the foot of the altar are these words: 'In memory of the woman who unbent the backs of our people.' And in front of the shrine there is a stack of the old short reeds which we used to use" (*UA*, 238). The parable of the broom confirms Schlesinger's vision of Asian villages as storehouses of pent-up energy awaiting liberation by modern technology, while Emma's near apotheosis serves to sacralize technological innovation as a universal principle capable of synthesizing tradition and modernity in specific local contexts.

These simple morality tales cannot be dismissed as mere masks for imperial domination. The ideal of intercultural mediation persisted in the discourse of Southeast Asia not simply as a clever tool to manipulate consent but as the bearer of an ideal of individual liberation that must be taken seriously as a force in the shaping of U.S. foreign policy. *The Ugly American* offers technology much as *The Chrysanthemum and the Sword* presents selfhood—a neutral, transcultural norm capable of integrating non-Western cultures into the neutral and necessary process of modernization. The sinister read of *The Ugly American* and its real-life referents such as Lansdale implies that the United States did know, or could have known, the true will of the Vietnamese people but simply chose to ignore it for reasons of political and economic interest; moreover, this interpretation too often assumes the possibility of some authentically consensual, emancipatory course of development. The insistence on the value of consent, which cuts across the political spectrum, obscures or evades the inherently violent and nonconsensual nature of modernization itself: one need look no further than the extermination of the native peoples of North America, European imperialism, and the mass starvations induced by the various collectivizing schemes of communist China and the Soviet Union.

Modernization is always violent and is never really indigenous in the way often fantasized by progressive policy makers and oppositional radicals. Communism was no more native to Vietnam than capitalism or democracy. There is an undeniable heroism in the struggle of the Viet Minh, but Ho Chi Minh's consolidation of ethnic, regional, and religious factions into a single nation-state would have involved much violence and bloodshed even without U.S. intervention. There simply was no single people, and thus no single consent, to win over in Vietnam. I read the persistent reflection on culture less as a mask for military and economic interests and more as an ideological interest in its own right: the demand that the world conform to a single ideal of the divided consciousness of the modern Western intellectual.

Defeat in Vietnam called forth the same interpretation as victory in Japan. Frances Fitzgerald's 1972 work *Fire in the Lake* marks the end point of this cultural reflection on U.S. foreign policy. Subtitled "The Vietnamese and the Americans in Vietnam," *Fire in the Lake* argues that the failure of U.S. policy stemmed from, of all things, the failure of Americans to understand Vietnamese culture. Like Benedict's *The Chrysanthemum and the Sword*, Fitzgerald's book reveals more about America than about the Asian "other." Anthropological accuracy aside, it struck a deep chord with the arbiters of American culture, winning the Pulitzer Prize, the National Book Award, and the Bancroft Prize for History. By 1972, the American reading public appeared willing to concede that the war in Vietnam could not be explained in the conventional political terms of communism and democracy. According to Fitzgerald,

> Since the Second World War the Vietnamese have been waging a struggle not merely over the form of their state but over the nature of Vietnamese society, the very identity of the Vietnamese. It is the grandeur of the stakes involved that has made the struggle at once so intense and so opaque to Westerners.[16]

By offering yet another exposé of the West's failure to understand the non-Western other, Fitzgerald reinforces the deeper Western opacity that sees in every culture a quest for "identity." *Fire in the Lake* reads the Vietnam War as a tragic episode in the necessary, inevitable, and progressive "struggle . . . to adapt a largely traditional society to the modern world" (*FL,* 7). Political independence appears as a surface means to a deep cultural autonomy, conceived not in terms of preserving any distinct indigenous tradition but of controlling the process of modernization.

Fitzgerald writes with an intellectual hubris equal to the military and political hubris of the U.S. policy makers. She consistently invokes the explanatory key of "culture" even as she acknowledges the consistent role of cultural analysis in the formulation of U.S. policy during the 1950s and 1960s. Fitzgerald reports that Dr. Wesley Fishel of Michigan State University, a key adviser to South Vietnamese president Ngo Dinh Diem, repeatedly insisted that "one had to know the whole history and culture of a country in order to understand its process of political and economic development." Under Fishel's supervision, "groups of social scientists set out to research the economics and sociology of the Vietnamese village as well as every aspect of Vietnamese government operations" (*FL,* 107–8). She further cites in-depth sociological studies conducted by the RAND corporation which, as early as 1965, revealed widespread hostility to U.S. policies among the Vietnamese people. Often Fitzgerald interprets the failure of these studies to issue in a more culturally sensitive policy as a matter of power: U.S. officials ignored these studies because they had no interest in democracy and saw the Vietnamese simply as cogs in a "military machine . . . to fight the Communists" (*FL,* 152). More often, she suggests that this failure was a problem of knowledge. The official studies failed to accomplish the "leap of perspective," the "effort of translation" necessary to capture the true nature of Vietnamese culture (*FL,* 5). Analyzing the civilian relocation programs the U.S. devised to create solidly anticommunist population concentrations, Fitzgerald concludes:

> Many American officials understood that the land and the graves of the ancestors were important to the Vietnamese. Had they understood exactly why, they might not have looked upon the wholesale creation of refugees as a "rational" method of defeating Communism. (*FL,* 11–12)

Much of Fitzgerald's analysis proceeds by such a move from surface to depth, from the "why" to the "exactly why." The above passage presents this move as a shift from American presuppositions to Vietnamese reality. By Fitzgerald's own account, however, this reality is filtered through yet another social-scientific account of Vietnamese culture, the French anthropologist Paul Mus's work, *Sociolgie d'une guerre.* In *Fire in the Lake,* the Vietnam War becomes yet another occasion for social-scientific revision: Fitzgerald, with the assistance of Mus, will accomplish the "leap of perspective" that proved too great for the army of social scientists enlisted by the U.S. government. By explaining the devastation wrought by the war as a failure of cultural understanding, Fitzgerald argues for a proper cultural understanding capable of directing authentically progressive social development.

Fitzgerald's new anthropology proceeds from the very old anthropological contrast between tradition and modernity. Vietnam and the United States stand for "two different dimensions, two different epochs of history" (*FL,* 4). In Fitzgerald's account, the "whole indivisible culture" of Vietnam appears as a slightly more agrarian, peasant version of Benedict's traditional Japanese culture. With "a stable technology and a limited amount of land the traditional Vietnamese lived by constant repetition, by the sowing and reaping of rice and by the perpetuation of customary law" (*FL,* 10). Land is not owned as private property but is held in trust to be passed on to future generations. Duties take priority over rights, family obligations over the freedom of the individual. At one point, Fitzgerald even compares the "Confucian" worldview of the Vietnamese to "a Japanese garden where every rock, opaque and indifferent in itself, takes on significance from its relationship to the surrounding objects" (*FL,* 28). From this characterization of a holistic culture flow the inevitable contrasts with the United States: "As Americans are, so to speak, canted towards the future, the traditional Vietnamese were directed towards the past." Similarly, "Americans live in a society of replaceable parts—in theory anyone can become President or sanitary inspector—but the Vietnamese lived in a society of particular people, all of whom knew each other by their place in the landscape" (*FL*, 14, 12). Fitzgerald, like Benedict, writes with great sympathy for traditional culture. Still, as in Benedict, the contrast between tradition and modernity slides inexorably into an argument for the necessary transition from tradition to modernity.

Fitzgerald reads North and South Vietnam as representing two contrasting paths to modernity, the popular and the authoritarian. The paths taken reflect the personalities of the respective leaders who came to power following the withdrawal of the French in 1954: Ngo Dinh Diem, the U.S.–backed president of South Vietnam, and Ho Chi Minh, the Chinese-backed head of state in communist North Vietnam. A conservative Catholic, Diem could not cope with modernity. Despite his Western education, he "had absorbed nothing of the scientific, positivist outlook of the West . . . [he] knew nothing about management, even less about economics" (*FL*, 149, 126). Diem likewise fails by the standard of tradition: "Diem was not truly a traditional leader—he was a reactionary, and like so many reactionaries, he idealized the past and misconceived the present" (*FL*, 125). Completely out of touch with the culture of the people, Diem, with U.S. support, continued the French "centralized strategy for modernization" that had disrupted traditional Vietnamese village life and incited previous anticolonial revolts. Displacing people to the cities, Diem's plan for "national development constituted little more than a refugee program" (*FL*, 180–81).

Unlike leaders of the South, who served as puppets for U.S. interests, Ho followed a centuries-old Vietnamese tradition of resisting Chinese political domination by asserting the distinctiveness of Vietnamese "habits and customs." Ho conceived his country's relation to Communist China in terms of the application of "the universal truth of Marxism-Leninism" to the particular situation of Vietnam (*FL*, 47–48). Ho, more than "all the analyses of the American social scientists," understood the need for Vietnamese solutions to Vietnamese problems (*FL*, 134). Ho, more than his "democratic" counterparts in the South, understood that the path to modernity must begin with the people in the villages.

Fitzgerald attributes much of the failure of U.S. military efforts to the cultural "Politics of the Earth" practiced by the National Liberation Front, the South Vietnamese communist insurgent organization inspired and supported by Ho's regime in the North. Following Ho's example, NLF insurgents

> built from the base of the country up, beginning among the ruins of the villages and with the dispossessed masses of the people. Because the landlords and the sol-

diers with their foreign airplanes owned the surface of the earth, the guerillas went underground in both the literal and the metaphorical sense. Settling down among the people who lived outside the sphere of modern technology, they dug tunnels beneath the villages, giving the people a new defensive distance from the powers which reigned outside the village. The earth itself became their protection—the Confucian "face" which the village had lost when for the last time, its hedges had been torn down. (*FL,* 181)

Politically provocative as this favorable read of the NLF may have been in 1972, it speaks to the same populist, participatory values celebrated in *The Ugly American.* The growing sympathy among liberal intellectuals for the communist cause suggests less an ideological shift from democracy to communism than a perceived shift in the locus of a populist historical agency that transcends narrow ideological divisions.

The historical agency that Fitzgerald locates in the NLF represents an ideal synthesis of tradition and modernity:

As an archeologist might conclude from examination of the NLF's goods and tools, the guerrillas were attempting not to restore the old village but rather to make some connection between the world of the village and that of the cities. The land mine was in itself the synthesis. Made of high explosives and scrap metal—the waste of foreign cities—it could be manufactured by an artisan with the simplest of skills. A technically comprehensible object, it could be used for the absolutely comprehensible purpose of blowing the enemy soldiers off the face of the village earth. Having themselves manufactured a land mine, the villagers had a new source of power—an inner life to their community. In burying it—a machine—into the earth, they infused a new meaning into the old image of their society. The Diem regime had shown a few of them a way out of the village. The NLF had shown all of them a way back in, to remake the village with the techniques of the outside world. "Socialism"—xa hoi, as the Viet Minh and the NLF translated it—indicated to the Vietnamese peasantry that the revolution would entail no traumatic break with the past, no abandonment of the village earth and the ancestors. Instead of a leap into the terrifying unknown, it would be a fulfillment of the local village traditions that the foreigners had attempted to destroy. (*FL,* 181–82)

Here the land mine appears as a real-life manifestation of the fictional synthesis of technology and culture represented by Jeepo's water pump. For Fitzgerald, as for Lederer and Burdick, technology mediates between tradition and modernity and transforms peasants into creative historical agents.

The achievement of agency demanded a deeper intervention into the life of the village than that ventured by Diem or his U.S.–backed successors. Top-down modernization destroyed villages; bottom-up modernization remade villagers. Like European revolutionaries of the nineteenth century, the NLF faced the problem of traditional peasant fatalism. According to Fitzgerald, "the

Communists alone recognized this political passivity as a *psychological* problem amenable to a psychological solution" (*FL,* 211). The effort to "turn the
villagers into loyal partisans of the NLF was . . . a long project requiring political education and organization" (*FL,* 197). No simple exercise in mass
propaganda, this reeducation was a distinctly individualizing process imple-
mented through small group self-criticism sessions (*FL,* 256). The NLF understood that "to change a Vietnamese peasant into a soldier . . . was to change
the entire pattern of his life" (*FL,* 251). Accepting the dislocations of modernization, "the Front was not merely trying to restore the old villages. It was attempting to create a community of individuals rather than of families" (*FL,*
237). The NLF used this process of individuation to transform peasant energy
into a creative force with a distinctly modern locus of authority—the will of
the people (*FL,* 215). As a collective of self-authorizing subjects, Vietnamese
peasants entered "a new kind of family, a new form of social security" (*FL,*
237). For Fitzgerald, the political revolution in Vietnam flows from this more
basic cultural revolution in social identity.

Between these two paths to modernity represented by North and South Vietnam, Fitzgerald's sympathies clearly lie with the path pursued by Ho and the
NLF. *Fire in the Lake,* however, mirrors the divisions of Vietnam itself. Fitzgerald gives the final word not to the heroic cultural reintegration represented by
the NLF, but to the devastating cultural disintegration bequeathed by the U.S.
presence. Moving from the anthropology of Mus to the sociology of Zola,
Fitzgerald concludes her study with an apocalyptic vision of Saigon, an urban
wasteland of shantytowns, rag pickers, street urchins, and prostitutes. Bui Phat,
one of the oldest refugee quarters in Saigon, stands for the general cultural anarchy brought on by the war:

> Most of Bui Phat lives beyond the law, the electricity lines, and the water system. . . .
> On the streets of tin shacks that run straight as a surrealist's line past the runways and
> into the sand, babies play naked in the dust and rows of green combat fatigues hang
> over the barbed wire like dead soldiers. (*FL,* 534–35)

French colonialism destroyed the Vietnamese state and disrupted village life,
but the American war destroyed the land and the family. This "social death," more
so than the "physical death" of material devastation, marks the true significance
of the war:

> An American in Vietnam observes only the most superficial results of this sudden
> shift of population: the disease, the filth, the stealing, the air of disorientation about
> the people of the camps and the towns. What he cannot see are the connections
> within the mind and spirit that have been broken to create this human swamp. The

connections between the society and its product, between one man and another, between the nation and its own history—these are lost for these refugees. (*FL,* 538)

For these farmers, as for their distant ancestors, to leave the hamlet was to step off the brink of the known world. Brought up as the sons of Mr. X or Mr. Y, the inhabitants of such a place, they suddenly found themselves nameless people in a nameless mass where no laws held. They survived, and as the war went on outside their control, they brought up their children in this anarchic crowd. (*FL,* 539)

As rootless, alienated city dwellers, the refugees of Saigon embody the character traits of the protagonist of a nineteenth-century French novel, or a twentieth-century American intellectual, for that matter. No mere unfortunate consequence of the war, this personality type ultimately appears as a positive achievement in its own right.

In advancing the positive value of alienation, Fitzgerald moves from a critique of U.S. imperialism to a critique of the idiocy of rural life:

It was not, of course, the cities themselves that were at fault. To leave the village for the towns was for many Vietnamese far from a personal tragedy. In the 1940s and 1950s the enterprising young men left their villages voluntarily to join the armies or to find some employment in the towns. The balance of village life had long ago been destroyed, and, in any case, who was to say that the constant toil and small entertainment of a peasant's life was preferable even to the harshest existences in a city? To join the army was in fact to see the world; to move to a town was to leave a life of inevitability for one of possibility. Though, or perhaps because, the hold of the family and the land was so strong, it contained also its contradiction—the desire for escape, for the death of the father and the end of all the burdensome family obligations. (*FL,* 540)

Ironically, the very cultural blindness of American policy makers appears to have achieved the cultural ideal imagined by more sociologically sensitive commentators. It has, effectively if not efficiently, released those "energies so long pent up in the villages of Asia." For Fitzgerald, the "tragedy" of the Vietnam War lies in the violent means, not the modernist end.

In classic modernist fashion, this "end" is no real end but is itself a means. In the modern world, all is process. Fitzgerald conceives the shift from tradition to modernity as a move from "inevitability" to "possibility." The reintegration fostered by the NLF appears naive and simplistic compared to the bracing uncertainty of life among the street gangs and prostitutes of Saigon. Nameless people in a nameless mass, these rootless urban dwellers lack the comfort and security of the NLF. Naked and alone, they must name themselves for themselves. In this sense, the refugees of Saigon best approximate the existential subjectivity promoted by the cold war intellectual elite as the highest level of human consciousness. Of these brave new subjects, Fitzgerald concludes:

> Brought up to regard themselves as part of a larger enterprise—brought up to a world that would seem oppressive to most Westerners—they experience the life of the cities as a profound alienation, a division of self. "Even the bar girl," said one Vietnamese intellectual, "even the bar girl who now has the money, who lives in the city and no longer wants to return to the country, who is accustomed to independence and gets along very well, even she feels guilty. At bottom she does not feel easy with herself, even after five or ten years of such work. She feels there is something missing. To find it she will give up her independence and all the advantages she now possesses." (*FL,* 553–54)

Fitzgerald sees in Vietnam what Schlesinger saw in America: "a highly unstable condition—a vacuum that craves the oxygen of organized society." Her endorsement of "the discipline of the revolutionary community" against the available liberal alternatives should not obscure the more basic rejection of traditional social organization in favor of "independence" that links her work to the cold war liberal consensus (*FL,* 554). The "independent" Saigon bar girl is but a slightly earthier version of Benedict's westernized Japanese coeds—between two worlds, at home in neither.

Fitzgerald's conclusion reveals this alienation itself to be the common goal of revolution and development. Like Benedict, Fitzgerald draws on indigenous cultural symbols to naturalize a fundamentally Western conception of freedom. Fitzgerald takes her title from the *I Ching,* the Chinese Book of Changes, in which fire in the lake serves as "the image of revolution," or "the mental picture of change within the society." She concludes that "the moment has arrived for the narrow flame of revolution to cleanse the lake of Vietnamese society from the corruption and disorder of the American war." It is no small point that Fitzgerald here conflates the traditional meaning of revolution as circular movement, or restoration of order, with the modern linear sense of revolution as the creation of a new order. The Vietnamese do not "restore their country and their history to themselves" so much as they enter into the endless flux of history as a product of human making (*FL,* 554). Benedict at least explicitly acknowledges the manipulations involved in her rehabilitation of the Japanese symbols of the chrysanthemum and the sword. Fitzgerald here presents modern revolution as a timeless principle rooted in traditional Vietnamese culture itself. *Fire in the Lake,* even more than *The Chrysanthemum and the Sword,* reflects the enduring blindness of Western intellectuals who see their own ideal of freedom as latent in all peoples and cultures throughout the world.

2

Culture and Counterculture

Liberals and radicals alike saw in modernization the promise of an unprecedented expansion of human agency as well as the threat of unprecedented domination through large-scale, centralized bureaucracies. On the domestic front, this intellectual tension manifested itself most clearly in the widespread postwar discourse on "conformity." An analysis of two key texts from the cold war era reveals a general consensus against conformity that links the liberal "culture" of the 1950s to the radical "counterculture" of the 1960s. David Riesman's *The Lonely Crowd* (1950) presents the classic defense of the possibility of individual autonomy within modern mass society. Theodore Roszak's *The Making of a Counter Culture* (1969) presents the classic case for communal autonomy from the totalizing trends of modern mass society. Both works turn to cultural modernism as an antidote to vulgar social and economic modernization. Within this consensus on cultural modernism, the common privileging of the human subject as the locus of authority links the seemingly divergent trends of rationalism and mysticism to each other, as well as to the economic ideologies from which these aesthetic ideologies sought to distance themselves. Viewed in these terms, the vaunted generational revolt from the 1950s to the 1960s appears less the assertion of a whole new way of life than an insistence on the right to control the particular formulation of a shared value of autonomy.

The adjective "liberal" has given the consensus culture of the 1950s a political inflection that its leading proponents themselves consistently downplayed. At their most Manichean, liberal anticommunists refused to see the cold war in explicitly ideological terms. The alternatives facing the world were stark—freedom versus tyranny—but they were not ideological, in the sense of capitalism versus communism. Daniel Bell's 1960 essay, "The End of Ideology in the West," summed up a whole generation's thinking on the "political" stakes of the cold war. Bell's essay suggests less a consensus against communism than a consensus against politics. Bell writes in the mode of epitaph rather than polemic: "The end of ideology closes the book, intellectually speaking, on an era, the one of easy 'left' formulae for social change." Marxism bears the brunt of his postmortem only in that it was the dominant left formula of an era that has decidedly passed. Bell sees the end of ideology not only in the futility of the American communist left, but even in the official state socialism of the Soviet Union, China, and the new nations emerging from the breakup of the European colonial empires. The Soviet Union and China may serve as models for Third World liberation movements, but the "fascination these countries exert is no longer the old idea of the free society, but the new one of economic growth. . . . For the newly-risen countries, the debate is not over the merits of Communism—the content of that doctrine has long been forgotten by friends and foes alike."[1]

Still, Bell cautions against capitalist triumphalism, warning that "for some of the liberals of the West, 'economic development' has become a new ideology that washes away the memory of old disillusionments." The end of ideology marks the end of an older liberal progressivism as well. As Marxists must give up the romance of revolution, so liberals must give up the dream "that one can set down 'blueprints' and through 'social engineering' bring about a new utopia of social harmony."[2] At the dawn of a new era, Marxists and liberals alike must learn to live with disillusionment.

Bell's critique extends from politics to knowledge. He sees in the passing of ideology the end of not only the quasi-religious hope for world transformation but also the quasi-religious dependency on an "all inclusive system of comprehensive reality." The appeal of Marxism stands as only the most extreme case of a broader modern search for a "secular religion," an escape from freedom that relieves people of the responsibility "to confront individual issues on their individual merits." Such worldviews have proven to function as "ideological vending machine[s]" capable only of spitting out "the prepared formula." Against this "faith ladder" to social progress, Bell demands a more modest, empirical ladder: "a utopia has to specify *where* one wants to go, *how* to get there, the costs of the enterprise, and some realization of, and justification for, the determination of *who* is to pay." The subordination of utopian passion to bureaucratic proceduralism confounds the ideological claims of Marxists, free market liberals, and social planners alike. Bell presents the postwar Western consensus—"the acceptance of a Welfare State; the desireability of decentralized power; a system of mixed economy and of political pluralism"—as the residue of reality that remains after the elimination of all ideological distortions.[3] Postutopian, it is also, in a sense, postpolitical.

The adjective "liberal" reflects less a political than a moral heritage. The key "individual issue" for Bell is the issue of the individual. As Bell looks beyond the

West to the Third World, he retains the freedom of the individual as the single article of faith admissible to the empirical ladder of economic development. Thus, he reads the future of the non-Western world through the classical liberal alternatives of consent and coercion: "whether new societies can grow by building democratic institutions and allowing people to make choices—and sacrifices—voluntarily, or whether the new elites, heady with power, will impose totalitarian means to transform their countries." Bell locates the primary threat to this freedom not in communism but in the "new ideologies" of "Pan-Arabism, color, and nationalism." Waxing nostalgic, he concedes that the old ideologies such as Marxism at least spoke the language of universal freedom and equality; in contrast, the new "mass ideologies of Asia and Africa are parochial, instrumental, and created by political leaders."[4] The appeal to ancient blood ties and symbolic associations renders these ideologies dangerously immune to appeals based on the universal ideals of the Enlightenment.

Bell's account of ideology points to a broader ambivalence concerning the concept of culture. Cold war intellectuals promoted culture as a benign alternative to ideology, but both concepts clearly suggest the idea of an "all-inclusive system of comprehensive reality."[5] Distinctions between the "soft" conditioning power of culture and the "hard" controlling power of ideology employed by intellectuals of the time failed to hold up to close scrutiny. Bell's suspicion of Third World nationalism reflects a domestic concern among U.S. intellectuals for the revival of American nationalism in the general postwar celebration of the "American way of life." The popular appeal of Joseph McCarthy suggested a fascist potential in the patriotism reinvigorated by America's new role as leader of the free world. Less extreme, but more pervasive, the equation of the "American way of life" with the consumer paradise of middle-class suburbia suggested that cultural unity came at the cost of individual conformity. The white-collar white male skewered in popular works such as William Whyte's *The Organization Man* (1956) bore the symbolic brunt of the assault, but intellectuals across the political spectrum found conformity creeping into every aspect of American life. Ironically, these critics often traced the roots of this cultural conformity to economic affluence, that is, to the very economic development that intellectuals such as Bell proposed as an antidote to the irrational nationalisms of the Third World. With varying degrees of discontent, most intellectuals nonetheless affirmed a real moral distinction between conformist culture and totalitarian ideology and allowed for the possibility of individual freedom within the larger unity of American culture.

David Riesman's *The Lonely Crowd* (1950) remains the most ambitious and enduring of all the postwar commentaries on the problem of conformity in American life. A collaborative, "big science" attempt to bring empirical rigor to the study of the American character, the book nonetheless received praise from no less a critic than Lionel Trilling as a literary achievement surpassing most of the novels of the day. Universally praised by intellectual elites, it also became a popular best-seller, earning Riesman the cover of *Time* magazine in conjunction with the release of the paperback edition in 1954.[6] Riesman's contrast of the "inner-directed" and "other-directed" character types stands as the definitive formulation of two key analytic categories that still structure much historical and sociological writing on American culture. Initially misread as a lament for the passing of individualism and subsequently misread as a naive endorsement of the continuing possibilities for individualism, the book is best read as a sociological expression of the stoic, existential progressivism characteristic of the most sophisticated midcentury modernist intellectuals. Ambivalent as to the actual state of "the changing American character," Riesman argues for awareness of the fundamental instability of all modern social relations as a mode of consciousness that transcends the ironies and complexities of any particular national character.

Normatively and analytically, Riesman writes very much in the Boasian humanist tradition of Margaret Mead and Ruth Benedict. Moral as well as intellectual imperatives drove Riesman to begin the work that would become *The Lonely Crowd*. With America at war with the avowedly racist and anti-Semitic regime of Nazi Germany, Riesman, like many concerned intellectuals, turned to social science to explain, in the jargon of the times, "the social psychology of defamation."[7] Psychologists working in this field turned to Boasian anthropology not only because cultural relativism provided a powerful argument for social tolerance but also because the concept of cultural patterning suggested a fruitful way of connecting individual psychology to a broader social environment.

The claim that each cultural part illuminates a cultural whole easily slid into the notion that each part stands for the whole. The "Culture and Personality" school of social psychology thus took the individual as a microcosm of the whole culture. Social scientists of this school took the term "character," previously applied mainly to the individual, and transferred it to culture; thus, the "American culture" and "American character" concepts came to be used interchangeably. During the mid-1940s, Riesman adopted the culture-and-personality approach as the basis for a unified, interdisciplinary curriculum that he helped design for the social science program at the College of the University of Chicago. Moving to Yale in 1947, he assembled a team of like-minded social scientists, including Nathan Glazer and Reuel Denney, dedicated to bringing this interdisciplinary perspective to bear on a solidly empirical study of contemporary American life.

The organizing category of "social character" most clearly betrays *The Lonely Crowd's* debt to the Culture and Personality school. Riesman defines social character as "the more or less permanent socially and historically conditioned organization of an individual's drives and satisfactions—the kind of 'set' with which he approaches the world and people" (*LC,* 4). He departs from previous national character studies by his emphasis on historical change, presenting three distinct character types reflecting three distinct historical epochs. The first, the "tradition-directed" character, stands for the "set" of the preindustrial West and the underdeveloped regions of contemporary Asia, Africa, and Latin America. The individual in such traditional cultures "learns to understand and appreciate patterns which have endured for centuries." Traditional cultures orient the individual to these "unchanging values" through "ritual, routine, and religion." The individual in these cultures "tends to reflect his membership in a particular age-grade, clan, or caste" and does not generally seek to develop any unique individuality (*LC,* 11).

The second, the "inner-directed" character, stands for the individuals of nineteenth-century Europe and America who forsook the "rigid social organization" of traditional societies for the "highly individualized character" of modern bourgeois societies. According to Riesman, "*the source of direction for the individual is 'inner' in the sense that it is implanted early in life by elders and directed toward generalized but nonetheless inescapably destined goals*" (*LC,* 15). The individual in such a society has greater freedom to choose goals, provided he pursues those goals with the ferocious, procedural discipline best captured by Max Weber's concept of the Protestant work ethic. The third type, the "other-directed" character, stands for the contemporary West, in particular the white American middle class. For this character, fixed goals and self-control give way to multiple goals and social control: "*What is common to all the other-directed people is that their contemporaries are the source of direction for the individual,*" and the "*goals toward which the other-directed person strives shift with that guidance.*" In such a culture, "*the process of striving itself and the process of paying close attention to the signals from others*" provides the only constant in the life of the individual (*LC,* 21).

True to the book's stated focus on "Western man since the Middle Ages," the tradition-directed type quickly drops out of the analysis (*LC,* 6). Most of the book focuses on the shift from the inner-directed to the other-directed through a variety of colorful, lively case studies drawn from contemporary American life, particularly the turbulent world of the adolescent peer group. From these studies flow a series of transitions—from morality to morale, from the invisible hand to the glad hand, etc.—that have entered into the common vocabulary of educated Americans.

Universally well received, the book was generally misperceived as a lament for the passing of a solid, productive individualism in the face of a fluid, consumer conformism. Riesman vigorously denied this "moral" interpretation and reasserted the analytic neutrality of the character orientations. The misinterpretation reflects popular anxiety concerning conformity more than any willful ambiguity in the text. Riesman insists early on that each neutral character type contains the more normatively weighted possibilities of conformity and creativity (*LC*, 6). Riesman clearly favors creativity over conformity and believes it to be just as possible in contemporary other-directed societies as in earlier inner-directed ones. He supplements his three character types with three subtypes that exist as possibilities within each general orientation. The first subtype, the "adjusted," refers to individuals "who reflect their society . . . with the least distortion." Such persons "fit the culture as though they were made for it" (*LC*, 241–42). The adjusted come closest to the popular understanding of conformity. The second, the "anomic," refers to those who do not conform to the dominant character type and also appear "constitutionally and psychologically unable to conform or feel comfortable in the roles such a society assigns to its regularly recurring deviants" (*LC*, 42–43). Nonconformist to the point of alienation, the anomic often descend into socially pathological behavior. The third type, the "autonomous," "may or may not conform outwardly, but whatever his choice, he pays less of a price, and he has a choice: he can meet both the culture's definitions of adequacy and those which (to a still culturally determined degree) slightly transcend the norms for the adjusted" (*LC*, 242–43).

Through most of the book, Riesman remains genuinely sanguine about the possibilities of autonomy for the contemporary other-directed individual; at one point he even praises the increased mechanization of consumption represented by the vending machine as an emancipatory antidote to the manipulative tendencies of other-directed, "glad-handing" salesmen (*LC*, 271–72). Still, most readers equated autonomy with inner-direction and saw Riesman's selective endorsement of contemporary consumerism as a desperate contradiction of his account of the triumph of conformity over individualism.

The conflicting interpretations of Riesman reflect his own conflicting interpretations of American culture. Against cultural elitism, Riesman defends the "creative although as yet uncodified elements in American popular culture." Against cultural populism, he warns of "the danger that *The Lonely Crowd* could be read as an invitation to intellectuals to go slumming in the mass media, and to patronize rather than seek to alter the folksy pursuits of the semi-educated" (*LC*, xiii). I read these seeming contradictions less as evidence of Riesman's personal ambivalence than as symptomatic of a dialectical mode of reasoning that structures most of *The Lonely Crowd*. In one of the more ironic, self-reflexive instances of this dialectical structure, Riesman introduces a chapter on "obstacles to autonomy in play" with the suggestion that the chapter itself may be one such obstacle:

Is it sensible to suggest research into play when it is possible that it would lead to increasing public and systematic interference with an area that ideally deserves privacy and lack of system? Perhaps a conspiracy of silence about leisure and play is its best protection? (*LC*, 277)

And perhaps not, for Riesman of course goes on to break the very silence he suggests. Were the above passage a sign of a serious crisis of conscience, Riesman could not have written so fine a work of sociology.

The seeming contradictions that frustrated contemporary critics appear on closer examination to be a consistent strategy of ironic juxtaposition that itself stands as a sign of autonomy.[8] Riesman never acknowledges this strategy as clearly as he identifies his categories. Still, his questioning of the very attempt to study popular culture reflects his own criteria for other-directed autonomy. For Riesman, "the autonomous at all times have been questioners." The autonomous among the inner-directed had only to question received traditions, whereas "the autonomous among the other-directed live in a milieu in which people systematically question themselves in anticipation of the questions of others." Thus, "someone who today refuses 'to bend the knee to custom' is tempted to ask himself: 'Is this what I really want? Perhaps I only want it because . . .'" (*LC,* 256). Critics tended to view such passages as expressions of despair. Riesman, in contrast, clearly endorses such hyper self-reflexivity as a positive advance to a new level of self-awareness.

Riesman enacts this autonomous self-questioning nowhere more than in his retrospective assessment of *The Lonely Crowd*. In the preface to the 1961 paperback edition, he concedes any and all criticisms of the original study: his national character approach did tend to encourage overgeneralization, and his conclusions, to the extent that they were valid at all, applied mainly to the white, salaried, professional middle class. His emphasis on culture unjustly minimized the persistence of inequities of political power, and he drastically underestimated the ability of the struggle for racial justice to provide a "cause" for which to take a passionate political stand (*LC,* xvii, xxxv, xlvii). These concessions made, Riesman defends his general approach against any specific conclusions. The scientific community must inevitably move beyond his earlier conclusions, but *The Lonely Crowd* still merits recognition for its contribution to the general advance of knowledge. Adopting the role of an aging pioneer, Riesman counts himself among those "brave adventurers," like Margaret Mead and Ruth Benedict, who sought to bring holistic thinking to bear on the study of modern society (*LC,* xii).[9] Anthropology and psychology proved appealing for the attention they gave to "previously neglected or underprivileged data," the stuff of everyday life (*LC,* xiv). The "massiveness of process and output" of contemporary social science represents a logical development of Riesman's earlier search for new data, but it has also worked to undermine his earlier search for holistic generalizations (*LC,* xii).

Riesman's quick run through the previous fifteen years of social science is a model of the comfortable, progressive nihilism of so many cold war intellectuals. He recounts how he turned to Freudian psychology to augment the deficiencies

of history, political science, and economics with respect to the role of psychological factors in social change. Freudian psychoanalysis, however, "assumed too
readily . . . what is basic or 'primary' in a particular culture," so Riesman turned
to the neo-Freudian work of Erich Fromm, which applied "a socially oriented
psychoanalytic characterology to problems of historical change" (*LC,* xiv). This
neo-Freudian influence manifested itself most significantly in Riesman's turn
from issues of infantile sexuality to the role of the adolescent peer group in the
shaping of character. In retrospect, this revision appears to Riesman as yet another simplistic determinism: "*The Lonely Crowd*, emphasizing as it does the role
of the peer group and the school in adolescence in the formation of character, perhaps itself underestimates the possibility of change as the result of the experience
of adulthood" (*LC,* xv).

Against this increasingly fluid conception of character, even a constant such as
human nature appears as a constraint. Thus, he accepts that "we may indeed be
coming to the end of the human story," with little choice but "to get rid of the
'problem of man' in the social sciences" (*LC,* xxv).[10] Riesman deflects this ni-
hilist trajectory less with assurances concerning the future than with a commitment, in the present, to "openness, pluralism, and empiricism" against "dogmatism and fanaticism," an ability to maintain a critical tension between overarching
concepts and the integrity of individual experience (*LC,* xxxiii, xvii).

The common criticisms of *The Lonely Crowd*, and Riesman's response to them,
reveal a consensus deeper than that suggested by the bland liberal value of mod-
eration. The "bias" of *The Lonely Crowd* is nothing less than the bias of modernity against tradition. Though initially presented as a major analytic category, the
"tradition-directed" character receives very little attention from Riesman and was
virtually ignored in the general public debate over his assessment of conformity.[11]
The descriptive irony that Riesman maintains in the face of the consumer regimentation of the peer group gives way to finger-wagging moralism in those few
instances when he actually addresses the persistence of relatively more traditional
social relations such as the ethnic group and the family. He reserves his harshest
criticism for the "neo-traditionalists" who "would like to freeze people into communities in which friendships will be based largely on propinquity" (*LC,* 278). He
allows for a thin cultural pluralism in which ethnics "add to the variety of the nation by retaining the colorful flavors of their 'racial heritages'" but attacks those
ethnic leaders who would restrict the social life of their constituencies "to a single culture" (*LC,* 284). This thick cultural pluralism amounts to an attempt "to
force roots upon the masses" and deny them "the privileges of modern life" (*LC,*
264, 278). Such "enforced privatization" threatens autonomy by imposing "restrictions . . . that keep people from adequate opportunities for leisure, including
friendships" (*LC,* 264).

The family looms large as another potential site of enforced privatization. Much as Betty Friedan would later argue in *The Feminine Mystique,* Riesman criticizes the isolation of the suburban home for cutting women off from "friendship markets" and for generally stunting the personal and intellectual development that would enhance their compatibility with their more worldly husbands (*LC,* 283). Traditional family life must give way to "a new model of marriage that finds its opportunity precisely in the choices that a free-divorce, leisure society opens up" (*LC,* 281). Freedom from these traditional constraints serves as a necessary, if not sufficient, precondition for autonomy.

This bias against tradition should be understood in structural rather than personal terms. Its source lies less in Riesman's particular prejudices than in his fundamentally sociological understanding of contemporary life: "The problem for people in America today is other people . . . other figures in the landscape—nature itself, the cosmos, the Deity—have retreated to the background or disappeared" (*LC,* xxi). That Riesman assumes rather than proves the marginal social status of these "other figures" is beside the point; the questionable status of autonomy as a social "fact" in no way diminishes its status as a social "value" to be pursued with all of the methodological rigor available to the modern social sciences. Autonomy, and the problem of conformity, become central social "facts" only after one accepts the value of the death of God and nature. This death gave birth to sociology, which replaced the sacred story of pilgrimage toward God with the secular story of the progress of man. Riesman allows for a potentially infinite variety of paths to autonomy, provided these paths lead away from traditional orientations toward God and nature. Sociology as a discipline contains "openness, pluralism, and empiricism" only within the confines of this narrative of the ascent from tradition to modernity. Tradition thus marks the limit of liberal tolerance.

The normative trajectory of autonomy becomes clear when Riesman turns his sociological gaze to "a world unsettled by the drastic message written in the sky above all countries: 'You, too, can be modern and industrial'" (*LC,* xxiii). Much like Benedict on Japan, Riesman allows the comparatively traditional societies of the non-Western world the freedom to develop in ways consistent with their indigenous traditions. Unlike Benedict, he warns:

> This is not to say that those leaders of the "developing" peoples are correct who believe that they can retain their unique cultural or racial tradition while also going "modern"; as many are poignantly aware, the effective means they employ tend to become their own ends, so that one can foresee eventual supersession of the regionally distinct religions and cultures which once were created and carried, if not unequivocally cherished, by people of very different social character. Against these means and against the hope of power and plenty (and at times as revenge against those who had previously monopolized these), traditional values fight everywhere a

rearguard action, buttressed by decaying institutions and the ineffectively recalcitrant social character of the older generation. (*LC,* xxiv)

Like Bell, Riesman views the Third World in terms of nationalism and modernization rather than communism and democracy; unlike Bell, he has more confidence in the inexorable progress of modernity. With more than a little irony, Riesman observes that

> relics of parochialism can persist—although as soon as a group or tribe seeks to protect its unique historical legacy by a nativist or revivalist movement, this very effort betokens the end of unself-conscious, taken-for-granted rituals, and hence paradoxically speeds initiation into the modern world. . . . Modernization thus appears to proceed with an almost irreversible impact, and no tribe or nation has found a place to hide. (*LC,* xxviii–xxix)

Beyond their own inherent logical contradictions, neotraditionalism and nationalism suffer from the irresistible appeal of explicitly nontraditional, modern materialism:

> To repeat: the most important passion left in the world is not for distinctive practices, cultures, and beliefs, but for certain achievements—the technology and organization of the West—whose immediate consequence is the dissolution of all distinctive practices, cultures, and beliefs. (*LC,* xxviii)

Riesman here rewrites a nineteenth-century imperial narrative of progress in a distinctly twentieth-century, social-scientific idiom. The West leads no longer through distinctive-yet-universal values but through distinctive-yet-universal techniques that undermine all distinctive, particular values. Within the global consensus on modernity, "technology and organization" unite East and West in a common assault on their respective traditions. National character, the modern successor to tradition as the bearer of cultural distinction, now faces a similar assault. Given the inexorable logic of modernization, "it is possible that the cast of national characters is finished" (*LC,* xxviii). Even as Riesman reaffirms the liberal vision of a world made safe for differences, the locus of difference increasingly recedes from view.

For Riesman, the passing of national character leaves the personal quest for identity as the primary site for the flourishing of pluralism and tolerance. Riesman sees in "the current preoccupation with identity in this country (notable in the great impact of Erik H. Erikson's work)" the stirrings of a freedom beyond all "characterological necessity" (*LC,* xlviii). The passing of "the widely variegated *social* character types of an un-unified world" signals the dawn of a new era of "the even more widely divergent *individual* character of a unified but less oppressive world" (*LC,* xxv). The quest for identity combines the solid, producerist virtues of inner-direction with the fluid, consumerist values of other-direction; it offers an opportunity "to focus on individual character development the puritan demands no longer needed to spur industrial and political organization," yet allows "individuals to shape their own character by their selection among models and experiences," particularly those that liberate them from "the provinciality of being born to a particular family in a particular place" (*LC,* 297, xlviii). This individual ethic of disciplined choice provides the basis for a broader social transformation from traditional ties "of blood and soil" to modern "ties based on conscious relatedness" (*LC,* xlviii). The popular success of *The Lonely Crowd* points to social science, now "part of our common understanding," as the empirical ladder of ascent to this social ideal (*LC,* xxix, xiii).

Then as now, dispute over the role of social science in the practical achievement of this ideal has obscured the consequences of the underlying shared consensus on the value of autonomy as a social ideal. C. Wright Mills, the leading American radical voice of the 1950s, proved incapable of imagining an alternative to the vision of economic and personal development promoted by liberals such as Bell and Riesman. His *White Collar* (1951) marked one of the angriest entries into the debate on conformity, while his *The Power Elite* (1956) reminded complacent pluralists of the persistence of dangerous inequities of political power.[12] Despairing of radical change in America, Mills eventually placed his hopes in the liberation movements of the Third World, particularly the Cuban revolution led by Fidel Castro. Politically provocative as his support for Marxist regimes may have been in the heat of the cold war, his social vision appears, in retrospect, indistinguishable from that of the hated liberal consensus: for Mills, Third World revolution pointed the way toward a "properly developing society" that would make possible "a variety of human beings, of styles of life, perhaps never before seen in human history."[13] Despite his untimely death in 1962, Mills inspired a new generation of student activists to put his "radical" critique into practice.

The New Left of the 1960s followed Mills all too well in failing to transcend the social categories of the much maligned liberal consensus. The 1962 Port Huron Statement, issued by the Students for a Democratic Society (SDS), attacked "the depersonalization that reduces human beings to the status of things" in the name of the quite conventionally liberal values of "human independence" and freedom to pursue "a meaning in life that is personally authentic." The vaunted ideal of "participatory democracy"—the insistence "that the individual share in those social decisions determining the quality and direction of his life"—appears in retrospect as a more stridently individualistic formulation of an otherwise conventional pluralist procedural norm.[14] The New Left followed Mills in the move from social criticism to political revolution, but the endorsement of violent means did little to alter the essentially liberal ends of economic development and individual liberation.

Still, the 1960s clearly *look* different from the 1950s. The difference, however, flows less from the political radicalism of the New Left than from the related, yet distinct, cultural radicalism of the "counterculture." The radical cultural movements of the 1960s had their roots in the 1950s as well but drew on literary and religious sources marginal to the dominant rationalism of the liberal/radical consensus. Beat Generation writers such as Allen Ginsberg and Jack Kerouac rejected the rigid formalism of the newly orthodox high modernism in favor of an ideal of spontaneous literary expression modeled on the improvisational style of African-American jazz musicians. The Beats extended the revolt against conformity to a deeper assault on the intellectual foundations of modernity, embracing the mystical traditions of Eastern religions as an alternative to the scientific rationalism of the West. This turn to the East received a more rigorous philosophical explication in a series of books on Zen Buddhism by the psychologist and Asian scholar Alan Watts.

The literary/religious assault on reason received further impetus from the discovery of psychedelic drugs that opened the "doors of perception" (in Aldous Huxley's famous phrase) to an experiential world that could not be contained within the boundaries of even the most radical political program. In the early 1960s, the author Ken Kesey began his West Coast experiments in utopian community living organized around LSD and rock music. Kesey's radicalism had very little to do with the social justice idealism of the early New Left, and the Dadaist tactics of his "Merry Pranksters" led to hostile confrontations with SDS–style activists at the few protests he chose to attend.[15] As the 1960s wore on, the rational, political New Left splintered into warring factions while the intentionally splintering, apolitical counterculture spread across America and promised a new mystical unity based on sex, drugs, and rock 'n' roll.

Critical intellectuals accustomed to bemoaning conformity quickly rushed in to explain this apparent outbreak of mass nonconformity. The counterculture found its most sophisticated and sympathetic defender in Theodore Roszak. In *The Making of a Counter Culture* (1969), Roszak dissents from the general intellectual skepticism of his peers to argue for the counterculture as an authentic and necessary rebellion against the oppressive rationalism of modern "technocratic society."[16] No mere generational revolt, the "youthful opposition" of the counterculture marks an epochal shift away from the modern scientific worldview that Roszak brands the "myth of objective consciousness" (*MCC*, 205). What begins as a reawakening to God, however, ends as a reaffirmation of man. Roszak rescues nature from the objective consciousness of science only to subject it to a "*consciousness* consciousness" which, as much as modern science, recognizes no limits to the existential act of self creation (*MCC,* 62).

From the start, Roszak's formulation of the problem of technocracy betrays his debt to his consensus adversaries. Technocracy appears as the evil twin of modernization:

> By the technocracy, I mean that social form in which an industrial society reaches the peak of its organizational integration. It is the ideal men usually have in mind when they speak of modernizing, up-dating, rationalizing, planning. Drawing upon such unquestionable imperatives as the demand for efficiency, for social security, for large-scale co-ordination of men and resources, for ever higher levels of affluence and ever more impressive manifestations of collective human power, the technocracy works to knit together the anachronistic gaps and fissures of the industrial society . . . . Politics, education, leisure, entertainment, culture as a whole, the unconscious drives, and even . . . protest against the technocracy itself: all these become the subjects of purely technical scrutiny and purely technical manipulations. (*MCC,* 5–6)

In Roszak's account, the beneficent social scientist of *The Lonely Crowd* becomes the authoritarian expert seeking to extend technical control into "even the most seemingly personal aspects of life" (*MCC,* 7). The ideal of enlightened individual autonomy masks a sinister reality of social control. Against this technical ideal, Roszak proclaims the obsolescence of all political ideologies. He declares Marxism to be "the mirror image of bourgeois industrialism," to the detriment of both (*MCC,* 100). All class-based political movements fail to transcend the economic logic of mass production and consumption. Race, the leading candidate for successor to class, offers no alternative. The civil rights movement has degenerated into a "forceful, indignant campaign fixated on the issue of integrating the excluded into the general affluence" (*MCC,* 13). Its "radical" successor, black power, has proven itself to be "as culturally old-fashioned as the nationalist mythopoesis of the nineteenth century," offering no more than rearguard resistance to the industrial status quo (*MCC,* xii). Acknowledging the seriousness of racial inequality, poverty, and the Vietnam War, Roszak nonetheless rejects the standard New Left response to these problems as itself complicit in the logic of technocracy.

Like his technocratic opponents, Roszak reserves some of his harshest criticisms for Marxism. In reviewing the available resources for the development of an authentic counterculture, Roszak first addresses the work of the leading Marxist intellectual of the postwar era, Herbert Marcuse. Marcuse's sophisticated synthesis of Marx and Freud proved particularly appealing to the middle-class, existential rebels of the New Left. His concept of "repressive tolerance" provided a rallying slogan for the critique of a liberal ideal of freedom that "encourages nonconformity and letting-go in ways which leave the real engines of repression in the society entirely intact."[17] Roszak concedes his own debt to Marcuse's work and cites approvingly Marcuse's critique of, among other practices, a *Playboy*-style sexual liberation that infantilizes women and promotes middle-class consumerism (*MCC*, 14–15).

On closer examination, however, Roszak finds that "Marcuse's hope for a non-repressive civilization derives from the growing affluence of industrial society" (*MCC*, 108). Like any good Victorian, Marcuse accepts that some individual repression is necessary for social order and progress; similarly, he attacks "surplus repression" in the name of a conception of freedom ultimately indistinguishable from "John Stuart Mill's notion of civil liberty" (*MCC*, 112–13). Marcuse's encounter with the dark forces of the Freudian unconscious, in turn, amounts to "little more than filling in the psychological totals in the same old political ledger" (*MCC*, 117). For Marcuse as much as for Mill, politics is "the struggle against injustice, against oppression, against privilege," and psychoanalysis only serves to remind us "that injustice is mental, as well as physical, cruelty" (*MCC*, 117). According to Roszak, Marcuse's concern for social justice legitimizes the spread of technocratic domination through expanded mental health services (*MCC*, 118–19).

Roszak departs from consensus thinkers by attacking this kind of Marxist critique not for its quasi-religious, millennial utopianism but for its "adamant secularism." Marcuse stands accused of complicity in technocracy by virtue of "the stubbornly and conventionally secular character of his thinking," his near total "opposition to any religious conception of transcendence" (*MCC*, 118). His Victorian-rationalist suspicion of "any form of transcendence that threatens to flee the glaring oppressions and long-suffering of mankind" allows for no cultural alternative to the technical, problem-solving orientation of technocracy itself. The rejection of transcendence denies the "ever-present sacramental dimension of life" and reduces the natural and social world to mere instrumentalities subject to the arbitrary manipulations of experts (*MCC*, 119).

The critical standard of religious transcendence shifts the critique of technocracy from surface social institutions to a deep, underlying, intellectual structure of thought: the scientific worldview. Roszak insists that "technocracy is not simply a power structure wielding vast material influence; it is the expression of a grand cultural imperative, a veritable mystique that is deeply endorsed by the populace" (*MCC*, xiv). This imperative, which Roszak names "the myth of objective consciousness," claims that there "is but one way of gaining access to reality . . . and this is to cultivate a state of consciousness cleansed of all subjective distortion, all personal involvement" (*MCC*, 208). Inseparable from modern philosophy in general, the myth of objective consciousness "begins in the spirit of the Cartesian zero, with the doubting away of all inherited knowledge in favor of an entirely new *method* of knowing, which, whether it proceeds on rationalist or empiricist lines, purports to begin from scratch free of all homage to authority" (*MCC,* 213).

Less a worldview than a way of viewing the world, objective consciousness rejects all normative ordering principles in nature for three procedural norms imposed on the perceiving subject. The first norm, the "alienative dichotomy," requires the thinker "to know without becoming involved in or committed to that which is being known." The second, "the invidious hierarchy," sees the subjective mind of the knower as "the center of reliable knowledge" over against the world, which must be approached "*as if* it were completely stupid . . . without intention or wisdom or purposeful pattern," knowable only in terms of what can be "observed, measured, and—ideally—formulated into articulate, demonstrable propositions for experimental verification." Finally, the third norm, "the mechanistic imperative," demands the reduction of life to clock-like routine and regularity in the service of maximum control (*MCC,* 217–18, 221–22, 227–28). Against the secular rationalist critique of technocracy as a corruption of the emancipatory potential of objective consciousness, Roszak critiques technocracy as the logical consequence of "two centuries of aggressive secular skepticism" inspired by the scientific revolution (*MCC,* 13).

Roszak sees the counterculture as a fundamentally religious revolt, an attempt to reconnect the social world to "the traditionally transcendent ends of life" banished from view by objective consciousness (*MCC,* 13). Unlike previous religious revivals in America, however, the counterculture is decidedly non-Christian. Roszak accepts the secular Enlightenment critique of "institutionalized religion" and confidently asserts: "Indeed, we are a post-Christian era" (*MCC,* 262, 138). He sees in the counterculture a "new, eclectic religious revival" that draws inspiration primarily from the mystical traditions of Eastern religions and the new experiments with psychedelic drugs (*MCC,* 138). Roszak acknowledges the "fraudulence and folly" of much of the counterculture's pop mysticism: the "wise silence" counseled by Zen Buddhism "can easily ally with the moody inarticulateness of youth," while drugs such as LSD can promote a kind of push-button substitute for genuine enlightenment (*MCC,* 38, 134). Cautious and tentative in his assessment of particular religious experiments, he locates the significance of the counterculture in its general reorientation of the terms of cultural revolt:

For all its frequently mindless vulgarity, for all its tendency to get lost amid the exotic clutter, there is a powerful and important force at work in this wholesale willingness of the young to scrap our culture's entrenched prejudice against myth, religion, and ritual. (*MCC,* 145)

> For what they are groping their way toward through all their murky religiosity is an absolutely critical distinction. The truth of the matter is: no society, not even our severely secularized technocracy, can ever dispense with mystery and magical ritual. These are the very bonds of social life, the inarticulate assumptions and motivations that weave together the collective fabric of society and which require periodic collective affirmation. (*MCC,* 148)

Unlike the comparatively esoteric mysticism of the Beats, the religiosity of the counterculture seeks to be inclusive and communal. The "sheer size of the population it potentially involves" suggests "a significant new culture a-borning among our youth" (*MCC,* 38). The old mysticism may have been counter, but the new mysticism is a culture.

Roszak's explicit rejection of Christianity and science belies the fundamentally Western and modern nature of his religious revivalism. The Reformation began the assault on "myth" and ritual within Christianity.[18] The secular Enlightenment extended this assault to encompass the lingering magical elements within Protestantism, only to have its stringent rationalism called into question by the Romantic movement. Even as Romantic thinkers questioned the Enlightenment assault on myth, they accepted the Enlightenment ideal of man as the maker of his world; thus, Romantics recovered the meanings and values of the premodern world as raw material for their own personal acts of self-creation. Post-Romantic attempts to reenchant the world have repeatedly issued in a similar enchantment of the self.

Roszak's contrast between the "bad" magic of technocracy and the "good" magic of the counterculture suggests the persistence of this pattern:

> There is one magic that seeks to open and vitalize the mind, another that seeks to diminish and delude. There are rituals which are imposed from on high for the sake of invidious manipulation; there are other rituals in which men participate democratically for the purpose of freeing the imagination and exploring self-expression. There are mysteries which, like the mysteries of state, are no better than dirty secrets; but there are also mysteries which are encountered by the community (if such exists) in a stance of radical equality, and which are meant to be shared in for the purpose of enriching life by experiences of awe and splendor. (*MCC,* 148)

Here the evaluative criteria lie not in the substantive truth embodied in a particular ritual or mystery, but in the quality of the conditions for the creation of and participation in any ritual or mystery. For Roszak, authentic ritual involves democratic participation; authentic mystery requires "a stance of radical equality." The goal of authentic ritual and mystery is "to open and vitalize the mind" and free "the imagination." Ultimately, Roszak's attempt to summon divine otherness through repeated evocations of "experiences of awe and splendor" falters on his repeated translations of ancient mysticism into the modern, secular idiom of egalitarian "self-expression." The spiritual turn to non-Western religions, like the earlier anthropological turn to non-Western cultures, merely serves to revitalize a very Western Romantic individualism.

The Romantic trajectory of Roszak's argument is implicit in his evasive agnosticism toward the account of the physical world presented by modern science. Drawing on Thomas Kuhn's *The Structure of Scientific Revolutions,* Roszak historicizes, and thus relativizes, scientific objectivity. More so than Kuhn, he sees the demythologizing animus of science as itself a mythology, "an arbitrary construct in which a given society in a given historical situation has invested its sense of meaningfulness and value" (*MCC,* 215). Still, awareness of the contingency of science points Roszak not to the world but to the self: "it is the psychology and not the epistemology of science that urgently requires our critical attention; for it is primarily at this level that the most consequential deficiencies and imbalances of the technocracy are revealed" (*MCC,* 217). Roszak traces the distortions of the scientific worldview to "the deep personality structure of the ideal scientist," the basic incapacity of the scientist to experience "joy" and "intensive personal involvement" (*MCC,* 215, 229).

As worldview becomes a matter of personality, so culture becomes merely a matter of consciousness. Roszak speaks of the rise of the counterculture as a shift from "an egocentric and cerebral mode of consciousness" to "a new culture in which the non-intellective capacities of the personality—those capacities that take fire from visionary splendor and the experience of human communion—become the arbiters of the good, the true, and the beautiful" (*MCC,* 50–51). A move from surface to depth, from quantity to quality, Roszak's formulation of transition fails to articulate any normative framework within which to judge the good, the true, and the beautiful. All but conceding the disenchantment of the world, Roszak, as much as any secular modernist, looks to the self as the source of "transcendent" truth.

True to Roszak's anthropocentric orientation, his quest for an alternative way of life takes him from cosmology to sociology. Roszak traces the revolt against the scientific worldview through the rise of psychoanalysis, mysticism, and psychedelic drugs, but he gives pride of place to the "visionary sociology" of Paul Goodman (*MCC,* 178). Goodman is both an obvious and curious choice for leading prophet of the counterculture. Of all the radical critics of the 1950s, he most directly and consistently conceived of the problem of conformity as a problem of youth. His best-known work, *Growing Up Absurd: Problems of Youth in the Organized System* (1960), proved prophetic in its anticipation of youth as the new

vanguard for radical social change; still, it offers a conventionally, even strenu-
ously, modern account of that social change. Goodman insists that the problems
of American society "are by no means inherent in modern technological or eco-
logical conditions" but follow "from the betrayal and neglect of the old radical-
liberal program."[19] Like most radicals of the time, he supplements this old program with the new themes of alienation and authenticity; unlike many of his
fellow critics, however, he does look beyond individual autonomy to "the miss-
ing community" as a necessary support for the existential search for meaning. For
Roszak, "it is Goodman's communitarianism which is, finally, his greatest and
most directly appreciated contribution to contemporary youth culture" (*MCC*,
200). If the counterculture is to establish itself as a whole way of life, its "fren-
zied and often pathetic experiments in community will simply have to succeed"
(*MCC*, 204). In Roszak's account; however, community suffers the same trajectory as mysticism—from the other to the self.

Goodman's visionary sociology appears little more than a reflection of his visionary personality. In keeping with his preference for the "non-intellective capacities of the personality," Roszak explicates Goodman's vision through his fiction rather than his more conventionally sociological studies such as *Growing Up
Absurd*. The following rhapsodic appreciation suggests awe before the creative
act of fiction itself, apart from any specific fiction created:

> It is essentially from his literary background that Goodman brings the gift of vision to
> his criticism, the inexhaustible capacity to imagine new social possibilities. Where our
> conventional sociology settles, in an attitude of premature senility, for analyzing struc-
> tures and rearranging functions, Goodman restores social innovation to a position of
> pre-eminence. It is hardly surprising that one who thinks as a novelist and poet should
> do so. The artist who sets about making a critique of social ills is bound to play the role
> of utopian: one who cannot, like the academic sociologist, allow the grim tyranny of
> established fact to monopolize the discussion of human potentialities. (*MCC*, 182)

Like objective consciousness, this aestheticism suggests less a worldview than a
way of viewing the world. As much as any scientist, the artist sees a world in motion, a world of "social innovation" and "new social possibilities." The artist, like
the scientist, sees this motion as relentless, potentially "inexhaustible." Goodman's
communitarianism amounts to an insistence on the need to create community, as reflected in a passage from his novel, *Making Do*: "If there is no community for you,
young man, young man make it yourself" (*MCC*, 204). These final words in
Roszak's chapter on Goodman also stand as Roszak's final words on community.
The surface shift from the quantitative thought of the academic sociologist to the
qualitative vision of the literary artist obscures a deep, underlying consensus on the
primacy of the instrumental imperatives to do and to make. The very title of

Roszak's book, *The Making of a Counter Culture*, reflects his own commitment to process over substance, a commitment central to technocratic culture itself.

In cosmology and sociology, Roszak offers a vision of constant flux guided only by "the sensibility of the artist" (*MCC*, 197). This utopian ideal embodies values that span the entire history of the modern concept of culture. From Romantic poetry, Roszak draws the image of the poet-legislator, most clearly articulated in Shelley's "A Defense of Poetry." From cultural anthropology, he dresses this poet in the exotic drag of the non-Western holy man or shaman. Thus, Roszak writes:

> When we look more closely at the shaman, we discover that the contribution this exotic character has made to human culture is nearly inestimable. Indeed, the shaman might properly lay claim to being the culture hero *par excellence,* for through him creative forces that approach the superhuman seem to have been called into play. In the shaman, the first figure to have established himself in human society as an individual personality, several great talents were inextricably combined that have since become specialized professions. (*MCC*, 243)

Following the technocratic internalization of authority, the position of the priest as mediator between God and man becomes a "position of talented uniqueness" (*MCC*, 236). The significance of the priest/shaman lies in his "creative powers," his "great talents," and of course, his "individual personality." Roszak's analogy to professional competence suggests more than a rather prosaic choice of words: he explicitly presents the shaman figure as a model for a new elite cultural vanguard. Against the bad magic of the technocratic elites, however, "good magic—magic as it is practiced by the shaman and the artist . . . seeks always to make available to all the full power of the magician's experience" (*MCC*, 260). At its most egalitarian, Roszak's shamanism thus draws on the very middle-class ideology of service that secular intellectuals used to justify their newfound authority in the postwar "consensus" world order.

No less than the technocratic architects of the Vietnam War, Roszak looked to the East and found only a mirror of America. This common misperception flowed from a common commitment to the ultimate value of personality. Like Bell, Roszak dismissed "ideological politics" for its "total subordination of the person to party and doctrine" (*MCC*, 59). Riesman's insistence "that each life is an emergency, which only happens once, and the 'saving' of which, in terms of character, justifies care and effort," found its counterculture equivalent in Roszak's insistence that "one must care for the uniqueness and the dignity of each individual and yield to what his conscience demands in the existential moment"(*MCC*, 61).[20] Locating the essence of the counterculture in its "profoundly personalist sense of community," Roszak only reinforced the orthodox social science reduction of culture to personality (*MCC, 206*).

3

The Negro Dilemma

As leader of the "free world," the United States felt special international political pressure to confront the most glaring domestic abuse of freedom: the denial of basic civil rights to African Americans through Jim Crow segregation. In 1944, Gunnar Myrdal published his massive study of American race relations, *An American Dilemma*. Financed by the Carnegie Corporation, *An American Dilemma* provided a state-of-the-art, empirical social-scientific argument for the economic and moral necessity of racial equality: segregation represented a feudal drag on a developing American economy, as well as an intolerable moral contradiction in the value system of a fundamentally egalitarian American culture. The *Brown* decision in 1954 declaring school segregation unconstitutional drew heavily on the social-scientific arguments of Myrdal and his colleagues.

The Supreme Court victory, and the general integrationist agenda of the civil rights movement that followed in its wake, brought with it its own dilemma, one that would explode with the rise of the black power movement in the 1960s: how could African Americans achieve *social* integration and still maintain the *cultural* difference made possible in many ways by the very segregation now rejected as racist? A reading of two significant politically opposed texts, Ralph Ellison's generally integrationist novel, *Invisible Man,* and Harold Cruse's generally nationalist intellectual history, *The Crisis of the Negro Intellectual,* shows how both the American dilemma of social equality and what I call the Negro dilemma of cultural difference found their resolution in a single narrative of modernization, in which economic development would provide the material base for the instrumentalization of culture in the service of individual liberation. Historians have presented the shift from integration to nationalism as a shift from a politics of individual rights to a politics of class and race. A reading of the works of Ellison and Cruse reveals a common insight into the class dimensions of racial oppression, as well as a common blindness to culture as anything more than fodder for the construction of individual identity.

Long before he achieved fame with the publication of *Invisible Man*, Ralph Ellison entered the debate on American race relations with a scathing review of none other than Gunnar Myrdal's *An American Dilemma*. Written in 1944 and included in Ellison's 1964 collection of essays, *Shadow and Act,* the review spans the most important years of the civil rights movement and makes it impossible to dismiss Ellison as a naive integrationist. Ellison praises Myrdal for dispelling many of the old racial "myths" of American sociology and confronting white America with its historical denial of democracy to the Negro; he then proceeds to attack American social science in general as inextricably bound up, since its inception, with the subordination of the Negro in America. Ellison singles out the University of Chicago sociologist Robert Park, in particular, for his conception of the Negro as "the lady among the races."[1] Park was the leading sociologist of his generation. Prior to his appointment at Chicago, he collaborated with Booker T. Washington on devising educational strategies for Negro improvement, and his urban ethnographies in Chicago placed race and ethnicity at the center of sociological inquiry. The infamous quote cited by Ellison aside, Park was, by the standards of his time, a liberal on race matters and drew on Boasian cultural relativism to refute older biological understandings of race.[2] Still, Ellison goes so far as to compare Park's propagation of his ideas at Washington's Tuskegee Institute to the propaganda work of Goebbels for Hitler. Ellison sees the American reaction to the rise of fascism in Nazi Germany as a kind of shock of recognition that has forced America to confront its own brand of fascism: the racial subordination of the Negro.

Ellison exempts Myrdal from the blatant racism of Park but then proceeds to expose the deeper class and cultural biases of even so "progressive" a work of social science as *An American Dilemma.* Sounding much like the C. Wright Mills of *The Sociological Imagination*, Ellison accuses Myrdal's work of a fundamental methodological ambiguity: a liberal stress on interdependence and multicausal explanation that effectively evades any analysis of structural relations of power and class conflict. Seeing the American dilemma as fundamentally a dilemma of conscience, Myrdal reduces the question of power to racism and then reduces racism to ignorance fostered by southern economic backwardness. Following this logic, *An American Dilemma* becomes little more than a brief for economic modernization, or in Ellison's formulation, a *"blueprint for a more effective exploitation of the South's natural, industrial and human resources"* by northern capitalists. Ellison links this class bias to a cultural bias that sees Negro life in the South only in terms of victimization. Anticipating the black radical response to the "culture of poverty" analysis of black urban life during the 1960s, Ellison affirms the creativity of black culture against Myrdal's social-scientific pathology: "Are American Negroes simply the creation of white men, or have they at least helped to create themselves out of what they found around them? Men have made a way of life in caves and upon cliffs, why cannot Negroes have made a life upon the horns of the white man's dilemma?"[3]

Expressing quasi-nationalist sentiments, Ellison goes on to suggest that Negroes have deliberately rejected aspects of white American culture as inferior to their own, and he calls for "the creation of a democracy in which the Negro will be free to define himself for what he is and, within the large framework of that democracy, for what he desires to be."[4] Ultimately, Ellison sees Myrdal's antidote to be as deadly as the disease it seeks to cure. The reduction of Negro life to pathology, the denial of Negro agency, and the demand for assimilation into the standards of mainstream white American society together pose as great a threat to Negro freedom as the more obvious restrictions of segregation.

Ellison's short, obscure review contains every major criticism that the Left would level against orthodox social science in the years following its rise to dominance in the academy after World War II. Like these critiques, however, Ellison criticizes social science only in the name of what he calls "a deeper science." Ellison tempers his critique of the modernizing agenda of *An American Dilemma* with the standard humanist distinction between positive and negative development: "In the positive sense it is the key to a more democratic and fruitful usage of the South's natural and human resources . . . in the negative, it is the plan for a more efficient and subtle manipulation of black and white relations."[5]

Ellison distinguishes the "fruitful" from the merely "efficient" in terms of the degree of creative participation by African Americans in the democratic development of American society as a whole. This critique assumes and affirms the modernist (and modernizing) definition of culture as process rather than substance. Ellison's critique, and the literary expression of this "deeper science," *Invisible Man,* affirm the process of self-definition over any particular substantive definition of self. The significance of Ellison's work lies most profoundly in its integration of African-American cultural discourse into a larger Anglo-American narrative of modernization.

The roots of this integration may be traced back to the Harlem Renaissance of the 1920s. Primarily an aesthetic movement, the Harlem Renaissance marked the arrival of the first generation of African Americans to engage in intellectual activity as a group outside of the traditional constraints of white philanthropy and the black church. Despite continued dependence on white patrons, the Harlem intellectuals developed a historically unprecedented self-consciousness as a distinct and relatively autonomous class within the African-American community at large. In the 1925 manifesto, "The New Negro," Alain Locke spoke for this generation of artists by rejecting the old conception of the Negro as "a social ward or minor" for a new conception of the Negro as a "personality" capable of a "fuller, truer self-expression." In rejecting the old leadership of Victorian ministers and sociologists, however, Locke uncritically endorsed the new leadership of modernist artists and anthropologists. Thus in "The New Negro," Locke attacks the notion of the Negro as "a chronic patient for the sociological clinic," only to call for more serious study in the "new scientific rather than the old sentimental interest." This new scientific approach understands the life of the Negro in terms of the industrial development of American society as a whole, what Locke describes as "a deliberate flight not only from countryside to city, but from medieval America to modern."[6]

The drama of modernization unites intellectuals and the masses in a single emancipatory great leap forward:

> The migrant masses, shifting from countryside to city, hurdle several generations of experience at a leap, but more important, the same thing happens spiritually in the life attitudes and self-expression of the Young Negro, in his poetry, his art, his education and his new outlook, with additional advantage, of course, of the poise and greater certainty of knowing what it is all about.[7]

Embracing the modern, the Harlem intellectuals also followed a tradition of Anglo-American primitivism by recovering the folk and African roots of modern Negro culture. Anthropology, particularly the cultural relativism propagated by Columbia professor Franz Boas and his students Ruth Benedict and Margaret Mead, provided an alternative to the harsh modernization of most sociological models by allowing for the persistence of folk and "primitive" values as resources for coping with the dislocations of modernity.

The Harlem Renaissance in many ways anticipated the discovery of the folk culture that would sweep mainstream Anglo-American culture, as well as a young, aspiring African-American writer named Ralph Ellison, during the 1930s. Like many other writers of the time, Ellison looked to the cultural agencies of the New Deal for an opportunity to pursue his interest in folk culture. Ellison had been deeply influenced by the work of the white folklorist Constance Rourke, whose 1931 *American Humor* had the distinction of being one of the earliest works to apply Boas's anthropological theories directly to the study of American culture; he was particularly impressed by Rourke's emphasis on the contributions of African Americans to American folk culture in general, and he continued to cite Rourke's work as a model of proper social science well into the 1960s. In 1938, Ellison obtained a position with the Federal Writer's Project, working under Sterling A. Brown, the project's editor of Negro affairs. Brown assigned Ellison to the Living Lore Unit, a group of twenty-seven writers charged with documenting New York City's urban and industrial folklore.

Since Warren Susman's seminal work on the culture concept in the 1930s, historians have come to see this turn toward the folk as the "soft" side of an era also known as the "hard" Red Decade.[8] This now commonplace historical opposition received an earlier formulation in a midcentury literary controversy, in which left-leaning literary critics compared Ellison unfavorably to his Marxist African-American counterpart at the Federal Writer's Project, Richard Wright. In the 1950s, Ellison responded to these criticisms with a series of attacks on "sociological" novel writing and a defense of psychological depth in characterization. The distinction between the liberal "folk" and the Marxist "masses" has, however, obscured the larger class issue of intellectual vanguardism and the larger cultural issue of the objectification of culture as a resource for development.

For all the literary differences between the two writers, nothing in Ellison's published writing suggests any objection to Wright's assertion in his 1937 manifesto, "A Blueprint for Negro Writing," that "every first rate novel, poem, or play lifts the level of consciousness higher" and that intellectuals have a duty to "create the myths and symbols that inspire a faith in life."[9] Similarly, Wright could not object to Ellison's assertion that "only through a skillful and wise manipulation of these centers of repressed social energy will Negro resentment, self-pity and indignation be channelized . . . and become transformed into positive action."[10] Wright and Ellison agreed on manipulation; they differed only on what they felt to be skillful and wise. Wright felt that art should raise awareness of the social forces at work upon the individual, an awareness he himself gained first from the liberal sociology of the "racist" Robert Park; Ellison sought to develop an African-American character that could serve as a center of consciousness able to comprehend the social relations of modern society, an ideal certainly compatible with Marxism.[11] The significance of the novels of Wright and Ellison lies not in their disparate politics but in their common incorporation of African-American life into what Ellison called "a literary form which has time and social change as its special province." The central place given these works in African-American intellectual history reflects the naturalization of a modernizing, novelistic "restless mobility" as the reference point for debates on African-American culture in general.[12]

Invisible Man is both the deeper literature and the deeper science that Ellison advocated in his criticism during the 1940s. It is, as Ellison often described it, the story of "a young Negro's quest for identity."[13] It is also a nearly total history of African-American life since emancipation, a history shaped by violence and deception, but ultimately a story of evolution and development. Ellison takes his nameless protagonist from the rural South to the urban North—from

the conservative, Booker T. Washington ethic of the Negro college to the revolutionary communistic ideology of the Brotherhood—and explores every available avenue for an African-American male to exist in white America. Against
Marxism, Ellison traces the development of historical consciousness in an individual, not a class; against liberalism, he presents this development as anything
but orderly and rational. The spatial/temporal journey of the novel serves as the
social/historical context for a psychological journey toward self-understanding,
and psychological insight never comes without a thorough engagement with the
very material world of social institutions.

Ellison's protagonist, the Invisible Man, begins his journey following the classic bourgeois path toward self-determination—education. The protagonist soon
finds himself expelled from his southern Negro college and banished to the North
by the college president for an inadvertent breach of racial etiquette. Rejected by
the world of the southern black bourgeoisie, Ellison's protagonist nonetheless
continues along the respectable bourgeois path of independence through work; he
soon finds himself at the mercy of a maniacal black machinist who blows up a
paint factory rather than join a union that might threaten the measure of control
he has achieved through his mastery of a paint processing machine. Recovering
from the explosion, the Invisible Man rejects the bourgeois ethic of self-control
and embraces a radical ideology of social control through revolution, only to find
himself yet again a pawn in the game of black-white power relations. Far from
blind to social power relations, the novel very nearly reduces social life to a
Hobbesian war of all against all, which finds the delusional naivete of the controlled matched only by the delusional hubris of the controllers. Dr. Bledsoe, the
Negro college president, fancies himself a hard-boiled, realistic power broker in
race relations and boasts, "This is a power set-up, son, and I'm at the controls"
(*IM,* 142); however, he deferentially accepts the Atlanta Compromise of segregation. Lucius Brockway, the machinist at the paint factory, likewise declares his
control over whites, boasting, "They got all this machinery, but . . . *we the machines inside the machines.*" Still, he works in a basement making white paint and
celebrates this whiteness by creating a successful advertising slogan, "If It's
Optic White, It's the Right White" (*IM,* 217).

The Invisible Man himself ultimately succumbs to the illusion of control. Re-
alizing that the Brotherhood has no real concern for blacks beyond their role as
cogs in the revolutionary machine of history, the Invisible Man devises an ironic
strategy of playing the game of rationalism with the white Brotherhood in hopes
of fostering the irrational elements within the black community: "my task would
be to deny the unpredictable human element of all Harlem so that they could ignore it when it in any way interfered with their plans" (*IM,* 514). The novel con-

cludes with a seemingly spontaneous uprising of blacks in protest against the killing of a black man by a white police officer. First believing the riot to be a result of his strategy, he soon discovers it to be the work of the Brotherhood itself: "The committee had planned it. And I had helped, had been a tool. A tool just at the very moment I had thought myself free. By pretending to agree I *had* indeed agreed" (*IM*, 553). With this epiphany, the Invisible Man attains a "new sense of self" and disappears down a coal chute.

The novel ends where it begins, with the Invisible Man in his underground sanctuary, though now strangely celebrating an American pluralism completely at odds with the reality presented in the novel. This disjunction serves to caution the reader about the actual practice of pluralism even as it uncritically affirms the theory of pluralism:

Must I strive toward colorlessness? But seriously, and without snobbery, think of what the world would lose if that should happen. America is woven of many strands; I would recognize them and let it so remain. It's "winner take nothing" that is the great truth of our country or of any country. Life is to be lived, not controlled; and humanity is won by continuing to play in face of certain defeat. Our fate is to become one, and yet many—This is not prophecy, but description. Thus one of the greatest jokes in the world is the spectacle of the whites busy escaping blackness and becoming blacker every day, and the blacks striving toward whiteness, becoming quite dull and gray. None of us seems to know who he is or where he's going. (*IM*, 577)

This plural society requires a plural self or, more properly, a dual self. The Invisible Man listens to Louis Armstrong on a phonograph player powered by electricity he has drained off free from the Monopolated Light and Power Company. Affirming white light and black heat, the Invisible Man declares himself "in the great American tradition of tinkers. That makes me kin to Ford, Edison and Franklin. Call me, since I have a theory and a concept, a 'thinker-tinker'" (*IM*, 7). In the utopian space of this underground retreat, Ellison inverts the dominant values of the real world: the equation of folk culture with backwardness and the machine with domination. Invoking Armstrong and Edison, Ellison affirms a vision of American freedom based on black culture and white technology.

Against the vulgar modernization of *An American Dilemma, Invisible Man* offers a vision of progress that affirms both tradition and modernity. The ecstasy of affirmation that frames the novel obscures, however, a subtle instrumentalization of culture at odds with the folk values that receive so much sympathy throughout the novel. Ellison constructs the key transformation of the novel—the Invisible Man's acceptance of the Brotherhood—in a way that highlights the contrast between black folk culture and both the pretensions of the black bourgeoisie and the

arrogance of white radicals. On being released from the hospital following the explosion at the paint factory, Ellison's protagonist decides to forsake his bourgeois
aspirations, symbolized by his place of residence, Men's House:

> The lobby was the meeting place for various groups still caught up in the illusions
> that had just been boomeranged out of my head: college boys working to return to
> school down South; older advocates of racial progress with utopian schemes for
> building black business empires; preachers ordained by no authority except their
> own, without church or congregation . . . the pathetic ones who possessed nothing
> beyond their dreams of being gentlemen . . . the "actors" who sought to achieve the
> status of brokers through imagination alone, a group of janitors and messengers who
> spent most of their wages on clothing such as was fashionable among Wall Street
> brokers, with their Brooks Brothers suits and bowler hats, English umbrellas, black
> calf-skin shoes and yellow gloves. (*IM,* 256)

Leaving Men's House, the Invisible Man rents a room from a simple country
woman named Mary. Kind, generous, and "exceedingly irritating to listen to,"
Mary stands as "a force, a stable, familiar force like something out of my past
which kept me from whirling off into some unknown which I dared not face" (*IM,*
258). During his time at Mary's, the Invisible Man returns to his country roots,
experiencing the pure joy of country food, without having "to worry about who
saw me or about what was proper" (*IM,* 264).

The folk serves as a refuge from the black bourgeoisie, yet it also provides the
occasion for initiation into white radicalism. Wandering through Harlem exulting
in fresh cooked sweet potatoes, Ellison's protagonist confronts the dark fate of the
folk in the modern world, the eviction of an elderly couple from their apartment:

> I turned aside and looked at the clutter of household objects which the two men con-
> tinued to pile on the walk. And as the crowd pushed me I looked down to see look-
> ing out of an oval frame a portrait of the old couple when young, seeing the sad, stiff
> dignity of the faces there; feeling strange memories awakening that began an echo-
> ing in my head like that of a hysterical voice stuttering in a dark street. Seeing them
> look back at me as though even then in that nineteenth-century day they had expected
> little, and this with a grim, unillusioned pride that suddenly seemed to me both a re-
> proach and a warning. My eyes fell upon a pair of crudely carved and polished bones,
> 'knocking bones,' used to accompany music at country dances, used in black-face
> minstrels . . . a straightening comb, switches of false hair, a curling iron . . . nuggets
> of High John the Conqueror, the lucky stone . . . a small Ethiopian flag, a faded tin-
> type of Abraham Lincoln, and the smiling image of a Hollywood star torn from a
> magazine. (*IM,* 271)

Simultaneously repulsed by and attracted to this pastiche of folk detritus and bourgeois aspiration, the Invisible Man cannot help but identify with the old couple:

And it was as though I myself was being dispossessed of some painful yet precious thing which I could not bear to lose; something confounding, like a rotted tooth one would rather suffer indefinitely than endure the short, violent eruption of pain that would mark its removal. And with this sense of dispossession came a pang of vague recognition: this junk, these shabby chairs, these heavy, old-fashioned pressing irons, zinc wash tubs with dented bottoms—all throbbed within me more meaning than there should have been. (*IM*, 273).

The Invisible Man then makes a speech calling on his "Black Brothers" to defend the elderly couple, and eventually the onlookers defy the white authorities and return the couple's belongings to their apartment. The police finally arrive to break up the protest.

The Invisible Man flees the police, only to be trailed by a mysterious white woman. The woman praises his speech and introduces him to a white man named Jack, the leader of the Brotherhood, a radical organization dedicated to proletarian revolution. Brother Jack too praises the Invisible Man on his leadership qualities but instructs him on the true significance of the eviction:

They're agrarian types, you know. Being ground up by industrial conditions. . . . It's sad, yes. But they're already dead, defunct. History has passed them by. . . . All they have left is their religion. That's all they can think about. So they'll be cast aside. They're dead, you see, because they're incapable of rising to the necessity of the historical situation. (*IM*, 290–91)

Confused by this rhetoric, the Invisible Man offers his own, more visceral reading of the old couple: "But I *like* them . . . they reminded me of folks I know down South. It's taken me a long time to feel it, but they're folks just like me, except that I've been to school a few years" (*IM*, 291). This exchange establishes the dynamic for the Invisible Man's stormy relationship with the Brotherhood: as the Brotherhood tries to fit every aspect of experience into a scientific logic of history, so the Invisible Man looks for inspiration in those vital elements of black culture outside of history, first in folk culture and later in the urban hipster culture of the zoot-suiter Rinehart.

The Invisible Man's experience with the Brotherhood ultimately propels him beyond culture and history to an ideal realm of the self. Having escaped the race riot, he reflects, "My problem was that I always tried to go in everyone's way but my own" (*IM*, 573). This awareness of self proceeds to distance him from both the folk and the modern: "And now I realized that I couldn't return to Mary's, or to any part of my old life. I could approach it only from the outside, and I had been as invisible to Mary as I had been to the Brotherhood" (*IM*, 571). The detachment of his underground retreat serves as the free space from which to undertake an engagement with both tradition and modernity—now on his own terms, the terms of selfhood and identity.

The great weakness of the novel lies precisely in this spatial/temporal evasion: the construction of "identity" as a neutral language between tradition and modernity, rather than a distinctly modern language in its own right. The detachment of Ellison's ideal outsider perspective fosters an objectification of culture no less rigorous than the scientific theories satirized in his portrayal of the Brotherhood. The sympathy with which Ellison engages the folk preserves certain folk practices only to transform them into commodities for consumption in the production of a unique self. The Invisible Man's rediscovery of the folk brings not an initiation into a whole way of life but merely regret over missed opportunities for invigorating experiences. After his sweet potato epiphany, for example, he muses, "What and how much had I lost by trying to do only what was expected of me instead of what I myself had wished to do?" (*IM,* 266). In the larger narrative context of the novel, the eating of sweet potatoes becomes an affirmation of choice, not of culture. Significantly, in the utopian space of his underground retreat, the Invisible Man experiences the folk in its industrialized, commodified form: a Louis Armstrong record played on an electric phonograph. In this scenario, technology produces culture yet reduces a communal ritual to an individual experience. Ellison's construction of a space beyond tradition and modernity ultimately affirms the dominance of modernity over tradition.

Ellison's nonfiction writing during the 1940s and 1950s confirms the dominance implicit in *Invisible Man*. In "Richard Wright's Blues" (1945), Ellison suspends his regular animus toward sociological writing and hails *Black Boy* as a scathing indictment of both white and Negro backwardness in the South. Sounding much like the Gunnar Myrdal of *An American Dilemma,* Ellison praises Wright for exposing the South as a society that denies "those forms of human relationships achievable only in the most highly developed areas of civilization."[14] As evidence of southern backwardness, Ellison cites the superior performance on IQ tests by northern over southern Negroes.

"Harlem Is Nowhere" (1948), an essay praised by some historians as a rare instance of Ellison engaging in tough-minded, materialist social analysis, again provides a brief for modernization straight from the pages of *An American Dilemma*. The essay praises the work of the Lafarge Psychiatric Clinic, a clinic headed by Dr. Frederick Werthem (who would later achieve fame for *The Seduction of the Innocents*, a study of the psychological effects of mass culture on children), dedicated to making psychological counseling available to the residents of Harlem on a mass scale. Ellison sees the clinic as evidence of nothing less than a full-scale cultural transformation in the life of the American Negro:

> For if Harlem is the scene of the folk-Negro's death agony, it is also the setting of his transcendence. Here it is possible for talented youths to leap through the development of decades in a brief twenty years, while beside them white-haired adults crawl

in the feudal darkness of their childhood. Here a former cotton picker develops the sensitive hands of a surgeon, and men whose grandparents still believe in magic prepare optimistically to become atomic scientists.[15]

Ellison avoids a simple-minded progressivism only by conceding the persistence of power relations despite general social development: "It is not industrial progress per se which damages peoples or cultures, it is the exploitation of peoples in order to keep the machines fed with raw materials."[16] Anticipating his great novel, these statements stand as a slightly more prosaic explication of the ideology rendered narratively in *Invisible Man*.

The intellectual roots of this ideology lie in the strain of left-liberal Anglo-American social criticism stretching from Thorstein Veblen to C. Wright Mills, a tradition that sees progress in terms of the liberation of the forces of production from the oppressive relations of production. In a 1958 interview, Ellison states, "It seems to me that the whole world is moving toward some new cultural synthesis, and partially through the discipline imposed by technology." Here technological development serves as both a means of and a metaphor for a larger process of human evolution. Commenting on the civil rights "struggle for full participation in American life," Ellison cautions that the Negro people "dare not fail to adapt to changed conditions lest we destroy ourselves." Ellison concedes that the Negro people "suffer much from the rupture of tradition" and criticizes "the entertainment industry . . . which thrives on the exploitation and debasement of all folk materials."[17] Still, he measures the costs of such cultural rupture against the benefits of material prosperity made possible by technology.

Ultimately, Ellison justifies the embrace of change not in terms of material compensation for cultural loss but in terms of expanded opportunity for cultural choice: "we haven't had a chance to discover what in our own background is really worth preserving. For the first time we are given a choice, we are making a choice."[18] *Invisible Man* provides a model for this new cultural consumerism by rejecting the folk background symbolized by life with Mary while retaining an artifact of that background, the music of Louis Armstrong.

Insisting on choice, Ellison himself nonetheless came to regret many of the choices made. He placed Louis Armstrong in the coal chute with his protagonist because he believed that music, more than any other "group expression" of African-American culture, had the power to overcome the rupture of tradition brought on by industrialization. Ellison wrote enthusiastically about jazz as one who had experienced the birth of swing firsthand. A fan more than a critic, he had little patience for anthropological or sociological accounts that sought to "explain" the music in broader social terms. Still, Ellison subjected jazz musicians to the same sociological imperatives he imposed on Negroes in general: "all are faced with the humanist American necessity of finding the balance between progress and continuity; between tradition and experimentation." The linking of Armstrong and Edison in the utopian space of *Invisible Man* affirms this balance in theory, but Ellison's nonfiction writing on music casts doubts on the sustainability of this balance in practice. "Harlem Is Nowhere," the essay that praises the emergence of the Negro from feudal darkness made possible by urban migration, also laments that "even his art is transformed; the lyrical ritual elements of folk jazz . . . have given way to the near-themeless technical virtuosity of bebop, a further triumph of technology over humanism." Ellison's 1958 essay on blues great Jimmy Rushing recalls an earlier, simpler time in the history of jazz: "The blues, the singer, the band and the dancers formed the vital whole of jazz as an institutional form, and even today neither part is quite complete without the rest. The thinness of much of the so-called 'modern jazz' is especially reflective of this loss of wholeness."[19] Ellison himself concedes this to be a "shamelessly nostalgic outburst," but the rest of his music writing follows this basic declension narrative of the fall from swing to bop.

Ellison's pastoral lament in no way challenges the basic progressive narrative within which he writes. At least since the 1930s, left-liberal intellectuals have incorporated respect for premodern cultures into their basically modernizing agenda; Robert Lynd's studies of industrialization in Muncie, Indiana, show how even the harsh technophilia of the Veblenian tradition of social science can accommodate pastoral lament.[20] Ellison the modernist writer approaches music much as modern city people approach the country. Music serves as a retreat, a firm base from which to confront the exhilarating but often bewildering complexity of modern life. Seeing music as a repository of cultural tradition, Ellison denies it the very freedom he claims for himself as a writer (think of how often modern literature has been attacked for a "near-themeless" technical virtuosity). In his essay "On Bird, Bird-Watching, and Jazz," Ellison attacks Charlie Parker for rejecting his folk roots, cultivating a detached persona, and appealing primarily to an audience of white intellectuals — in short, for doing in music what Ellison did in literature.

Ellison consistently argued against white critics who tried to place his work in an explicitly Negro cultural context. In "Change the Joke and Slip the Yoke," he criticizes Stanley Edgar Hyman's attempt to link the protagonist of *Invisible Man* to the West African trickster tradition; Ellison insists that his most immediate model was rather the "smart man playing dumb" tradition of Yankee-American literature. Acknowledging some folk influence, Ellison concedes that "I use folklore in my work not because I am Negro, but because writers like Eliot and Joyce made me conscious of the literary value of my folk inheritance."[21]

Ellison's modernist appropriation of the folk renders the folk indistinguishable from the modern. Ellison writes of the blues not as a structure of rhythm, harmony, and melody, but as a general attitude "less angry than ironic," a "refusal to offer solutions," a "near-tragic, near comic lyricism," or "an autobiographical chronicle of personal catastrophe expressed lyrically" (*IM,* xviii).[22] Ellison defines the blues so broadly as to include the writing of Ernest Hemingway, whose writing he finds "imbued with a spirit beyond the tragic" that approaches the blues. The blues functions in Ellison's nonfiction as an aesthetic ideal of individuality to be invoked in critical attacks on more sociologically oriented literature.

Ellison's understandable distaste for the literary style of most deliberately sociological writing blinded him to the individualistic bias of sociology as a discipline. Thus, Ellison attacks LeRoi Jones's *Blues People* for reducing the blues to sociology but neglects the extent to which Jones tells a story much in the spirit of *Invisible Man*, namely, the emergence of Negro modernism. Ellison clearly does not share Jones's appreciation for bebop, but Jones's characterization of bebop could stand as a description of *Invisible Man*: "It was the beginning of the Negro's fluency with some of the canons of formal Western nonconformity . . . the cult of redefinition."[23] *Blues People* and *Invisible Man,* each in its own way, provide a sociology of modern Negro individualism: *Blues People* sees this individualism transforming folk culture, whereas *Invisible Man* sees pure folk culture as a resource for individual identity.

It is difficult to accuse Ellison of inconsistency when, like his namesake Ralph Waldo Emerson, he affirmed contradiction as a positive strategy. Ellison has his protagonist declare that "all life is divided and . . . only in division is there true health" (*IM,* 576). Ellison's literary criticism, like his literature, denounces and defends, hates and loves. Some critics have attacked this ironic stance as politically irresponsible, but the greatest irony of all may be just how politically inspirational this attitude proved to be during the cold war era. The theologian Reinhold Niebuhr invested irony with an almost sacred aura that allowed for the persistence of individual morality despite the essentially immoral nature of society as a whole. At best, Niebuhr's irony inspired Martin Luther King with its insistence that the violence of racism could only be overcome through a strategy of nonviolent resistance; at worst, this irony justified a foreign policy "realism" that sought to promote political freedom through military and economic domination. The significance of Ellison's irony lies not in the political obligations it allowed him to dodge but in the cultural position it forced him to take. Inspired to create a literary alternative to social-scientific positivism, Ellison succeeded only in providing a humanist justification for the instrumentalization of culture in the service of social and economic development.

For all of its political militancy, the black power movement never seriously questioned this modernizing agenda. A SNCC position paper in 1966 stated: "We reject an American dream defined by white people and must work to construct an American reality defined by Afro-Americans."[24] Black power leaders often adopted the rhetoric and strategies of African anticolonial movements, but as many a cold war liberal liked to gloat, most of these movements wanted merely their fair share of the benefits of Western prosperity. In their manifesto *Black Power*, Stokely Carmichael (Kwame Ture) and Charles Hamilton state: "Black people must refine themselves, and only *they* can do that."[25] As wanting to be boss does not make a worker a revolutionary, so demanding self-determination does not determine an alternative self.

Leaving aside the ideological purity of black power in interracial politics, the consensus on modernization contained a more significant and clearly identifiable political divide within the black community itself. In retrospect, the riots following the passage of major civil rights legislation make more sense than black power leaders calling the civil rights establishment a bunch of Uncle Toms. Again, the issue was largely a matter of control, with black radicals accusing civil rights leaders of relying too heavily on white liberal charity. Again, political confrontation facilitated a process of cultural integration, in this case integration into the cultural narrative of generational revolt recently revived by white student radicals. There have always been political divisions within the African-American community, most notably the Washington-DuBois split of the early twentieth century. Unlike previous divisions, the civil rights–black power split made political positions not so much a matter of wrong and right, but of old and new; in effect, black power brought the New Negro rhetoric of generational revolt out of aesthetics and into politics. As the tradition of the new fragmented the arts, so too would it fragment politics. Apart from external repression by police and government officials, black radicalism of the post–civil rights era followed the same internal logic of white radicalism, from bourgeois individualism to an antinomian collectivism of one.

No text of the black power era exemplifies this logic more than Harold Cruse's 1967 work, *The Crisis of the Negro Intellectual*. Though historians have come to see Cruse's book as a key statement of Marxist black nationalism, the text defies any easy classification. If it is Marxist, then it is Marxism without a party; if it is nationalist, than it is nationalism without a nation. Largely ignored by the mainstream press, it tended to provoke strong responses from those who took the time to read it. In the words of one reviewer, it is "a book that will infuriate almost everyone. . . . Almost six hundred pages of polemic, this is an intellectual history of the American Negro in this century which dismisses practically every thinker as 'a retarded child.' "[26] The book begins with what was by 1967 a fairly conventional attack on the NAACP but curiously ends with a dismissal of black power militancy as "part and parcel of the very gradualism of the NAACP."[27]

At a time when SNCC leader H. Rap Brown called on blacks to "get you some guns" and "kill the honkies," Cruse could write that

> a closer examination of every analysis by each Black Power exponent from SNCC and CORE reveals that while the slogan cast a revolutionary *sounding* theme and a threat of more intense revolt across the land, the *substance* was, in fact, a methodological retreat to black social reforms. (*CNI*, 545)

Cruse supports this sweeping claim by addressing specific programs and strategies employed by black power activists; however, he reads all the deficiencies of these specific strategies as symptomatic of a single "Dialogue Between Shadow and Substance." Washington and DuBois debated the relative merits of economic self-sufficiency versus political equality; in a sharp departure from this level of specificity, the abstract dialogue between shadow and substance enables Cruse to dismiss all existing positions, whether nationalist or integrationist, as counterrevolutionary reformism. Shadow/substance, like reform/revolution, invests African-American politics with a surface/depth historical dynamic previously lacking. For the old alternatives of nationalism and integration, Cruse substitutes a new politics of transition, from surface to depth, from shadow to substance, from reform to revolution.

Despite Cruse's revolutionary rhetoric, his transition fails to provide any ideological alternative to political orthodoxy. Mainstream Anglo-American intellectuals since the nineteenth century have seen radical change as central to the promise of American life. Ellison's *Invisible Man*, the greatest literary expression of the African-American struggle for integration into that promise, similarly argues for constant transition as an emancipatory social ethic. Politically opposed in many ways, *Invisible Man* and *The Crisis of the Negro Intellectual* nonetheless produce the same set of social relations: both works ultimately take the individual, as either Invisible Man or a Negro intellectual, as the fundamental unit of social analysis.

Cruse's book begins where Ellison's book ends, in a liminal space between black and white. What Ellison celebrates as synthesis Cruse indicts as crisis. Ellison sees liminality providing African-Americans with equal access to Thomas Edison and Louis Armstrong, whereas Cruse sees it as alienation from both of these worlds:

> in the detached social world of the intellectuals, a considerable amount of racial integration and ethnic intermingling does take place on a social level. While the Negro intellectual is not fully integrated into the intellectual class stratum, he is, in the main, socially detached from his own Negro ethnic world. (*CNI*, 9)

Both Ellison and Cruse take the individual/intellectual as a synecdoche for the African-American community, which in turn becomes a synecdoche for America as a whole. According to Cruse, the Negro intellectual "is left in the limbo of social marginality, alienated and directionless on the landscape of America, in a variegated nation of whites who have not yet decided their own identity" (*CNI*, 13). In this respect, African Americans share much the same cultural predicament as the children and grandchildren of European American immigrants. Acknowledging his debt to an earlier discourse of ethnic pluralism, Cruse calls on African Americans to forge a distinct cultural identity within a broader American culture, a task he sees as the "great promise" of a "new nation of nations." Ultimately Cruse, like Ellison, accepts the quest for identity as the defining trope of American culture, as well as the guiding trope for the Negro within that culture (*CNI*, 565).

Cruse simply cannot be read as a nationalist in any strong, separatist sense of that term. To be sure, he provides ample opportunity for misreading. Cruse begins his book with an obligatory nationalist attack on the NAACP. He asserts that the "basic impulse behind all creativity is national or ethnic-group identity" and, against all civil rights orthodoxy, warns that "in the process of racial integration the Negro creative intelligentsia sheds this identity day by day" (*CNI*, 221). Much of the book is indeed an attack on the cooptation of black intellectuals by white liberals and radicals—most notoriously, an attack on cooptation by Jewish liberals and radicals in particular. What Cruse says of the writers and artists of the Harlem Renaissance, he says of just about every other group of black intellectuals: "the Harlem intellectuals were so overwhelmed at being 'discovered' and courted, that they allowed a *bona fide* cultural movement, which issued from the social system as naturally as a gushing spring, to degenerate into a pampered and paternalized vogue" (*CNI*, 51–52).

Cruse attacks Negro intellectuals not for failing to produce specific works of artistic merit, but for failing to "wed . . . ideas to institutional forms" (*CNI*, 37). Cruse sees proper institutional forms as ethnic, controlled by Negroes, and in this sense nationalistic. Still, against cultural nationalism Cruse dismisses "the readiness of most Black Nationalist trends, to lean heavily on the African past and the African image" as "nothing but a convenient cover-up for an inability to come to terms with the complex demands of the American reality." Moreover, against political nationalism he criticizes that "school of Harlem thought that condemns *any* effort on the part of the American Negro to seek racial equality within the American system" (*CNI*, 554, 552). Cruse's radical bluster obscures a fair, but also fairly unobjectionable, evaluation that "integrationism . . . has met an impasse," and "the black intelligentsia . . . must more and more shift its allegiances to the nationalist cause" (*CNI*, 259).

The significance of Cruse's book lies in knowledge, not politics. *The Crisis of the Negro Intellectual* argues not for any particular nationalist or integrationist program, but for a particular approach to the problem of nationalism and integration.

That approach is historical. Assessing the crisis of the Negro intellectual, Cruse states that "the worst effect of his American conditioning is not his color-complex about blackness, but that it renders him unable to look at his own history and influence in America objectively and understand it scientifically" (*CNI*, 559–60).

Cruse singles out black power intellectuals in particular for being "false to history" and for lacking "a social theory based on the living ingredients of Afro-American history" (*CNI*, 558, 557). Cruse explains the various nationalist and integrationist intellectuals by a common failure to understand African-American history. What is this history? According to Cruse:

> American Negro history is basically a history of the conflict between integrationist and nationalist forces in politics, economics, and culture, no matter what leaders are involved and what slogans are used. . . . The pendulum swings back and forth, but the men who swing it always fail to synthesize composite trends. (*CNI*, 564)

Unobjectionable as a description, this reading hardly explains anything. Curiously, Cruse repeatedly invests it with explanatory power. Analyzing the problem of how the NAACP and the black power movement can both claim Frederick Douglass for their own, Cruse concludes that

> so how then, do divergent integrationist and nationalist trends wind up honoring the same hero? Because neither integrationists nor nationalists truly understand the crucial impact of the integrationist vs. nationalist conflict within the contours of American Negro history. (*CNI*, 563)

Cruse invokes the same "explanation" for black power's acceptance of Malcolm X, who broke with the separatism of Elijah Muhammad, and its rejection of W. E. B. DuBois, who broke with the separatism of Booker T. Washington: "The only way to understand this process is not to be led astray by mere slogans, but to see the fundamentals at work: the underlying conflict between integrationist and nationalist tendencies" (*CNI*, 563).

Here, as elsewhere, Cruse "explains" present confusion as a consequence of past confusion. This explanation affirms neither integration nor nationalism, but rather *the conflict between* integration and nationalism. The crisis of the Negro intellectual stems from an intellectual alienation from history conceived as dialectical struggle. The resolution of the crisis lies not in achieving utopia but in placing the struggle for utopia on the proper historical footing.

In narrative terms, Cruse's argument may be read as a secular, quasi-Marxist translation of the American Puritan jeremiad tradition. On one level, Cruse calls on African-American intellectuals to return to the wisdom of past leaders such as Washington, DuBois, and Garvey; on a deeper level, Cruse's social-scientific framework replaces the substance of the Fathers with the process of history. The master tropes of Cruse's narrative turn out to be not integration and nationalism but stasis and dynamism. Cruse praises Malcolm X for leaving "the Nation of Islam because this type of black power lacked a dynamic, was static and aloof to the broad struggle" (*CNI*, 548). The great promise of Malcolm X lay not in a new nationalism but in a new coalitionism: "He proposed to create another movement (the Organization for Afro-American Unity, OAAU) and link up with all the direct actionists and even passive resisters, believing that one must be involved in all forms of struggle wherever they are on all fronts" (*CNI*, 548).

Cruse's historical dialectic ultimately pits narrow nationalism and integration versus broad nationalism and integration. In a kind of black radical version of the cold war intellectual cult of complexity, Cruse sees historical progress lying in an abstract, generalized movement from the narrow to the broad. Cruse indicts white racism and black politics for betraying the promise of American life in practice, but like any cold war pluralist he affirms the virtues of the "Open Society" in theory. Having reduced black politics to a history of slogans, Cruse concludes his jeremiad with the slogan of history: "Those who cannot remember the past are condemned to repeat it" (*CNI*, 565). Ironically, Cruse remembers his American past all too well and for that very reason is condemned merely to repeat it.

Cruse's book proves itself incapable of escaping the antinomies of American pluralism. American intellectuals have always conceived of America as an open society. Intellectuals have located the closed "other" variously in Catholicism, monarchism, savagery, or communism, but the fundamental opposition of open versus closed has remained. In the middle decades of the twentieth century, the anthropological concept of culture entered mainstream American intellectual discourse. The open/closed antinomy helped transform "culture" from a substantive, whole way of life to a process of creating and re-creating a whole way of life. Intellectuals came to see cultural freedom in terms of the democratic distribution of control over this process rather than the substance of any particular cultural value. In this tradition, Cruse largely avoids the substantive issue of Negro culture. He concentrates on determining the degree of autonomy from white intellectuals possessed by various Negro arts organizations and sees this autonomy as the first step in the movement out to the broader struggle for cultural identity that burdens Americans of all cultural groups. For Cruse, as for Ellison, culture serves as raw material for the creation of individual and group identity. Taken together, *Invisible Man* and *The Crisis of the Negro Intellectual* show that during the cold war era, intellectuals on opposite sides of a political divide found a common enemy in a fugitive and cloistered culture unwilling to accept the necessity of cultural change.

4

Beyond the Unmeltable Ethnics

As racial discourse moved toward Marxist radicalism, ethnic discourse moved toward Catholic conservatism. Generally thought to have assimilated into affluent middle-class quietude during the 1950s, white ethnics surprised liberal policy makers by violently resisting school and residential integration in the name of an almost tribal, communal localism. By the late 1960s, the urban, working-class, white ethnic had replaced the small-town southern sheriff as the symbolic embodiment of the racism inherent in American society as a whole; by the early 1970s, white ethnics had transformed their resistance to integration into a positive reassertion of cultural distinctiveness. In the wake of these developments, intellectuals attempted to rethink their understanding of the place of ethnicity in American society. In this chapter, I examine the two works that best capture the contradictions of this rethinking: Nathan Glazer and Daniel Patrick Moynihan's *Beyond the Melting Pot: The Negroes, Puerto Ricans, Jews, Italians, and Irish of New York City* (1963) and Michael Novak's *The Rise of the Unmeltable Ethnics: Politics and Culture in the Seventies* (1972). The centrality of religion to the discourse of ethnicity introduced a genuinely alternative conceptual framework into the general discussion of cultural difference in the postwar years. Ultimately, however, the sociological terms of the engagement transformed the sacred into yet another resource for self-development.

The influx of European immigrant groups in the middle of the nineteenth century marked the beginning of a persistent WASP fear of subversion of republican institutions by a dangerous "other" internal to American society. The second wave of immigration in the early twentieth century led Anglo intellectuals beyond fear of subversion to hope for assimilation, through either a "melting pot" ideal of transforming immigrants into good Americans or an ideal of cultural pluralism that saw America as a "nation of nations" able to accommodate differences among a variety of national groups. By midcentury, the conflict between melting pot and pluralist understandings of the place of ethnicity in American life had resolved itself in favor of an official affirmation of a kind of melting pot pluralism. The war against fascism abroad became a war for diversity at home—an ideal most popularly represented by the multiethnic platoon films that Hollywood produced as part of its contribution to wartime propaganda efforts. Ironically, at the very moment that politicians and intellectuals were affirming diversity as a value, it seemed to be disappearing as a fact. Suburbanization broke up many of the old ethnic neighborhoods, and the descendants of European immigrants seemed destined to blend into a homogeneous mass of affluent whiteness. Only African Americans appeared exempt from this homogenizing trend. The political urgency of African-American integration combined with the trend toward suburbanization to marginalize European ethnicity as a concern in mainstream cultural discourse.

The expanding knowledge industry of the postwar American university refused to let ethnicity disappear completely. The academy, perhaps more than any other single institution, seemed best to embody the new commitment to ethnic pluralism. In the years following World War II, the ethnic makeup of the American university was dramatically transformed by the sudden influx of a new generation of young Jewish-American intellectuals. This transformation was particularly striking in that last bastion of WASP cultural authority, the Ivy League university. The leading public intellectuals of the 1950s—Daniel Bell, Richard Hofstadter, David Riesman, and Seymor Martin Lipset—were all of Jewish descent and were all tenured at Ivy League institutions. These newly arrived Jewish-American intellectuals neither asserted nor denied their ethnic heritage; rather, they took their own acceptance into elite WASP cultural institutions as evidence of the general decline of both ethnic discrimination and ethnic particularity in American life. At a time when educational institutions took on a new significance, both as a vehicle for upward mobility and a laboratory for racial integration, the Jewish "passion for education" made Jews "paradoxically the most 'American' of all the ethnic groups."[1] Constituting only 2 percent of the population, Jews were nonetheless representative of that to which all Americans should aspire.

Despite a general agreement that strong ethnic distinctions had disappeared from the American present, intellectuals accorded ethnicity a new prominence in the American past. In his Pulitzer Prize–winning book *The Uprooted* (1951), Jewish-American historian Oscar Handlin argued that far from being merely an aspect of American history, "the immigrants *were* American history." Handlin describes immigration less as a geographical phenomenon than a psychological experience. Immigrants were uprooted not merely from their local villages but from the centuries-old traditions that had shaped their understanding of the world. The initial "shock of alienation" that "forever snapped the ancient ties" proved, however, to be "an act of liberation." Handlin concludes in an almost confessional tone, adopting a first-person narrative voice to proclaim that "in our flight, unattached, we discovered what it was to be an individual, a man apart from place and station." The immigrant emerges from Handlin's book as the representative man of modernity, and the birth of this existential subject redeems the dislocations of modernization. Often melodramatically sympathetic to the suffering of the immigrants, Handlin nonetheless sees traditional ethnic cultures merely as "a platform from which to launch new ascensions that will extend the discoveries of the immigrants whose painful break with their past is our past." Handlin concludes with his ideal of the proper relation of the modern to the traditional: "We will justify their pitiable struggle for dignity and meaning by extending it in our lives toward an end they had not the opportunity to envision."[2]

Will Herberg's *Protestant, Catholic, Jew* (1955) provided the sociological counterpart to Handlin's history. Herberg differs from Handlin only in arguing for the persistence of religious affiliation as the last residue of living ethnic traditions. Though more sympathetic than Handlin to the substance of the tradition whose passing he analyzes, Herberg reformulates the last tradition, religion, as yet another manifestation of the existential search for meaning. True, authentic religion is the "striving to find a center of life beyond life, a larger whole transcending the self in which to ground the meaning and security of existence." Herberg modifies earlier melting pot theories of assimilation to argue for America as a "triple melting pot" of three distinct faith traditions: Protestantism, Catholicism, and Judaism. Even these distinctions fade upon closer examination: at best, the three groupings provide little more than a setting, a "platform" in Handlin's sense, for the exercise of authentic religion, now redefined in antitraditional, existential terms; at worst, they offer little more than minor variations on a common "American way of life."[3]

Relatively benign when viewed historically, ethnic cultures appeared much more sinister when viewed as a living reality. Even as social scientists celebrated tolerance and diversity, they tended to trace the roots of intolerance to the very ethnic cultures that were supposed to be celebrated and tolerated. In the wake of the Holocaust, the American Jewish Committee sponsored a series of studies on the social origins of prejudice. The most significant book in the series, *The Authoritarian Personality* (1950), was written under the direction of Theodor W. Adorno, himself a German-Jewish refugee from Nazi Germany. Adorno and his associates traced the rise of anti-Semitism to the "irrational remnants of ancient racial and religious hatreds" among the European masses.[4] Unable to cope with the economic and social dislocations of the Great War, rural peasants and the urban lower-middle-class scapegoated Jews as the source of social problems and looked to an authoritarian leader to restore order. As this explanation became orthodoxy, social scientists began to equate "ancient" and "religious" with the "irrational" and "hatred." The authoritarianism of German culture became merely an extreme case of a broader authoritarianism, the desire to "escape from freedom" that infected all traditional ethnic cultures.

This reading of European anti-Semitism profoundly shaped the understanding of what appeared to many as a homegrown American fascism, the anticommunist witch hunt led by Senator Joseph McCarthy. One major line of sociological analysis traced McCarthy's appeal to his ethnicity. An Irish Catholic, McCarthy supposedly spoke to the anxieties of American ethnics unsure of their status in American society and overwhelmed by the social dislocations of modern life; communism provided a scapegoat for these anxieties, and anticommunism served as a means to assert the ethnic's true Americanism. Given its original concerns to explain and refute anti-Semitism, the analysis of the "authoritarian personality" tended to exempt Jewish ethnic culture from this characterization; further, the urban American context to which intellectuals most often applied this analysis tended to dilute authoritarianism of any specifically German character. Consequently, the burden of the dark side of ethnicity fell on the high-profile urban Catholic ethnic groups—the Irish and the Italians.

Despite persistent concern for ethnicity through the 1950s, no major work specifically addressed the state of ethnic groups in contemporary America until Glazer and Moynihan's *Beyond the Melting Pot* (1963). Still very much a work of the "consensus" era, *Beyond the Melting Pot* reads less as a response to the literature on ethnic assimilation and more as a continuation of the 1950s discourse of interest-group pluralism. By the mid-1950s, the pluralist discourse that had grown out of the second wave of European immigration had shifted its locus from ethnicity to politics. Having established that American culture bound citizens together through a common faith in democracy, social scientists proceeded to prove that this faith was grounded in an accurate assessment of empirical reality. Works such as John Kenneth Galbraith's *American Capitalism: The Theory of Countervailing Power* (1950) sought to steer a middle path between the naive individualism of classical liberalism and the cynical bipolar class antagonisms of classical Marxism. Drawing on Tocqueville's notion of the voluntary association, many social scientists argued that democracy in America should be understood in terms of the interaction of a variety of social and economic "interest groups" that mediated between the individual and the state. Empirical case studies, most notably Robert A. Dahl's *Who Governs?: Democracy and Power in an American City* (1961), consistently argued that despite some lingering economic inequality, political power was fairly evenly distributed among a variety of groups, with no single group having inordinate power over other groups for any significant period of time. *Beyond the Melting Pot* works best at this level, arguing for distinct ethnic voting patterns and thus distinct ethnic interest groups in New York City politics.

The book nonetheless makes larger cultural claims. Its title explicitly invokes the early twentieth century debate over the status of ethnic cultures in the United States. Glazer and Moynihan argue not only that "the ethnic pattern is still so strong in New York City" but also that the "the melting pot . . . did not happen" (*BMP,* 291, 290). To go beyond the melting pot is also to go beyond the interest group, a political category, to the ethnic group, a cultural category. The understanding of culture at work in the analysis is, however, somewhat contradictory. Glazer and Moynihan assert that from "the beginning, our society and our politics have been at least as much concerned with values as with interests," yet they downplay the normative cultural continuities within ethnic groups across generations (*BMP,* v, 313). The "ethnic group" is *"not a survival from the age of mass immigration but a new social form"* (*BMP,* 16).

A hybrid form, the ethnic group floats in a liminal space between the cultural and the social, between pluralism and assimilation:

> It is true that language and culture are very largely lost in the first and second generations, and this makes the dream of "cultural pluralism"—of a new Italy or Germany or Ireland in America, a League of Nations established in the New World—as unlikely as the hope of a "melting pot." But as the groups were transformed by influences in American society, stripped of their original attributes, they were recreated as something new, but still as identifiable groups. Concretely, persons think of themselves as members of that group, with that name; they are thought of by others as members of the group by new attributes that the original immigrants would never have recognized as identifying their groups, but which nevertheless serve to mark them off, by more than simply name and association, in the third generation and even beyond. (*BMP,* 13)

The cautious tone of this formulation contrasts sharply with the confident assertion of the book's title. Glazer and Moynihan constantly assert the persistence of cultural difference yet qualify the substance of this difference out of existence. They declare ethnics to be "still, in many essential ways, as different from one another as their grandfathers had been" yet concede that the descendents of the various immigrant groups live as "Americans, in the same dress, with the same language, using the same artifacts, troubled by the same things" (*BMP,* 14). At the level of culture, this kind of dialectic threatens to reduce ethnicity to the perception of ethnicity. Ethnic cultural difference would seem to consist in the general sense or feeling of ethnicity, the enduring tendency of people to make ethnic generalizations. The authors want to argue strongly that "the distinctions are important, and . . . they consist of more than the amusing differences of accent and taste in food and drink," but the only substantial cultural difference they examine—"different ideas about education and sex"—also divides members of the WASP mainstream (*BMP,* 21).

Glazer and Moynihan resort to no such dialectics in their assessment of the relations among the various ethnic groups of New York. Against the egalitarian orientation of much of 1950s pluralist analysis, the authors frankly order the ethnic groups they study into a social class hierarchy based on achievement and merit: Jews at the top, Italians and Irish in the middle, and Negroes and Puerto Ricans at the bottom. Asking "a measure of forgiveness for taking up a subject which needs to be discussed, but which cannot be aired without giving pain to some," they forge on with an impartial assessment of "the unevenness of achievement" among the groups (*BMP,* vi). Their account of Negroes and Puerto Ricans owes much to Oscar Lewis's "culture of poverty" thesis, which argues that the material conditions of poverty induce values (laziness, profligacy, etc.) that keep people impoverished even after external constraints to advancement (i.e., racism) have been removed. Glazer and Moynihan concede the persistence of racism as a factor in the persistence of poverty, yet this qualification at best merely victimizes Negroes and Puerto Ricans, absolving them from responsibility for their actions. The authors indulge in no such sentimentality with regard to non-Jewish white ethnics. Though economically more successful than Negroes and Puerto Ricans, "white Catholics . . . have the least positive attitude toward work of any of the major groups" (*BMP,* 259). The Italians and the Irish suffer from not only a culture of poverty but from what amounts to a poverty of culture. The urban poor suffer from rootlessness and lack of social organization, while the urban ethnic lower-middle class suffers from too much rootedness and organization. Glazer's account of the Italians and Moynihan's chapter on the Irish both stress the debilitating effects of the persistence of premodern traditions, the tendency of each group to attempt to recreate the "conservative village" in "an urban environment" (*BMP,* 188). This conservative continuity provided a stability that enabled the Italians and the Irish to secure a foothold in the lower middle class, yet it has hindered their advancement into the professions and, more alarmingly, fostered a hostility toward progressive political change.

This poverty of culture thesis receives its sharpest formulation when the authors compare ethnic Catholics to Jews. Glazer concludes that "mobility for Italians has to be individual mobility, because the group moves slowly and is conservative in its outlook and habits." However, "Jewish mobility is a mass phenomenon" because of the Jewish "passion for education" and general culture of achievement (*BMP,* 198, 155). Moynihan similarly writes of the "relative failure of the Irish to rise socially" as compared to the Jews (*BMP,* 258). Ironically, Jews serve as the heroes of *Beyond the Melting Pot* not because they have refused to melt but because they have melted more successfully than any other ethnic group: "with the powerful acculturative processes of American life, Jews will become like everyone else ... and one wonders whether the effect of social progress is to make Jews just like the upper-class Protestant denominations that they begin to approximate in wealth and occupation" (*BMP,* 159).

In many ways, the book is an attempt to answer the question, Why can't Negroes, Puerto Ricans, Italians, and Irish be more like Jews? The question is one of class, the answer one of culture. For Glazer and Moynihan, certain ethnic cultures lag behind others in adopting those values necessary for economic success and real cultural achievement. The concept of cultural lag allows Glazer and Moynihan to retain an enlightened suspicion of ethnicity as a potential social problem in need of social-scientific supervision while affirming ethnicity to the degree that it adapts properly to the demands of a modern, economically mobile society.

True to a kind of pluralism, Glazer and Moynihan recognize that this cultural lag manifests itself in distinct ways within distinct cultures. The "problem" of ethnic Italian culture is the family. Glazer interprets Italian-American culture through the lens of the concept of "amoral familialism" developed in the sociologist Edward C. Banfield's revealingly titled 1959 work, *The Moral Basis of a Backward Society.* The value system of amoral familialism assumes that "one owes nothing to anyone outside one's family, and effort should advance only the family" (*BMP,* 195). This strong sense of family obligation informs a distinctly Italian-American cultural ethos:

> The set of qualities that seems to distinguish Italian Americans include individuality, temperament, and ambition, all of which, however, are restricted by the culture and outlook of the family and neighborhood. This produces a tension, the most satisfying resolution of which is some form of worldly success that is admired by one's family and the friends of one's childhood. Perhaps the ideal is the entertainer—to give him a name, Frank Sinatra—who is an international celebrity, but still the big-hearted, generous, unchanged boy from the block. That form of individuality and ambition which is identified with Protestant and Anglo-Saxon culture, and for which the criteria of success are abstract and impersonal, is rare among American Italians (*BMP,* 194).

Glazer's account of ethnic Italian culture reproduces all of the classic dichotomies of social-scientific thought. Italian Americans are communal, whereas WASPs are individualistic. Their family life possesses a "heightened and uninhibited emotional quality" that contrasts sharply with the repressive rationality of the WASP family. Italian Americans exhibit a strong "desire for material goods and sensual satisfaction ... uninhibited by a Puritanical religion" (*BMP,* 197). An emotional, expressive people, Italian Americans "can make great efforts for a noble gesture" but have proven "incapable of creating institutions that work steadily for common ends" (*BMP,* 193). Mired in the primal unity of the family, ethnic Italians have been unable to imagine new organizational forms. Glazer acknowledges one exception to this rule—the Italian dominance of "organized" crime—but insists that this organization is best understood as an extension of the Italian family structure and should not be confused with the rational organization of modern bureaucracies (*BMP*, 196).

Glazer's chapter on Italian Americans amounts to a sociological meditation on backwardness, or "the burdens of Southern Italian culture" (*BMP*, 201). Nowhere is this backwardness more debilitating than in the area of education:

> To New York's public school administrator of twenty and thirty years ago the great burden was the "Italian problem," just as today it is the Negro and Puerto Rican problem. . . . The problems of present-day Negro and Puerto Rican children often stem from the weakness of the family, in which a single overburdened and resentful parent is unable to maintain an ordered home life for the child. By contrast, the problems of the Italian children stemmed from a too strong, too rigorously ordered family, which did not value education. (*BMP*, 200)

Ethnic Italians are American to the extent that they desire advancement, but still too peasant in their sacrifice of self-advancement to family advancement: "Under this (from an American viewpoint) topsy-turvy system of values, it was the 'bad' son who wanted to go to school instead of to work, the 'bad' daughter who wanted to remain in school instead of helping her mother" (*BMP*, 199). This communal ethic clashes with the individualizing discipline of the public school, and it deprives Italian-American children of opportunities for social advancement.

Indifference to education points to an even deeper cultural pathology, an overt hostility to individual self-development. Glazer concedes that Italian Americans appreciate the practical value of education "as a means of preparing for a profession—teaching for the girls, engineering or the free professions for the boys," but insists that their cultural background "does not incline them toward the more intellectual and speculative college curricula" (*BMP*, 202). Italians accept vocational training with clearly defined career goals, but their culture lacks a general "ideology of change." As a group, they continue to suffer from a peasant culture in which "intellectual curiosity and originality [are] ridiculed or suppressed. 'Do not make your child better than you are,' runs a South Italian proverb." Italian children underachieve in public schools not merely because of the primacy of family obligations but because at a deeper level they have "not been raised for new adventures" (*BMP*, 199). In technical terms Glazer draws from cultural anthropology, "the Italian family seems to be more interested in a child's being than his becoming, and the latter is sacrificed to the former" (*BMP*, 198). Italian children are "ill at ease" when "forced out of the close familiar family and into the school" and whenever they find themselves in fluid social situations demanding flexibility and adaptability to change (*BMP,* 199).

Ultimately, Glazer finds the clearest symptom of the poverty of Italian-American culture in its failure to nurture the dreams and ambitions of young Italian-American intellectuals:

> An Italian-American novel published in 1961 (*A Cup of the Sun* by Octavia Waldo) describes the problems of a young Italian American of great sensitivity who wants to become an artist or writer. She is as isolated in her community as she would be in a small Midwest town. She must go away to school, and she knows she will never have anything to come back to. Her development separates her decisively from the friends with whom she grew up. (*BMP*, 198)

Glazer here invokes the protagonist of *A Cup of the Sun* much as Ruth Benedict invokes Japanese writers in *The Chrysanthemum and the Sword*: Italian-American culture, like Japanese culture, appears to fail in its essential obligation to nurture the development of individual identity.

Despite a fair degree of economic success, Italian Americans have failed to internalize the expressive individualism that Glazer deems essential to the broader social and economic progress of America as a whole. This partial assimilation has left Italian Americans caught between two worlds with, in effect, the worst of both. Success in vocational education has pulled Italian Americans "from the working class to (in increasing measure) the middle class, from the city to the suburbs" (*BMP,* 216). This path of upward mobility, however, threatens to cut them off from the vital peasant element of their lower-class roots without providing the aesthetic compensation that sustains the more liberal and intellectual members of the middle class. Of this new middle class environment, Glazer concludes:

> Young Italian intellectuals do not find this a very congenial atmosphere. But there are as yet not enough of them to develop any steady criticism of the style of Italian-American life; and the few who might do this have neither the organs nor the audience that would make such an enterprise worthwhile. If they are novelists, they celebrate the rich content of the old proletarian, city life. They know this is disappearing, and is being replaced by a new middle-class style, which is American Catholic more than it is anything that may be called American Italian. But it is still too new to have found anyone to record it, to criticize it, and perhaps to transcend it. (*BMP,* 216)

This passage signifies an incorporation of Italian-American culture into the orthodox discourse of cultural individualism that dominated humanist social science in the postwar years. A healthy culture is one that not only encourages the development of individuality within itself but actually fosters its own transcendence. Culture must sacrifice its integrity to the perception of its integrity by critical, autonomous intellectuals. This perception will, moreover, always be a kind of backward glance, for it depends on a critical mass of detachment ("there are not yet enough of them to develop any steady criticism") to sustain the "organs" and provide the "audience that would make such an enterprise worthwhile." Italian-American culture has, by Glazer's account, clearly failed in its duty to individuals. The significance of Glazer's account lies less in his negative assessment of Italian-American realities than in his subjecting an ethnic Catholic culture to a basically WASP standard of judgment.

Irish America offers an even more extreme form of the cultural stagnation that results from incomplete assimilation. Glazer's charge that Italians are becoming American Catholic is, in effect, the charge that they are becoming American Irish. Throughout the cold war period, the Irish serve as the lowest common denominator of white ethnicity. Despite a creeping middle-class Catholicism, Italian-Americans still show a healthy interest in sex and proudly associate themselves with the continental Italian culture of fashion and film that shaped the cosmopolitan outlook of postwar Europe. The Irish, in contrast, remain sexually repressed and long ago passed up their opportunity for international cultural ascendancy by rejecting the secular modernism of Yeats, Joyce, and O'Casey (*BMP,* 202–5, 252, 247). Moynihan's chapter on the American Irish is a genuinely moving pastoral lament for the passing of the time when New York was Irish; it is also a scathing indictment of the pathology of lower-middle-class, petit bourgeois life. The Irish, even more than the Italians, remain beyond the melting pot by virtue of a Catholic anti-intellectualism that retards the proper ethnic development into the culture of the secular WASP middle class.

Reminiscent of Glazer's account of the Italians, Moynihan explains the deficiencies of the Irish in terms of the persistence of premodern values. Moynihan reads the Irish-American urban experience as a meeting of the "ancient world of folkways and the modern world of contracts" (*BMP,* 233). Leading the first major wave of immigration in the mid-nineteenth century, the Irish arrived in American cities with a habit of politics developed in Daniel O'Connell's Catholic Emancipation movement. As O'Connell's movement used modern organizational methods to ensure the survival of a premodern religious tradition, so the great institutional achievement of the Irish in America, "machine" politics, "resulted from a merger of rural Irish custom with urban American politics" (*BMP,* 223). According to Moynihan, this merger ultimately favored rural conservatism over urban dynamism: "the Irish just didn't know what to do with their opportunity. They never thought of politics as an instrument of social change—their kind of politics involved processes of a society that was not changing" (*BMP,* 229). Even in its prime, Irish political conservatism seemed to combine the worst of the old and the new. Ironically, the city machine was both hierarchical *and* impersonal:

> The stereotype of the Irish politician as a beer-guzzling back-slapper is nonsense. Croker, McLaughlin, and *Mister* Murphy were the least affable of men. Their task was not to charm but to administer with firmness and predictability a political bureaucracy in which the prerogatives of rank were carefully observed. The hierarchy had to be maintained. (*BMP*, 226–27)

According to Moynihan, this peasant conservatism reached its authoritarian nadir in Irish support for the anticommunism of Joseph McCarthy.

Still, the election of John F. Kennedy rescued the Irish from their darkest political hour and seemed to vindicate the urban liberalism of the first Irish Catholic presidential contender, Al Smith. At the time of Kennedy's assassination, Irish Catholics held all of the national leadership positions in the Democratic Party and sustained the party's commitment to the liberal agenda of the New Deal. Moynihan finds the deepest and most troubling expression of Irish conservatism not in politics, but in religion.

As Italians suffer from excessive loyalty to the family, so the Irish suffer from excessive loyalty to the Roman Catholic Church. For Moynihan, the Church is the glory and shame of the American Irish. It is "incomparably the most important thing they have done in America. But they have done it at a price." Support for the Church has diverted economic and cultural resources that would otherwise have lifted the Irish as a group into the middle class. Economically, a "good part of the surplus that might have gone into family property has gone to building the church." Culturally, the "celibacy of the Catholic clergy has . . . deprived the Irish of the class of ministers' sons which has contributed notably to the prosperity and distinction of the Protestant world" (*BMP,* 230). Moynihan places his sociological assessment of Irish Catholicism in the context of the contemporary debate over Catholic intellectual achievement. In his 1956 book, *American Catholics and Intellectual Life*, Monsignor John Tracy Ellis decried the lack of Catholic intellectual achievement, particularly when compared to American Jews who had become leaders in the secular and historically Protestant academy. Irish dominance of the church hierarchy left them with the burden of blame for this underachievement. For Moynihan, Irish Catholic anti-intellectualism appears even more embarrassing in light of highly vocal and costly commitment to a separate parochial school system on the part of the Irish clergy.

The acute cultural bathos of the American Irish derives not only from their high public profile in the present but also from their real achievements in the past. For all of his criticism of contemporary Irish anti-intellectualism, Moynihan nonetheless provides what is still one of the most lyrical accounts of the golden age of Irish-American popular culture:

> They became the playboys of this new Western World. "None can Love Like an Irishman" was a favorite song of Lincoln's day. By the turn of the century it had become equally clear that none could run like them, nor fight like them, nor drink as much, nor sing as well. When it came to diving off the Brooklyn Bridge or winning pennants for the Giants, it took an Irishman. And who could write such bittersweet songs as Victor Herbert? Or enjoy life like "Diamond Jim" Brady? All was "bliss and blarney." . . . When the movies began to fashion a composite picture of the American people, the New York Irishman was projected to the very center of the national image. . . . James Cagney (a New Yorker) was the quintessential figure: fists cocked, chin out, back straight, bouncing along on his heels. But also doomed: at the end of the movie he was usually dead. (*BMP*, 246–47)

In culture as in politics, the Irish simply did not know what to do with their opportunity. As they failed to develop a progressive politics, so they failed to develop a progressive culture. Contemporary Irish-American culture has little to offer beyond nostalgia for the glorious achievements of a proletarian past increasingly at odds with the dull reality of a lower-middle-class present (*BMP*, 251).

This historical contrast points to the developmental framework that provides the normative structure of *Beyond the Melting Pot*. The Irish have more or less entered the middle class economically, but they have failed to make any contribution to middle-class culture. Moynihan presents the rejection of Irish modernism as a sign of a larger arrested cultural development:

> *Reilly and the 400* was fun, but it was not *Riders to the Sea*. When it emerged that the American Irish did not see this, their opportunity to attain a degree of cultural ascendancy quite vanished. After that began a steady emigration from the Irish "community" of many of the strongest and best of the young. The migration was as devitalizing in America as it was to the Irish nation overseas. (*BMP*, 248)

The American Irish failed to produce any work of serious artistic merit and proved unwilling to nurture and support an intellectual class capable of appreciating the great works of art produced by international modernists. Moynihan concludes, "Excepting those with a strong religious vocation, the sensitive, perceptive children of the American Irish born early in the twentieth century found little to commend itself in the culture to which they were born" (*BMP*, 248). The Irish, like the Italians, failed to develop an intellectual class. The Irish control of the religious and political institutions that could have sustained such a class makes the Irish failure all the worse.

The accounts of the Italians and the Irish in *Beyond the Melting Pot* suggest less the persistence of a vital ethnic pluralism than the persistence of a Manichean intellectual dualism. Beneath the diffuse and local tensions of ethnic interest-group politics lies the long, twilight struggle between the enlightened and the unenlightened. Ultimately, Glazer and Moynihan redeem the pathology of ethno-religious culture by decoupling the ethnic from the religious. Acknowledging the racial divisions of American society in their accounts of the Negroes and Puerto Ricans, they nonetheless conceive of the future of American politics primarily in terms of the conflict between a general ethnic ethos and a general religious ethos:

> Thus a Jewish ethos and a Catholic ethos emerge . . . two subcultures, two value systems, shaped and defined certainly in part by religious practice and experience and organization but by now supported by the existence of two communities. . . . One is secular in its attitudes, liberal in its outlook on sexual life and divorce, positive about science and social science. The other is religious in its outlook, resists the growing liberalization in sexual mores and its reflection in cultural and family life, feels strongly the tension between moral values and modern science and technology. The conflict may be seen in many ways—not least in the fact that the new disciplines such as psychoanalysis, particularly in New York, are so largely staffed by Jews. (*BMP*, 298)

The authors are careful to present the terms "Jewish" and "Catholic" as neutral social-scientific shorthand for two broad yet distinct value orientations. Insisting that these values are "nurtured in the social groupings defined by religious affiliations," they still refuse to reduce these values to "purely the expression of the spirit of a religion" (*BMP*, 313, 298). The attempt to secure sufficient flexibility for these terms as analytic tools in no way diminishes the inflexibility of Glazer and Moynihan's general attitude toward religion. "Jewish" refers to an ethnic as well as a religious grouping; in *Beyond the Melting Pot*, Jewish achievement appears as a function of Jewish secularity, the distance of ethnic Jews from their religious roots. "Catholic" refers to a religious affiliation that encompasses many ethnic groups, including the Italians and the Irish; Glazer and Moynihan attempt to avoid invidious ethnic distinctions by grouping the most negative aspects of Italian and Irish ethnicity under a religious category. In the context of the book, the choice of the word "Jewish" to stand for the secular suggests not only the empirical reality of New York intellectual life but also the wish to associate enlightened secular intellectualism with the persistence of ethnic diversity; the choice of the word "Catholic" to stand for the religious speaks to the persistence of an American intellectual tradition that finds in the Catholic Church the source for all social and intellectual backwardness.

In the conclusion of *Beyond the Melting Pot*, ethnic pluralism ultimately triumphs over religious dualism. Glazer and Moynihan insist that the variety of subcommunities within the two broad value orientations ensures that neither orientation will achieve the institutional consolidation necessary to impose its will on the other. Subcommunities that share similar values may be divided over antagonistic interests. In classic pluralist fashion, the "group-forming characteristics of American social life" diffuse social conflict (*BMP,* 291). Indeed, ethnic groups owe their existence less to a shared culture or country of origin than to a "central tendency in the national ethos which structures people, whether those coming in afresh or the descendents of those who have been here for generations, into groups of different status and character" (*BMP,* 290–91). This same tendency promotes "the evolution of the American peoples" over time. In the conclusion of *Beyond the Melting Pot*, the sharp divide of fixed values gives way to an affirmation of faith in the process of creating values: "the American nationality is still forming: its processes are mysterious, and the final form, if there is ever to be a final form, is as yet unknown" (*BMP,* 315).

Following a narrative convention rooted in the Puritan jeremiad, Glazer and Moynihan resolve all doubts and uncertainties as to the substance of American nationality through a commitment to the reflection on the process of national development.[5] This language of process proves as evasive in its secular versions as in its earlier religious expressions. Despite their official pluralist silence as to specific ends, Glazer and Moynihan argue for a very specific final form for American nationality: ethnic groups must progress to the level of the social and cultural values of liberal intellectuals. The refusal of liberal intellectuals to acknowledge the particular interests served by their promotion of the "neutral" process of pluralism would contribute to the reassertion of ethnic culture on the part of ethnics themselves.

Glazer and Moynihan correctly perceived race and religion as the key categories of domestic politics in the 1960s. Urban ethnic Catholics resented having their schools and neighborhoods transformed into laboratories for progressive race relations. This resentment stemmed in no small part from an awareness that these experiments were designed primarily by WASP and Jewish academics safely removed from the violence provoked by forced integration. The liberal tendency to excuse urban rioting by African Americans as a logical (and morally justifiable) consequence of centuries of racial oppression seemed to confirm white ethnics' growing suspicion that they were to be the ones to pay the price for racial justice. Growing liberal sympathy for the antiwar movement, as well as the permissive counterculture associated with it, further sharpened the battle lines between white ethnics and liberal intellectuals: the sons of white ethnics went to war while the children of liberal intellectuals received college exemptions and spat on returning soldiers as "baby killers." The New Deal coalition of liberal intellectuals and working-class white ethnics finally collapsed at the 1968 Democratic National Convention in Chicago. With the blessing of Irish Catholic mayor Richard Daley, the Chicago police provoked a riot through their violent repression of antiwar protests outside convention headquarters. The nomination of Hubert Humphrey, an old labor Democrat, failed to rally the New Deal coalition, and the Republicans won the election.

Postmortem analyses quickly called attention to the specifically ethnic dimension of Nixon's electoral victory. In his highly influential 1969 work, *The Emerging Republican Majority,* Kevin Phillips argued that Nixon's "silent majority," the white conservative electorate that voted him into office, had "many ethnic strains" and could not be seen as "a white Anglo-Saxon Protestant monolith." Writing as a partisan Republican against Democratic commentators who equated the breakup of the New Deal coalition with the collapse of civilization, Phillips declared that "ethnic polarization is a longstanding hallmark of American politics, not an unprecedented and menacing development of 1968."[6] Phillips understood the ethnic divide of the 1968 election in terms of yet another enduring feature of American politics, the struggle between elitism and populism:

> Since the days of Alexander Hamilton and the Federalists, the United States—and the Northeast in particular—has periodically supported a privileged elite, blind to the needs and interests of the large national majority. The corporate welfarists, planners and academicians of the Liberal Establishment are the newest of these elites, and their interests—for one thing, a high and not necessarily too productive rate of government social, educational, scientific and research spending—are as vested as those of Coolidge-Hoover era financiers and industrialists. The great political upheaval of the Nineteen Sixties is . . . a populist revolt of the American masses who have been elevated by prosperity to middle-class status and conservatism. *Their* revolt is against the caste, policies and taxation of the Mandarins of Establishment liberalism.[7]

Broadening the Jewish–Catholic scheme of *Beyond the Melting Pot* to account for nonethnics, Phillips nonetheless insisted on the centrality of northeastern Catholics to the political realignment of 1968. Defining the new populist majority in terms of a hostility to "sociological jurisprudence, moral permissiveness, experimental residential welfare and educational programming," Phillips effectively translated the Jewish/Catholic moral divide of *Beyond the Melting Pot* into the Democratic/Republican divide of party politics.[8]

By the early 1970s, ethnic Catholic intellectuals themselves attempted to articulate the vanguard position ascribed to them by social scientists. Michael Novak's 1972 work *The Rise of the Unmeltable Ethnics* stands as the most significant attempt to transform the ethnic in-itself to an ethnic for-itself. Novak explicitly attacks the "authoritarian personality" interpretation of white ethnics as the bigotry of the intellectuals, and he defends ethnic respect for authority as a legitimate concern for social order and cultural continuity. In Novak's reading of ethnicity, the conservative/liberal divide of *Beyond the Melting Pot* becomes an epochal confrontation between tradition and modernity. Novak's understanding of the legitimate fears of white ethnics serves as an enduring antidote to the dismissive progressivism of Glazer and Moynihan's account. Ironically, Novak's defense of tradition in specifically ethnic rather than religious terms leads him back to the very social-scientific worldview so often the object of his critique. By looking to ethnic traditions to provide "a new direction for the Left," Novak engages in an act of self-objectification that incorporates Catholic ethnicity into a very WASPish tradition of sociological romanticism.[9]

At its best, Novak's appropriation of the sociological concept of modernization enables him to move beyond the relatively narrow political categories of Phillips's discussion of ethnicity. For Novak, debates over racial integration and government regulation obscure a fundamental consensus that unites liberals and conservatives: "'Modernization' is our project. Mass production, mass markets, centralized transport—everything favors dense metropolitan areas" (*RUE,* 240). Novak declares this "nationalizing, standardizing super-culture shaped by industry" to be the "most revolutionary force in American life for the past hundred years" (*RUE,* 122). This framework of modernization confounds the standard liberal/conservative dichotomy of American politics. In their defense of corporate capitalism, those "in America who call themselves conservative are the chief agents in the destruction of what they claim to value: old America and its simple, honest, rural values" (*RUE,* 122). The Left romance with the Viet Cong offers no real alternative: "the war in Indochina may be seen as a competition between two rival ways of legitimizing modernization" (*RUE,* 268). Faced with this global consensus on economic development, Novak proposes an alternative political framework: "Is not the chief political battle of our time drawn up between the enlightened and the unenlightened?" (*RUE,* xiii). Novak's sympathies lie with the unenlightened, and his book is in large part an attempt to fashion white ethnics into a political vanguard of counterenlightenment.

Against charges of nostalgia, Novak launches an antimodern critique of modernity's own evasion of the social consequences of progress. Conceding the achievements modernity claims as its own, he links them to an institutional violence that defenders of modernity consistently deny. The enlightened superculture of international corporations has indeed created "a world of expanded liberties and fruitful possibilities" (*RUE,* 160). Intellectuals and artists understandably prize "the excitement, stimulation, and variety of cities," yet Novak concludes sardonically that the "price of human suffering in New York seems a little high for the stimulation of so few" (*RUE,* 240). Novak refuses moderns the excuse of unintended consequences: from New York to Saigon, the suffering has been so persistent as to make the defense of rational, orderly social development the equivalent of a willful and manipulative obfuscation.

Novak also refuses to simply shift the locus of violence from ethnic "authoritarianism" to WASP rationalism. He argues instead for the distinctly ideological nature of violence in the modern world. WASP violence, "the celebrated Yankee shrewdness," refuses to acknowledge itself as such. WASPs prefer to keep violence "at arm's length, invisible, conducted at a distance by intermediaries who merely follow orders. Ugly scenes and confrontations are not 'civil.' Other ethnic groups are not less violent, but they hide less from themselves" (*RUE,* 151).

The captains of industry killed more people through their violent repression of labor activism during the Gilded Age than Chicago bootleggers killed during the wars of Prohibition. However, even when figured as robber barons, WASPs are greedy, never violent, whereas the Italian Al Capone, despite his protestations of being a businessman, is always figured as a gangster. In perhaps his sharpest contrast of these "styles of violence," Novak observes, "Antipersonnel bombs were not invented by men on a construction gang; guys on a beer truck did not dream up napalm. Ph.D.'s from universities, who abhor bloodshed, thought them up" (*RUE,* 169). The Vietnam War has revealed that "cool rationality" may be "the most murderous passion of them all" (*RUE,* 174–75). Their self-imposed blindness to this violence, however, confirms WASPs in their own sense of moral superiority to ethnics.

Leveling the field on violence, Novak turns to questions of culture. White ethnics do not suffer from the burden of peasant cultural lag; rather, they have actively fought to maintain their premodern traditions. Ethnic hostility to liberal education stems not from any irrational anti-intellectualism but from a perfectly rational understanding of the nature of an education that "tends to separate children from their parents, from their roots, from their history, in the cause of a universal and superior religion" (*RUE,* 58). The ambitious educational initiatives of liberal intellectuals during the 1960s only confirms these suspicions:

> in recent years the threat to ethnics is as perceptible as the arrival of missionaries on South Sea islands, their hands full of brassieres. Intellectuals want the ethnics to become *enlightened,* to "become converted and live." And if ethnics don't want to become like intellectuals? (*RUE,* 18)

Seemingly neutral terms such as "humanism" and "progress" mask a will to power on the part of intellectuals who wish to incorporate ethnics into their own modernizing program—a program in which ethnics, if only by virtue of their late arrival, would always occupy a subordinate position. Ethnics see the drive for moral and intellectual improvement as "moral pressure to abandon their own traditions, their faith, their associations, in order to reap higher rewards in the culture of national corporations" (*RUE,* 38, 61). Ethnics not only value local associations over rootless mobility, they also harbor a deep, primordial suspicion of the liberal, enlightened view "that life is intended to be exciting, glamorous, or fun" (*RUE,* 203). Novak respects this peasant fatalism as a wisdom born of experience and sees it as a needed corrective to the hubris of modern enlightenment.

Intellectually daring as an intervention into American party politics, Novak's account of the WASP/ethnic split nonetheless remains heavily indebted to a sociological tradition that is itself the creation of the very modernizing elites he criticizes. In the language of German sociology, ethnics embody all the virtues of *Gemeinschaft,* whereas WASPs embody all the vices of *Geselleschaft.* The empirical accuracy of Novak's argument aside, the tools of analysis he adopts lead him away from the traditions he wishes to embrace. Ethnic cultures have no language of "ethnicity." By Novak's own account, they are, in a sense, instinctual—felt, lived, and experienced. Lacking self-consciousness as cultures, they have no traditions of specifically *cultural* self-reflection to draw on for Novak's brand of cultural politics. Novak is of Slovak descent and writes out of sympathy for ethnics, but he does not write from any distinctively ethnic literary or intellectual tradition; moreover, he explicitly subordinates the main intellectual tradition native to these ethnic cultures, Catholicism, to a more basic, primal ethnicity. Ironically, this move to the primitive, the move from religion to culture, leads Novak into the trap of sociological rationalism. Ultimately, *The Rise of the Unmeltable Ethnics* is not a premodern, ethnic story but a modern WASP story of an intellectual confronting culture.

For Novak, the personal is sociological. In wounded, indignant tones that anticipate contemporary multiculturalism, Novak complains that "nowhere in my schooling do I recall any attempt to put me in touch with my own history" (*RUE,* 55). At the level of institutions, Novak shares much of the basic liberal faith in the school as a place where children learn about themselves. At the deeper level of ideas, Novak still looks to the social sciences as a kind of technology of the self, a neutral tool capable of unlocking the hidden essence of ethnic experience. In a significantly autobiographical moment, Novak describes his own personal confrontation with modern reason:

> Imagine, then, an uncertain Slovak entering an Introductory Course in the Sociology of Religion at the nearby state university. Is he sent back to his Slovak roots, led to recover paths of experience latent in all his instincts and reflexes, given an image of

the life of his grandfather that suddenly, in recognition, brings tears to his eyes? Is he brought to a deeper appreciation of his Lutheran or Catholic heritage and its resonances with other bodies of religious experience? On the contrary, he is secretly taught disdain for what his grandfather *thought* he was doing when he acted or felt or imagined through religious forms. In the boy's psyche, a new religion is implanted: power over others, enlightenment, an atomic (rather than a communitarian) sensibility, a contempt for mystery, ritual, transcendence, soul, absurdity, and tragedy; and deep confidence in the possibilities of building a better world. Or, by way of reaction, the new myths of the counterculture, the new hopes of radical politics. He is led to feel ashamed for the statistical portrait of Slovak immigrants, which shows them to be conservative, authoritarian, not given to dissent, etc. His teachers instruct him with the purest intentions, in a way that is value free. (*RUE*, 66–67)

Even as this passage indicts the arrogance of sociological rationalism, it points to the promise of sociological humanism. The sociology that in practice breeds "disdain" for ethno-religious traditions can (and should) in theory connect the ethnic individual to "paths of experience latent in all his instincts and reflexes."

Novak's account obscures the history of a sociological practice that has in fact fostered both a "deeper appreciation" and a "contempt" for premodern cultures. At least since the Victorian era, intellectuals have been drawn to premodern and non-Western cultures precisely out of the longing for "mystery, ritual, transcendence" that draws Novak's "uncertain Slovak" to an introductory course in the sociology of religion. The tearful sociological epiphany that Novak expects of a properly conducted sociology of religion course is as much a symptom of enlightenment as the "deep confidence in the possibilities of building a better world" or the "new hopes of radical politics." The uncertain Slovak would not receive the traditions of his grandfather; rather, he would be "given an image of the life of his grandfather" and would be taught to understand that life in terms of "its resonances with other bodies of religious experience." Peasants, of course, do not see their culture as a culture and do not view their traditions in comparative terms. Sociological appreciation and sociological contempt share a common detachment alien to the ethnic culture under consideration. WASP form ultimately undermines ethnic content.

This contradiction between content and form is nowhere more evident than in Novak's appropriation of that most WASPish of literary forms, autobiography. Novak had available to him a substantial body of scholarship that had traced the origins of modern autobiography to the daily journals that formed the basis of Puritan conversion narratives; Max Weber's *The Protestant Ethic and the Spirit of Capitalism* had long since established the link between this Puritan self-scrutiny and the rationalization of society as a commonplace of sociological thought. Novak himself alludes to this tradition in his attack on WASP improvement ("Pilgrim's progress never ends . . . there seems to be no limit to their willingness to 'update' their moral sensibilities"), yet he fails to pursue this link beyond the level of polemic (*RUE,* xv). Autobiography, like sociology, becomes a neutral tool capable of providing an antidote to modern secular rationalism: "There is no other way but autobiography by which to cure oneself of too much objectivity. It is a cure many in America might profitably indulge" (*RUE,* 51). Of course, WASP Americans had been indulging in such a cure since the seventeenth century, producing that orgy of autobiography that is the uniquely confessional culture of the United States. Novak's misread of disease as cure speaks to the marginality of autobiography of his own ethnic Catholic tradition. Catholic ethnics had long resisted this autobiographical orientation precisely because of the communal values Novak praises. Novak's translation of the personal ties of ethnic community into the autobiographical perception of those ties itself marks his assimilation into WASP cultural norms.

The Rise of the Unmeltable Ethnics functions as a kind of sociological autobiography. The autobiographical dimension creates a distinct private self, while the sociological dimension relates that self to an objective other, society. Novak describes the book as "a struggle to discover the contours of my own sense of reality, stories, and symbols," yet he insists that this sense "is not only private . . . it is social" (*RUE,* xv, xvi). The relative weight given to the private or the social matters less than the establishment of the private/social dynamic as the foundation of Novak's "systematic treatment" of human experience:

> The nugget of my systematic idea has been with me as long as I can remember. It is to attend to the imaginative, perceptual, and affective sides of human consciousness, to what I have called "intelligent subjectivity." Over the years I have been slowly working out a language, poor and inadequate at best, for talking about what happens when human beings act. I am fascinated by instincts, emotions, images, hardly articulable ways of feeling, the movements of the stomach, habits, traditions: the organic networks of actual human life transmitted from generation to generation. (*RUE,* xv)

Novak presents his concept of "intelligent subjectivity" as a synthesis of reason and emotion: "the organic networks of actual human life" structure the "hardly articulable ways of feeling" that motivate individuals. This abstraction effectively flattens substantive normative distinctions among specific ethnic traditions and reduces those traditions to variations on a reason–emotion dialectic. Significantly, Novak gives no thick account of any particular ethnic culture, least of all his own Slovak tradition. He argues less for the substance of ethnic cultures than for a psychological process of ethnicity.

This psychological orientation transforms culture into consciousness. Novak takes the sociological fact of ethnic diversity in America as the normative basis for a reconceptualization of ethnic life in terms of existential decision:

> What is an ethnic group? It is a group with a historical memory, real or imaginary. One belongs to an ethnic group in part involuntarily, in part by choice. Given a grandparent or two, one chooses to shape one's consciousness by one history rather than another. Ethnic memory is not a set of events remembered, but rather a set of instincts, feelings, intimacies, expectations, patterns of emotion and behavior; a sense of reality; a set of stories for individuals—and for the people as a whole—to live out. (*RUE*, 47–48)

This definition of "ethnic group" appears surprisingly thin compared with Novak's tendency to associate ethnicity with instincts "so thick with life that they lie far beyond the power of consciousness" (*RUE*, xvi). No mere contradiction, thick/thin, like private/social, provides a tension point to drive the development of consciousness. Ethnicity is "part involuntary" and "part by choice," with both poles of this dialectic privileging the internal and subjective over the essential and objective. In the above passage, the attempt to move outward to a narrative conception of culture only reinforces the process of internalization. Ethnic memory is not a particular "set of events remembered" but a particular way of remembering anything, a "set of instincts" or "patterns of emotion." Novak's ethnics do not tell stories of people in the past; they "live out" stories of themselves in the present. Ethnicity is, in effect, a tool that "one chooses to shape one's consciousness."

The Rise of the Unmeltable Ethnics, no less than *Beyond the Melting Pot,* subordinates culture to the demands of individual choice. Both works argue for an autonomous, oppositional consciousness as the ideal mode of being in a pluralistic society. Glazer and Moynihan attack ethnic provincialism for failing to nurture the development of intellectuals with a heightened self-awareness, while Novak attacks intellectual cosmopolitanism as "dysfunctional since it detaches persons from the integration of personality that can be achieved only in historical symbolic communities" (*RUE*, 229). The intellectual and the ethnic move in different directions, but both move toward some heightened sense of self: movement itself matters more than any particular direction.

Novak insists that the "function of ethnic belonging is to integrate a person's sense of reality," but personality integration must always take priority over any possible restrictions entailed by ethnic belonging (*RUE*, 229). Even in the realm of ethnicity, choice is primary: "Individuals are and should be free to identify with the cultural sense of reality, stories, and symbols they prefer" (*RUE*, 32–33). True choice in turn requires real options. Like any good liberal, Novak looks to education to level the playing field of ethnic opportunity: "Education is best when it is a combination of ethnic and universal. Every child should have an education in his own ethnic tradition, and also an experimental exposure to the ethnic traditions of others" (*RUE,* 284). Novak argues not for the maintenance of traditional ethnic cultures but for the opportunity for individuals to experience ethnic diversity.

This brand of ethnic pluralism has been a consistent part of the "forced nationalization" of American culture throughout the twentieth century (*RUE,* 229). During the Progressive Era, some of the most articulate spokesmen (and women) for this pluralist nationalism were Jewish immigrants successfully Americanized by the public schools. Catholic ethnics, with their traditional suspicion of public education, resisted this assimilation longer, but by the time of Novak's writing they had, as a group, adopted this pluralist ideology. Attacking the straw man of liberal rationalism, Novak never addresses the role of "experimental exposure" itself in producing the bland superculture of corporate America. In pluralist rhetoric, the problem is never ethnic interaction but the failure of America to take "seriously our cultural pluralism" (*RUE,* 45–46).

Novak concedes that American society has allowed for the mixing of ethnic groups, but he insists it has yet to see the "establishment of systems of identity and self-respect" (*RUE,* 19). This systematic approach would ensure the flowering of all ethnic groups and the creation of a new America:

> The task is to discover what America is, or might yet be. No one, of course, can address that larger issue without coming to terms with his own ethnic particularity. No one ethnic group speaks for America. Each of us becomes aware of her own partial standpoint. For it is in possessing our own particularity that we come to feel at home with ourselves and are best able to enter into communion with others, freely and receiving of each other. The point of becoming ethnically alert and self-possessed is not self-enclosure; it is genuine community, honest and un-pretending. (*RUE,* xvi)

The melting pot, science, radicalism, and the superculture all stand as false, oppressive ordering principles against the emancipatory unity-in-diversity that is "America." This unity is, moreover, no stable entity but a fluid process: "There is a creativity and new release, there is liberation and there is hope. America is becoming America" (*RUE,* 291). Pluralism is, in this sense, always rising—always moving beyond the melting pot.

At his most political, Novak is at his most personal. His vision of a nation fully ethnic and fully American is an ideal synthesis of the two halves of his own divided self: "On the one hand American, enlightened, educated; on the other, stubbornly resistant, in love with values too dear to jettison, at home neither in the ethnic community nor in any intellectual group" (*RUE,* 62). The vitalities of family, neighborhood, and community serve Novak as a kind of Walden Pond, a personal retreat as prelude to a larger social engagement. For Novak, "ethnicity . . . offers resources to the imagination," yet the ultimate object of the imagination is America (*RUE,* 69). Novak's hope for an ethnic Democratic party marked the practical limits of his own brand of personal politics. In the 1972 election, Richard Nixon once again captured the white ethnic vote and rode it to a landslide victory over George McGovern. White ethnic support for Nixon only confirmed liberals in their equation of ethnicity with authoritarianism. The cultural divide between the enlightened and the unenlightened widened through the 1970s and set the terms for the culture wars of the 1980s.

5

The Feminist Mystique

Ideologues of integration differed in their coding of racial and ethnic difference in the open society, yet virtually all affirmed a positive difference between men and women. Rooted in the nineteenth-century ideology of "separate spheres," the domestic revival of the 1950s promoted a particularly stark version of the older dichotomy between public man and private woman. The moral superiority conferred on women in the nineteenth century had provided a rationale for breaking out of the domestic sphere to exert a positive influence on public life; in contrast, the legitimation of sexual pleasure and endorsement of high fertility that characterized the new domesticity of the "baby boom" era promised women total fulfillment through the role of wife and mother in the intensely private world of the family. The second-wave feminism of the 1960s rejected the "difference" of domesticity. It asserted a basic identity between men and women as the justification for women's full participation in a rational public sphere itself so profoundly shaped by the moral reform efforts of an earlier feminism.

Second-wave feminism rejected a residual Victorian sentimentalism only to assert an ever more rigorous Victorian rationalism. The feminist revival has generally been understood in terms of the shift from the liberal feminism of the early 1960s, which concentrated on women's "exclusion from the public sphere," to the radical feminism of the late 1960s, which "focused on the sexual politics of personal life."[1] A reading of two representative texts, *The Feminine Mystique,* Betty Friedan's groundbreaking manifesto of liberal feminism, and *Sexual Politics,* Kate Millett's best-selling 1970 manifesto of radical feminism, reveals that this conventional frame obscures significant continuities across the liberal/radical divide. Friedan's ideal of equal economic opportunity for women grows out of her belief in the centrality of work to personal identity; Millett's vision of sexual liberation requires a highly developed medical–industrial infrastructure to provide women the broadest range of reproductive and child care options. *The Feminine Mystique* and *Sexual Politics* both promote an ideal of woman as a rational, decision-making individual pursuing economic and sexual liberation in a society organized by rational bureaucratic institutions. This feminist mystique incorporates women into the public sphere only to extend the instrumental rationality of economics into the previously "separate" sphere of private life.

The Victorian consensus that unites Friedan and Millett points to the narrow middle-class orientation of postwar feminism. Unlike contemporary racial and ethnic nationalism, postwar feminism rarely looked to pre-bourgeois traditions for alternative social ideals. Feminist activists generally welcomed the dissolution of premodern "island communities," seeing in them only the most brutal and overt forms of gender inequality; feminist primitivism, a kind of neopagan nationalism based on the anthropological posit of an original, Edenic matriarchy, arose in the 1970s largely as an alternative to political activism. Acknowledging the passing of the premodern regime of coercion, feminists directed their critique toward the distinctly modern, middle-class regime of consent. Liberal and radical feminists alike rooted gender inequality in the power of male cultural ideals that infantilized women. Despite evidence that women accepted, and in many cases helped to create, these ideals, both liberals and radicals had to invest these ideals with a kind of coercive power. In postwar feminist thought, the critique of gender power relations became in large part an assault on the therapeutic authority of experts.

No single text better embodies the ambiguities of expert authority than the "bible" of the baby boom, Dr. Benjamin Spock's *The Common Sense Book of Baby and Child Care* (1946). The second best-selling book in American history (after the Bible), *Baby and Child Care* speaks not only to the intensity of the postwar revival of domesticity but also to an unprecedented acceptance of expert authority by the American reading public. From its opening admonition to "Trust Yourself," Spock's book confounds the "male-doctor-as-God" stereotype vilified by Friedan and other feminists.[2] A model of therapeutic, consensual authority, Spock continually cautions his readers against the advice of experts, neighbors, friends, and relatives, all in favor of the reader's own "common sense." A medical doctor, he criticizes modern medicine for putting "distance between mothers and their babies" and compares modern child-rearing practices unfavorably "to what comes naturally in simpler societies." Spock warns his readers "not [to] take too literally what is said in this book" and consistently argues against general theory in favor of the irreducible particularity of every parent, child, illness, and behavior problem. A model of progressive piety, Spock continually revised his book to accommodate the changing realities of family life, eliminating sexist language, addressing the special problems of working mothers, and even acknowledging the importance of the men's liberation movement. Through all these revisions, at least two goals remain constant: the need to foster "a more relaxed, more whole existence" in the private world of the family and the need to raise "idealistic children" devoted to service in the public world of society.[3] Subsequent feminist criticism would never seriously question the basic form and values of Spock's expertise.

Betty Friedan came of age in the social and intellectual world of *Baby and Child Care*. Like many middle-class women of her generation, she married young, moved to the suburbs, and devoted herself to child rearing. Unlike most women of her generation, however, Friedan had graduated from an elite, private liberal arts institution (Smith College), had planned a career as a professional psychologist, and actually wrote articles for the women's magazines she would attack in *The Feminine Mystique*. Only someone socialized in such proximity to the intellectual culture that produced *Baby and Child Care* could hear in Spock's "voice of gentle reassurance" the "condescendingly stern tones of medical authority."[4] Friedan is never so much a child of Spock as when she rejects his authority. As Spock counsels women to turn from the experts to their own common sense, so Friedan counsels women to turn from experts to their own "inner voice" (*FM*, 31). This inner voice, in turn, calls each woman to develop an idealistic, creative self capable of leading a productive life of service to others—the very kind of self promoted in *Baby and Child Care*.[5] Critics of conformity questioned the prospects for this self in the American man. Friedan wrote *The Feminine Mystique* to reassert this self as a legitimate aspiration for the American woman.

For women of the baby boom era, conformity was less a problem to solve than a problem to name. Friedan opens her book by naming "The Problem That Has No Name," the feminine mystique:

> The feminine mystique says that the highest value and the only commitment for women is the fulfillment of their own femininity. . . . The mistake, says the mystique, the root of women's troubles in the past is that women envied men, women tried to be like men, instead of accepting their own nature, which can find fulfillment only in sexual passivity, male domination, and nurturing maternal love. (*FM*, 43)

The qualities praised in the mystique as uniquely feminine appear, on closer examination, indistinguishable from those very qualities decried in the reigning critiques of male conformity:

> the apathetic, dependent, infantile, purposeless being, who seems so shockingly non-human when remarked as the emerging character of the new American man, is strangely reminiscent of the familiar "feminine" personality as defined by the mystique. Aren't the chief characteristics of femininity . . . passivity; a weak ego or sense

of self; a weak superego or human conscience; renunciation of active aims, ambitions, interests of one's own to live through others; incapacity for abstract thought;
retreat from activity directed outward to the world, in favor of activity directed in-
ward or phantasy? (*FM*, 286)

The "happy housewife" of the feminine mystique would appear to be little more
than the "cheerful robot" of corporate America in domestic drag.

The comparison made, Friedan must respond to those who would reply simply
that what is alarming in men is only natural in women. Proceeding in classic
social-scientific fashion, Friedan argues that current ideals of femininity are not
natural, but socially constructed. Though she refers to the isolated suburban home
as a "comfortable concentration camp," she does not invest it with the explanatory power bestowed on bureaucracy in the discourse of male conformity. Friedan
looks instead to the other major recognized instrument of conformity, the media:
"expectations of feminine fulfillment . . . are fed to women by magazines, television, movies, and books that popularize psychological half-truths, and by parents,
teachers and counselors who accept the feminine mystique" (*FM*, 77). This
broader cultural locus precludes any simple reform of domestic life, yet it also
tends to invest the feminine mystique with the character of a conspiracy so immense as to defy resistance. Friedan ultimately balances despair and hope
through a historical declension narrative that draws on ideals of the past as critical tools for evaluating the realities of the present.

Friedan follows her naming of women's crisis of identity with a chapter on the
rise and fall of feminism, "The Passionate Journey." The first generation of feminists during the nineteenth century, women such as Susan B. Anthony and Elizabeth Cady Stanton, were social revolutionaries fighting for women's right to
higher education, careers, and the vote. Driven by "the need for a new identity,"
nineteenth-century feminism found its most succinct formulation in the declaration of Ibsen's Nora: "I believe that before all else I am a reasonable human
being" (*FM*, 80, 83). Confronted by nearly universal opposition from the male
leaders of religion, business, and politics, nineteenth-century feminists forsook
their revolutionary egalitarianism for the single-minded drive to secure the vote.
With the achievement of suffrage in 1920, feminism floundered for lack of a distinct social vision. Male social scientists filled this ideological vacuum with a
new positive image of woman as a wholly sexual being. This new image, in turn,
reinforced the negative stereotype of radical nineteenth-century feminism as the
neurosis of man-hating, sex-starved spinsters.

To complicate this story, Friedan acknowledges at least one slight reprieve for
postsuffrage feminism. Friedan recalls a period within her own lifetime during
which the mass media promoted consistently positive images of women as

strong-willed and independent. Surveying the films and magazine stories of the 1930s, Friedan finds the typical heroine

> usually marching toward some goal or vision of their own, struggling with some problem of work or the world, when they found their man. . . . Her passionate involvement with the world, her own sense of herself as an individual, her self-reliance gave a different flavor to her relationship with the man. (*FM,* 38)

A reading of these same sources from the 1940s reveals a concerted effort on the part of social scientists, magazine editors, and filmmakers to redefine women as wholly sexual beings capable of fulfillment only through marriage and child rearing:

> The one "career woman" who was always welcome in the pages of the women's magazine was the actress. But her image also underwent a remarkable change: from a complex individual of fiery temper, inner depth, and a mysterious blend of spirit and sexuality, to a sexual object, a babyface bride, or a housewife. Think of Greta Garbo, for instance, and Marlene Dietrich, Bette Davis, Rosalind Russell, Katharine Hepburn. Then think of Marilyn Monroe, Debbie Reynolds, Brigitte Bardot, and "I Love Lucy." (*FM,* 53)

Ironically, the media that had provided the forum for feminism's last stand also served as the vanguard of the feminine mystique. The transformation in popular culture from the 1930s to the 1940s replicates in microcosm the larger intellectual shifts in feminism from the nineteenth to the twentieth century. Refusing to dismiss the feminine mystique as yet another banality of mass culture, Friedan traces its roots to perhaps the most revered figure of postwar intellectual life, Sigmund Freud.

Now a feminist commonplace, the assault on Freud is perhaps the boldest critique set forth in *The Feminine Mystique.* Friedan acknowledges Freudian psychology's status as "a new religion" for many postwar intellectuals and shows appropriate reverence (*FM,* 123). She insists that "Freud's discovery of the unconscious workings of the mind was one of the great breakthroughs in man's pursuit of knowledge. . . . No one can question the basic genius of Freud's discoveries, nor the contribution he has made to our culture." More specifically, Friedan is careful to acknowledge that "Freudian psychology, with its emphasis on freedom from a repressive morality to achieve sexual fulfillment, was part of the ideology of women's emancipation." She even allows that much of the negative influence of Freud has resulted from the distortion of his theories by "the popular magazines and the opinions and interpretations of so-called experts" (*FM,* 104). In attacking the Great Emancipator, Friedan is first careful to affirm the essential truth of emancipation.

Even in its purest expression, however, Freudian theory poses a serious threat to the emancipation of women:

> Freud's concept of the superego helped to free man of the tyranny of the "shoulds," the tyranny of the past, which prevents the child from becoming an adult. Yet Freudian thought helped create a new superego that paralyzes educated modern American women—a new tyranny of the "shoulds," which chains women to an old image, prohibits choice and growth, and denies them individual identity. (*FM*, 104)

Friedan assaults Freudian orthodoxy with the tools of another social-scientific orthodoxy: cultural relativism. Adopting the mode of criticism popularized by Mead and Benedict, Friedan explains Freud as "a prisoner of his own culture. As he was creating a new framework for our culture, he could not escape the framework of his own" (*FM*, 105). Freud the Emancipator could not transcend Freud the Victorian:

> The fact is that to Freud, even more to the magazine editor on Madison Avenue today, women were a strange, inferior, less-than-human species. He saw them as childlike dolls, who existed in terms only of man's love, to love man and serve his needs. It was the same kind of unconscious solipsism that made man for many centuries see the sun only as a bright object that revolved around the earth. Freud grew up with this attitude built in by his culture—not only the culture of Victorian Europe, but that Jewish culture in which men said the daily prayer: "I thank Thee, Lord, that Thou hast not created me a woman," and women prayed in submission: "I thank Thee, Lord, that Thou has created me according to Thy will." (*FM*, 108)

Friedan links Freud's misunderstanding of women to his acceptance of a biological determinism that merely reflects the narrow, mechanistic "approach to causation implicit in the scientific thought of his time." Reinforced by his medical training, this conception of causality led Freud "to translate all psychological phenomena into sexual terms, and to see all problems of adult personality as the effect of childhood sexual fixations." According to Friedan, "much of what Freud believed to be biological, instinctual, and changeless has been shown by modern research to be a result of specific cultural causes" (*FM*, 106). These studies, for example, reveal the supposed "penis envy" Freud observed in women to be not a timeless female desire to possess the male sex organ but a historically specific desire on the part of Victorian women to possess the social freedoms enjoyed by Victorian men (*FM*, 117–18). Firmly in the Mead-Benedict tradition, Friedan relativizes particular cultures only to essentialize culture against biology as an explanatory causal force.

Ironically, Friedan reserves her harshest criticism for the very culturalist tradition she draws on in her critique of Freud. Echoing the radical critique advanced by C. Wright Mills in *The Sociological Imagination,* Friedan argues that cultural consciousness, as much as Freudian biologism, has provided an "easy out" for avoiding the hard questions of gender inequality (*FM,* 134). Under the general rubric of "functionalism," sociologists and anthropologists have sought to understand society in terms of the organic interrelation of a multiplicity of distinct social roles, or functions. Despite an official posture of scientific neutrality, however, "the function is" has become "the function should be." By investing the prevailing Victorian views of women with "an absolute meaning and a sanctimonious value . . . functionalism put American women into a kind of deep freeze" (*FM,* 127). Functionalism found its Freud in none other than Benedict's fellow cultural relativist, Margaret Mead.

Friedan sees in Mead's influence none of the ironies or complexities that she concedes to popular Freudianism. At first glance, Mead would seem to merit a more sympathetic interpretation. She too was a Great Emancipator. Friedan acknowledges that Mead's breakthrough 1928 work, *Coming of Age in Samoa,* put forth a "vision of the infinite variety of sexual patterns and the enormous plasticity of human nature" (*FM,* 136). Herself a frequent contributor to women's magazines, Mead "might have passed on to the popular culture a truly revolutionary vision of women finally free to realize their full capabilities in a society which replaced arbitrary sexual definitions with a recognition of genuine individual gifts as they occur in either sex" (*FM,* 136).

According to Friedan, somewhere, somehow, something went wrong:

> Increasingly, in her own pages, her interpretation blurs, is subtly transformed, into a glorification of women in the female role—as defined by their sexual biological function. At times she seems to lose her own anthropological awareness of the malleability of human personality, and to look at anthropological data from the Freudian point of view—sexual biology determines all, anatomy is destiny. At times she seems to be arguing in functional terms, that while women's potential is as great and various as the unlimited human potential, it is better to preserve the sexual biological limitations established by a culture. (*FM,* 137)

Friedan refuses Mead the cultural excuse she grants Freud. Mead's ability to transcend Victorian ideals of womanhood in her own life as a female professional and as an intellectual invests her theories with an almost willful hypocrisy lacking in Freud's consistent sexism. Mead "was, and still is, the symbol of the woman thinker in America" (*FM,* 135). Her theories suggest not so much bias as betrayal. For Friedan, Mead stands as the great lost opportunity for feminism in the middle decades of the twentieth century.

For its time, Friedan's critique of sexism was radical. At any time, the critique of bias is simply in the nature of social-scientific revision. The role that *The Feminine Mystique* played in the revival of feminism during the 1960s has obscured the role it played, and has continued to play, in legitimating the authority of social science in American cultural life. Friedan's attack on Freud and Mead serves as prelude to her re-creation of herself as a truly enlightened, feminist expert. Following Freud, Friedan adopts the role of the radical scientist probing the depths of the human psyche in search of fundamental truths; following Mead, Friedan offers herself as a symbol of the woman thinker in America. Friedan reads Freud and Mead as cautionary tales of the "overvaluation of the power of social science not merely to interpret culture and personality, but to order our lives" (*FM*, 144). She writes *The Feminine Mystique* to bring about a "drastic reshaping of the cultural image" that assumes nothing if not an overvaluation of the power of social science to order people's lives (*FM*, 364).

Friedan follows Freud in both subject matter and method. Despite her own critique of Freud's cultural bias, she bases much of her argument on evidence from a similarly narrow middle-class milieu:

> I found many clues by talking to suburban doctors, gynecologists, obstetricians, child-guidance clinicians, pediatricians, high-school guidance counselors, college professors, marriage counselors, psychiatrists, and ministers—questioning them not on their theories, but on their actual experience in treating American women. I became aware of a growing body of evidence, much of which has not been reported publicly, because it does not fit current modes of thought about women—evidence which throws into question the standards of feminine normality, feminine adjustment, feminine fulfillment, and feminine maturity, by which most women are still trying to live. (*FM*, 31)

These psychotherapeutic professions are themselves a result of Freud's own encounter with a "growing body of evidence" that did "not fit . . . modes of thought about women" current to his time. Freud, for all of his supposed biologism, turned from "theories" to the "actual experience" of women in developing psychological explanations for seemingly physical ailments. If anything, the bias toward psychological "evidence" in Friedan's sources suggests an even less representative sampling than Freud's more broadly medical, pre-psychotherapeutic patient pool.

As Freud pierced through the "image" of female sexual purity to reveal the "reality" of female sexual frustration, so Friedan pierces through the image of female sexual fulfillment to reveal the reality of female psychological frustration:

> It is my thesis that the core of the problem for women today is not sexual but a problem of identity—a stunting or evasion of growth that is perpetuated by the feminine mystique. It is my thesis that as the Victorian culture did not permit women to accept or gratify their basic sexual needs, our culture does not permit women to accept or gratify their basic need to grow and fulfill their potentialities as human beings, a need which is not solely defined by their sexual role. (*FM*, 77)

Identity thus replaces sex as the new essence revealed by science. The nature of women consists in the "basic need to grow and fulfill their potentialities as human beings." By Friedan's own account, however, this new essence emerges not simply from the actual experience of women but from the theories of yet another male expert, the "brilliant psychoanalyst" Erik Erikson (*FM*, 77). Friedan is nowhere more the child of Freud than when she presents this move from the feminine mystique to identity as a move from theory to experience.

Friedan's turn to identity represents less a challenge to male authority than an incorporation of women more fully into a male, middle-class form of authority. Friedan explicitly models her account of the identity crisis in women on the "identity crisis, which has been noted by Erik Erikson and others in recent years in the American man" (*FM*, 334). The domestic woman, like the organization man, suffers from economic dependence, cultural conformity, and most of all a lack of meaningful work: "One sees the human significance of work—not merely as the means of biological survival, but as the giver of self and the transcender of self, as the creator of human identity and human evolution" (*FM*, 333). What Friedan presents as a breakthrough from economics to psychology is in fact little more than a "shopworn staple" of the American Protestant work ethic: work as a solution to a spiritual/social crisis. Significantly, Erikson's best-known "case study" of the problem of identity in the 1950s was his psychobiography of Martin Luther, *Young Man Luther.* The tropes of the comfortable concentration camp—its isolation, its routine, its "dailiness"—are the tropes of the Catholic monastery, and Friedan explicitly models her own emergence from the feminine mystique on Luther's emergence from medieval Catholicism (*FM*, 313, 78). Like newly liberated monks, women must seek transcendence in the world and in time. Friedan demands for women the freedom to exercise that "unique human capacity to transcend the present, to live one's life by purposes stretching into the future—to live not at the mercy of the world, but as a builder and designer of that world" (*FM*, 312). Friedan's "discovery" of identity as the basic human need reflects less a persistent psychological reality than an enduring cultural narrative of self.

Firmly within this narrative, the concept of identity overcomes the split between image and reality only to introduce a new tension between permanence and change. Friedan sees identity as, in one sense, "the firm core of self or 'I' without which a human being, man or woman, is not truly alive" (*FM*, 305). Like many male cultural critics of the 1950s, Friedan affirms this solid core of self as the best defense against "the dehumanizing aspects of modern mass culture." Moving to the broadest level of cultural criticism, Friedan asserts the need "for men and women to have a strong core of self, strong enough to retain human individuality through the frightening, unpredictable pressures of our changing environment" (*FM*, 305). A bulwark against uncontrollable change, identity also serves as a vehicle for controlled growth. Women who possess a solid core of self

also possess a "basic need to grow and fulfill their potentialities as human beings." Indeed, turning to the very biological language she rejected in Freud,
Friedan reports that "scientists of human behavior . . . in many fields . . . postu-
late some positive growth tendency within the organism, which, from within,
drives it to fuller development, to self-realization" *(FM,* 310). Anatomy would
once again appear to be destiny.

The concept of identity provides a secular substitute for an older religious
struggle for salvation. Like her Puritan predecessors, Friedan asserts the certainty
of salvation—the solid core of self—only to assert the need for continued self-
scrutiny, figured positively as growth: "The identity crisis in men and women . . .
must be faced continually, solved only to be faced again in the span of a single
lifetime. . . . No woman in America today who starts her search for identity can
be sure where it will take her" *(FM,* 377).

Friedan synthesizes the solid and fluid elements of identity through the process
of creating and re-creating a variety of solid cores of self. She codes this perpetual change positively as growth but refuses any explicit teleology. The authority
of identity operates within the classic antinomian opposition of "free to choose"
versus "bound by convention" *(FM,* 318). Friedan imposes not a substantive ideal
of self but a procedural norm of choice, the ideal that "a woman, as a man, has
the power to choose, and to make her own heaven or hell" *(FM,* 14). Under the
regime of identity, the necessity of motherhood gives way to the necessity of existential subjectivity.

This transformation of self entails a transformation of society. Authentic choice
requires enabling conditions for the exercise of freedom. In *The Feminine Mystique,* the establishment of these conditions takes on the character of a military
campaign. Friedan concludes her book by outlining "A New Life Plan for
Women" that depends on the full-scale mobilization of society in service to the
"inner voice" of women. She calls for the equivalent of the G.I. Bill or the Mar-
shall Plan, a "national program . . . which would first bring the housewife back
into the mainstream of thought with a concentrated six-week summer course, a
sort of intellectual 'shock therapy.'" At one level, Friedan looks to education as a
means of providing women with the training necessary to enter the workforce
outside the home. At another level, she intends this "shock therapy" as an initiation to a lifetime process of self-discovery:

> Colleges and universities also need a new life plan—to become lifetime institutions
> for their students; offer their guidance, take care of their records, and keep track of
> their advanced work or refresher courses, no matter where they are taken. . . . All col-
> leges could conduct summer institutes to keep alumnae abreast of developments in
> their fields during the years of young motherhood. They could accept part-time stu-
> dents and offer extension courses for the housewife who could not attend classes

regularly. They could advise her on reading programs, papers, or projects that could be done at home. They could also work out a system whereby projects done by their alumnae could be counted as equivalent credits toward a degree. Instead of collecting dimes, let women serve supervised professional apprenticeships and collect the credits that are recognized in lieu of pay for medical interns. Similarly, when a woman has taken courses at a number of different institutions, perhaps due to husband's geographical itinerary, and has earned her community credits from agency, hospital, library or laboratory, her college of origin, or some national center set up by several colleges, could give her the orals, the comprehensives, and the appropriate examinations for a degree. The concept of "continuing education" is already a reality for men in many fields. Why not for women? Not education for careers instead of motherhood, not education for temporary careers before motherhood, not education to make them "better wives and mothers," but an education they will use as full members of society. (*FM*, 372)

The humble "inner voice" of the isolated housewife would seem to require a highly sophisticated bureaucratic infrastructure for its articulation. Friedan's revolt against the feminine mystique ironically issues in a qualitative expansion of the very institutions that propagated the mystique. In the name of identity, these institutions would now assist women in translating their life experiences into quantifiable units or credits, which in turn translate into degrees, which by the above formulation serve as a kind of certificate of selfhood at various stages of development. Each stage is provisional, subject to that constant revision of self for which "continuing education" seems at best a euphemism. Through this process of revision, women must learn to structure their lives through a series of discrete papers, plans, and projects, all capable of being directed toward some new goal in the future. Despite Friedan's by-now-quaint allowance for marriage and young motherhood, it is difficult to see where spouses and children—or any nonprofessional relationship with other people—would fit into this constant round of self-improvement.

What Friedan asserts as a moral right, she argues for as a practical necessity. The denial of women's access to the means of personal identity threatens social order and national security. Drawing on an older feminist tradition of republican motherhood, Friedan argues that women who lack a solid core of self cannot pass on to their children the independence and self-possession required of citizens in a democracy. Linking her critique of the feminine mystique to contemporary concerns over juvenile delinquency, Friedan sees the "subtle and devastating change . . . in the character of American children" as merely "a more pathological form" of "the housewife's problem that has no name." The "new vacant, sleepwalking, playing-a-part quality of youngsters" merely reflects the same quality in their lobotomized mothers (*FM*, 285). Friedan draws extensively on studies that observe this same "collapse of identity" in many of the soldiers who fought in the Korean

War; she even goes so far as to suggest that the perpetuation of the feminine mystique will undermine the resolve needed in the struggle against international communism (*FM,* 285–86). Friedan concludes:

> The problem that has no name—which is simply the fact that American women are kept from growing to their full human capacities—is taking a far greater toll on the physical and mental health of our country than any known disease. . . . If we continue to produce millions of young mothers who stop their growth and education short of identity, without a strong core of human values to pass on to their children, we are committing quite simply genocide, starting with the mass burial of American women and ending with the progressive dehumanization of their sons and daughters. (*FM,* 364)

Here the moral and practical reveal themselves as variations on a more basic economic logic. The mass suicide of America can be avoided only by drawing on "the untapped reserves of women's intelligence" (*FM,* 370). Women are an underutilized resource that must be mobilized to ensure the development of the full productive capacity of the American economy. As women need work to achieve identity, so society needs identity to sustain growth.

The Feminine Mystique was an instant best-seller on its release in 1963 and, like Spock's book, benefited from the paperback revolution in publishing. The persuasiveness of Friedan's argument reflected not simply the widespread dissatisfaction of suburban housewives but also the persistence of feminist activism through the dark days of the baby boom. After the initial domestic retreat immediately following the war, women began a slow return to the workforce through the 1950s. By December 1961, women labor activists within the Democratic party had convinced President Kennedy to authorize a President's Commission on the Status of Women. In both its assumptions and conclusions, the commission was of a piece with Friedan's book: it sought ways for women "to continue their role as wives and mothers while making a maximum contribution to the world around them" and recommended career counseling and child care to enable women to balance home and work.[6]

Reading the report upon its release in 1965, Friedan did not object to the findings so much as she feared for the possibility of their implementation. Despite the inclusion of a sex discrimination clause in the Civil Rights Act of 1964, Friedan became convinced of the need for an NAACP–style women's group to lobby for women's issues. In 1966, Friedan and a group of Washington, D.C.–area feminists formed the National Organization for Women (NOW), with Friedan serving as its first president. Like the President's Commission, NOW stated as its purpose the promotion of "action to bring women into full participation in the mainstream of American society now . . . in truly equal partnership with men."[7] NOW differed from Washington's official position only in the seriousness of its commitment to achieve Washington's own stated goal of workplace equality for women.

As Friedan was establishing a liberal feminist orthodoxy in NOW, a second stream of feminism was developing in the student movement. Politicized through participation in the civil rights movement, radicalized by the black power movement and antiwar protests, women students began to reflect on the power relations of gender inequality. At the SDS Conference in 1967, feminist students organized a "Women's Liberation Workshop" to examine sexism not only in American society in general but within SDS itself. The workshop boldly concluded that "women are in a colonial relationship to men and we recognize ourselves as part of the Third World."[8] The male leaders of SDS generally dismissed sexism as a distraction from the real issues of race and class. The female leaders of NOW, on the other hand, were suspicious of the rhetoric of class conflict and the countercultural emphasis on sexual matters that seemed so prominent in the emerging women's liberation movement. Looking for allies, radical feminists were forced to choose adversaries. As radical feminists pursued an increasingly gender-specific agenda, they increasingly found themselves in bitter confrontations with liberal feminists.

The rise of radical feminism presents another case of generational conflict passing for ideological revolt. Despite the inspiration of black power, radical political feminism generally did not advocate armed struggle or any kind of separatist nationalism. Alice Echols, the leading historian of radical feminism, has characterized the generational revolt as follows: "while liberal feminists defined the problem as women's exclusion from the public sphere, radical feminists focused on the sexual politics of personal life."[9] Clearly feminists of the time perceived this shift in ideological terms. Friedan, in particular, spewed venom on radical feminists for conducting a "bedroom war" for sexual liberation that distracted from the real struggle for economic equality in the workplace. Despite her own extended reflections on identity and selfhood in *The Feminine Mystique,* Friedan attacked the consciousness-raising sessions of radical feminists as mere "navel-gazing." She was particularly hostile to what she called the "lavender menace" of lesbian feminism, which she feared would undermine the credibility of feminism as a whole.[10] Friedan consistently fought against the radical presence within NOW, to the point of accusing Gloria Steinem of being a CIA agent provocateur working to destabilize the organization.[11]

Kate Millett's *Sexual Politics*, the most widely read of the radical feminist manifestos, calls into question the interpretation that Friedan's response seems to confirm. The graphic sexuality and Marxist rhetoric of the book obscure a fairly conventional egalitarianism very much of the world of *The Feminine Mystique.* Attacked by Friedan for "extremist hate rhetoric," Millett simply argues for the extension of Friedan's bureaucratic new life plan for women to the final frontier of marriage and the family (*FM*, 389).

A cursory reading of *Sexual Politics* could lead to the conclusion that Friedan's hostility derived from a sense of plagiarism, not betrayal. Millett devotes roughly half her book to a history of feminism straight out of *The Feminine Mystique*. She traces the rise and fall of feminism from the sexual revolution of the nineteenth century to the counterrevolution of the twentieth. True, Millett draws on different sources: her preference for European, high-brow literature lends *Sexual Politics* a bohemian ambiance at odds with Friedan's suburban milieu; similarly, her choice of Friedrich Engels's *The Origin of the Family, Private Property, and the State* as the reference text for correct thinking on matters of sex appeared particularly confrontational at a time when the United States was fighting a war against communism in Vietnam. Still, her account of feminism follows Friedan, without so much as a footnote of acknowledgment.

According to Millett, the Victorian era, despite its naive sentimentalism and earnest rationalism, "was the first period in history that faced and tried to solve the issue of the double standard and the inhumanities of prostitution."[12] Millett champions the rationalism of John Stuart Mill's defense of women's equality against the sentimentalism of John Ruskin's ideal of women's moral superiority. She praises the fiction of the Bronte sisters for presenting strong, independent-minded female characters. Finally, she sees in Ibsen's Nora the culmination of the Victorian feminist struggle for equality, and the first public declaration of the sexual revolution (*SP*, 160). Like Friedan, she sees the revolution undermined by the very success of the suffrage movement. The narrow focus of feminist politics left the movement without a program once it had achieved the vote (*SP*, 120). The sexual experimentation that truly flourished in the early twentieth century soon floundered for lack of a theory to sustain it as a social practice.

Millett attacks the suffrage movement for its "bourgeois" indifference to the plight of working-class women but locates the failure of suffrage less in terms of social power than intellectual perspective:

> The chief weakness of the movement's concentration on suffrage . . . lay in its failure to challenge patriarchal ideology at a sufficiently deep and radical level to break the conditioning processes of status, temperament, and role. (*SP*, 121)

> The real causes of the counter-revolution . . . lie in the fact that the sexual revolution had, perhaps necessarily, even inevitably, concentrated on the superstructure of patriarchal policy, changing its legal forms, its more flagrant abuses, altering its formal educational patterns, but leaving the socialization processes of temperament and role differentiation intact. (*SP*, 240)

Millett here employs Marxist concepts such as "ideology" and "superstructure," as well as conventional Marxist political judgments, such as the dismissal of reform as counterrevolutionary. Her choice of the term "patriarchy," drawn from the anthropology of "primitive" societies, invests her argument with a world-historical scope clearly lacking in Friedan's humbler, more historically distinct concept of the feminine mystique. Still, Millett follows Friedan, as Marxism followed liberalism, by employing a surface/depth mode of analysis. As Friedan sees the surface image of the feminine mystique obscuring the deep reality of women's need for identity, so Millett sees the surface superstructure of reform obscuring the deep reality of patriarchal oppression. Both see social norms as "conditioning processes" that distort some authentic, pure, solid core of being, and both see politics as the liberation of self from repressive external conditions.

Millett's "deep and radical" analysis of the patriarchal counterrevolution targets the familiar enemies of Freud and functionalism. Freud once again appears as a man of his times unable to transcend his narrow Victorian prejudices: "Freud did not accept his patient's symptoms as evidence of a justified dissatisfaction with the limiting circumstances imposed on them by society, but as symptomatic of an independent and universal feminine tendency" (*SP*, 243). Freud "made a major and rather foolish confusion between biology and culture, anatomy and status," and thus misread power envy as penis envy (*SP*, 253). For Millett, as for Friedan, functionalism merely provides a sociological justification of Freudian prejudice:

> The main service of functionalism appears to reside in its justification of the systems it perceives and covertly identifies with, followed by prescriptive recommendations as how to "adjust" groups or individuals to this system. When it filters down to practical application in schools, industry, and popular media, it may simply become a form of cultural policing. (*SP*, 296)

This policing encourages in women the very values of submission and maternal nurturing that Friedan identified with the feminine mystique. Millett's critique of social science, like her history of feminism, was old news by 1970 and hardly merits so provocative a label as "sexual politics."

Millett earns her title at best through the graphic exploration of sexual modernism that frames her fairly conventional rewriting of *The Feminist Mystique*. The extremist hate rhetoric of *Sexual Politics* comes not from Millett but from the male literary prophets of sexual modernism: Henry Miller, D. H. Lawrence, Norman Mailer, and Jean Genet. Millett opens *Sexual Politics* with random passages drawn from these writers and devotes roughly the final third of the book to an in-depth analysis of their work. She argues convincingly that the sexual liberation of men has entailed the sexual domination of women, the reduction of women to "cunt" (*SP,* 390). Sex, by Millett's account, is profoundly unsexy; if her analysis of these sexual modernists constitutes a "bedroom war," then her battle cry would seem to be "retreat." Against Friedan's lingering sentimentalism concerning sexual bliss, Millett attacks sexual relations as the root of social inequality. For both Millett and Friedan, however, the real issue is still equality. The adjective "sexual" modifies the noun "politics."

Millett's politics, like Friedan's, begins with conformity and ends with autonomy. For Millett, "in the matter of conformity patriarchy is a governing ideology without peer; it is probable that no other system has ever exercised such a complete control over its subjects" (*SP,* 55). Millett ritualistically compares the condition of women with that of African Americans, going so far as to assert that "sexism may be more endemic in our own society than racism" (*SP,* 63). She updates this conventional feminist rhetoric with a more timely, Vietnam-era comparison to imperial domination: "In terms of industry and production, the situation of women is in many ways comparable both to colonial and to pre-industrial people" (*SP,* 66). These comparisons place feminism within a fairly conventional understanding of politics as "power-structured relationships, arrangements whereby one group of persons is controlled by another" (*SP,* 43–44). Millett, like Friedan, presents feminism as a move beyond conventional understandings of power: "It is opportune, perhaps today even mandatory, that we develop a more relevant psychology and philosophy of power relationships beyond the simple conceptual framework provided by our traditional formal politics" (*SP,* 44). As Friedan moves from surface to depth to uncover the root of emancipation in identity, so Millett moves from surface to depth to find the root of repression in sex.

Of the sexual modernists, only the homosexual Jean Genet transcends the power relations of sexual politics. Genet emerges as the hero of Millett's book not for any positive vision of sexual emancipation, but for his critical insight that "sex role is sex rank" (*SP,* 449). Much of Genet's fiction uses the single-sex world of the male prison as a way of exposing the link between sex role and social power. The transvestites and "female" homosexuals who fall at the bottom of the prison social hierarchy demonstrate "the utterly arbitrary and invidious nature of the sex role. Divorced from their usual justification in an assumed biological congruity masculine and feminine stand out as terms of praise and blame, authority and servitude, high and low, master and slave" (*SP,* 449).

In *The Balcony*, Genet extends this critique from the imperial West to the colonized Third World. Flying in the face of New Left pieties concerning revolution, Millett affirms Genet's assertion that anticolonial movements will inevitably reproduce the oppression of their oppressors "unless the ideology of real or fantasized virility is abandoned, unless the clinging to male supremacy as a birthright is finally foregone" (*SP,* 40).

Moving beyond the New Left, however, merely takes Millett back to liberalism. Millett's brutally searching exploration of Genet's brutally searching exploration of sexual domination leads her to conclude, "In Genet's analysis, it is fundamentally impossible to change society without changing personality, and sexual personality as it has generally existed must undergo the most drastic overhaul" (*SP*, 41). The goal of this personal-social transformation is simply "the arrangement of human life on agreeable and rational principles from whence the entire notion of power *over* others should be banished" (*SP*, 43-44). Sensitized to the contingency of all sexual roles, individuals in Millett's utopia would be able to explore their own personal sexual identity free from the constraints of coercive social norms. Ironically, Millett's tedious summaries of Victorian novels and treatises leave her with little energy or inspiration for developing anything like a sexual equivalent of Friedan's new life plan for women. *Sexual Politics* is in many ways much less a work of personal politics than *The Feminine Mystique*.

Millett's contribution to feminism lies in her simple assertion that women need a sexual new life plan in order to achieve social equality. Once again, the work of Erik Erikson provides the occasion for the most explicit articulation of feminist ideals. At first glance, Millett's response to Erikson would seem to indicate a decisive break with Friedan's affirmation of identity. Millett attacks Erikson as yet another patriarchal social scientist engaged in the "persistent error of mistaking learned behavior for biology" (*SP*, 289). Millett specifically criticizes Erikson's 1964 essay, "Womanhood and the Inner Space," for perpetuating sentimental Victorian ideals concerning gender difference. Erikson's critique of male aggression and sympathy for women's civilizing role serve only to essentialize traits that are in fact "culturally conditioned" and "depend upon . . . political relationships" (*SP*, 283). Millett rejects Erikson's seemingly humanist plea for gender diversity—his call for a "vital tension" between men and women—as yet another imposition of patriarchal domination (*SP*, 284).

Exposing Erikson's conclusions as a confirmation of his assumptions, Millett proposes an alternative:

> What might be more productive to study is the child who has broken the magic circle of programmed learning so that one could isolate elements which helped in transcending the cultural mode. How, for example, does a tomboy arrive at the positive "aggression" of an outdoor scene, or a boy arrive at a peaceful scene; the one escaping the doll house which has been successfully inflicted on her peers, the other the malevolence inflicted on his. (*SP*, 290)

Millett's new approach merely replaces one set of assumptions/conclusions with another. Her sexual egalitarianism, "an integration of the separate sexual subcultures, an assimilation by both sides of previously segregated human experience," finds its confirmation in the choice of role-transgressive children as the proper focus for social science research (*SP*, 92). Millett comforts her reader with the assurance that such important work is already being done at the California Gender Identity Center, whose research "not only suggests that the possibilities of innate temperamental differences seem more remote than ever, but even raises questions as to the validity and permanence of psycho-sexual identity" (*SP*, 50–51). In rebelling against conventions of sex, Millett merely conforms to conventions of identity. The fluidity she sees in sex roles is the same fluidity Friedan sees in the ceaseless growth of a properly aware solid core of self.

With sex, as with identity, the personal is economic. An understanding of sexual freedom begins with an awareness of sexual feudalism: "Woman is still denied sexual freedom and the biological control over her body through the cult of virginity, the double standard, the prescription against abortion, and in many places because contraception is physically or psychically unavailable to her" (*SP*, 83). As eighteenth-century political economists "discovered" the tremendous productive power of the free market repressed by feudal restrictions, so current sex researchers have discovered a "vast inherent potential of female sexuality . . . nearly totally obscured through cultural restraints" (*SP*, 165). Masters and Johnson's important work on multiple orgasms has revealed that while "the male's sexual potential is limited, the female's appears to be biologically nearly inexhaustible" (*SP*, 164).

Following the first stage of classic bourgeois economic development, Millett calls for the removal of all external constraints on the free market:

> A sexual revolution would require, perhaps first of all, an end of traditional sexual inhibitions and taboos, particularly those that most threaten patriarchal monogamous marriage: homosexuality, "illegitimacy," adolescent, pre- and extra-marital sexuality. The negative aura with which sexual activity has generally been surrounded would necessarily be eliminated, together with the double standard and prostitution. The goal of revolution would be a permissive single standard of sexual freedom, and one uncorrupted by the crass and exploitative economic bases of traditional sexual alliances. . . . Marriage might generally be replaced by voluntary association, if such is desired. (*SP*, 92)

Following the second stage of classic bourgeois economic development, Millett seeks to order this anarchy with rational bureaucratic structures:

> The collective professionalization (and consequent improvement) of the care of the young . . . would further undermine family structure while contributing to the freedom of women. (*SP*, 92)

The care of children, even from the period when their cognitive powers first emerge, is infinitely better left to the best-trained practitioners of both sexes who have chosen it as a vocation, rather than to harried and all to frequently unhappy persons with little time nor taste for the work of educating minds, however young or beloved. (*SP,* 175)

Having solved the nagging problem of child care, Millett's sexual revolution completes Friedan's new life plan for women. A comparative reading of *The Feminine Mystique* and *Sexual Politics* suggests that liberal and radical feminists differed slightly in their analysis of the problem but shared a common solution. Friedan reacted so violently to Millett's "bedroom war" not out of any failure of sexual nerve but from her conviction that sexual liberation itself had been used to discourage women from entering the public sphere. After her own experience with the feminine mystique, the idea of fulfillment through multiple orgasms must have seemed little more than an updated version of fulfillment through multiple childbirths. As Friedan broke through sex to get to economics, so Millett broke through economics to get to sex. Both shared a common narrative of transition from repression to liberation; neither proved successful in establishing feminism as a basis for group identity much beyond their own fairly narrow middle-class milieu.

The critique of the class bias of feminism has obscured the power relations of emancipation itself.[13] Millett opens her book with a critique of male sexual liberation that suggests some awareness of the persistence of domination within even the most vanguard emancipatory ideologies but concludes with a utopian vision that amounts to something like an egalitarian distribution of domination. Friedan, the mother of modern feminism, provides the most frighteningly naive affirmation of this emancipation:

This "will to power," "self-assertion," "dominance," or "autonomy," as it is variously called, does not imply aggression or competitive striving in the usual sense; it is the individual affirming his existence and his potentialities as a being in his own right; it is "the courage to be an individual." (*FM,* 310)

Feminism's vision of the individual is, moreover, very much in the American grain. As Friedan scours history for a usable feminist past, she settles on the classic site of American individualism, the frontier:

Until, and even into, the last century, capable women were needed to pioneer our new land; with their husbands, they ran the farms and plantations and Western homesteads. These women were respected and self-respecting members of a society whose pioneering purpose centered in the home. Strength and independence, responsibility and self-confidence, self-discipline and courage, freedom and equality were part of the American character for both men and women, in all the first generation. (*FM,* 334)

Alas, every frontier has its Indians. In the 1973 *Roe v. Wade* decision, the new feminist frontier found its Indians in the unborn. Despite its failure as a galvanizing, cross-class ideology, feminism helped to legitimate the most heinous social practice since slavery: the routine abortion of roughly 1.5 million children every year. Friedan continued to serve as the leading spokeswoman of mainstream feminism, but Millett provided feminism with its defining issue. Abortion, not workplace equality, became the litmus test for feminist, and even more broadly liberal, political orthodoxy.

6

Compulsory Sexuality

Kate Millett's turn to Genet proved prophetic. On June 27, 1969, gay men rioted against police harassment at the Stonewall Inn in New York's Greenwich Village, and "gay power" was born. In late 1970, amid the controversy surrounding the release of *Sexual Politics*, Millett publicly acknowledged her own bisexuality, exacerbating the straight–lesbian split within feminism.[1] The movement for gay and lesbian liberation is generally understood as the last great legacy of the counterculture, itself generally understood in terms of a broader modernist revolt against the sexual Victorianism of the 1950s.[2] But a closer reading of the popular intellectual debate over sexuality from the 1950s through the 1970s suggests a different story. At the peak of the revival of domesticity known as the baby boom, popular commentators wrote of a "sexual revolution" that was irreversibly altering traditional relations between men and women. Enlightened opinion of the 1950s promoted a new ethic of "permissiveness with affection," to which gay power appears, in retrospect, little more than a homosexual postscript. The heterosexual revolution of the 1950s and the homosexual revolution of the 1960s demanded a common understanding of "sexuality" as a neutral energy force, distinct from procreation, existing within each individual as a resource for self-development.[3] From the 1950s onward, this compulsory sexuality has manifested itself in a consistent and ever broadening assault on external constraints in favor of an internalized ethic of responsible sexual choice.

The revolt against Victorianism has proved to be the most resilient cultural narrative for understanding sex in twentieth-century America. As yesterday's liberation becomes today's repression, historians discover in every era since the Victorian era proper a new Victorianism. Admittedly, midcentury American popular culture could be interpreted as in some respects sexually conservative or "Victorian" in relation to the sexual "modernism" of the 1920s. The stock market crash, the coming of the "talkies," and a rising alarm among moral and religious leaders forced a revolution in self-censorship in the most powerful cultural force of the 1930s and 1940s, the Hollywood film industry. Pressured by the Catholic Legion of Decency and concerned not to offend potential customers, the studio executives appointed conservative Irish Catholic Joseph Breen to head the Production Code Administration in 1934. Under Breen's guidance, Hollywood reinforced nineteenth-century prohibitions against adultery and premarital sex (although, as even Betty Friedan conceded, it also promoted strong, independent women characters in some ways more "modern" than the sexually liberated divas of the late silent era).[4]

This moral consensus began to lose its hold on Hollywood in the years following World War II. The challenge of television and the breakup of the studio system led film producers to throw off the moral self-censorship of the production code that shaped the content of Hollywood's golden era. In their attempt to lure television viewers into theaters with ever more titillating subject matter, producers consistently won court battles against censorship. In the world of high art, literature professors canonized modernism while art critics hailed abstract expressionism as the representative art of a free and democratic society. Rock 'n' roll brought to popular music a raw sexual energy that the more pharmaceutically oriented noodling of 1960s rock would never match. The older moral code survived only in the new medium of television, which replaced film as the primary form of entertainment for the house-bound consumers of the postwar baby boom. Bracketing developments in film and popular music, historians constructing narratives of liberation tend to read the conservative sexual morality of television as the representative cultural standard of the 1950s.

Credit for the revolt against this Victorianism conventionally goes to a humble zoologist specializing in the taxonomy of the gall wasp. In January 1948, Alfred C. Kinsey released his massive *Sexual Behavior in the Human Male* to the shock and delight of the American reading public. *Time* magazine declared, "Not since *Gone with the Wind* had booksellers seen anything like it." *Newsweek* concurred by declaring the book "the season's most sensational best seller." Popularly known simply as the Kinsey Report, the book sold over 200,000 copies in the first two months following its release and spent over twenty-seven weeks on the *New York Times* best-seller list. The report also received middlebrow cultural sanction from the *Times,* whose reviewer praised it as an important contribution to science that would "promote tolerance and understanding and make us better 'world citizens.'"[5] The perception of the book as a tool for tolerance stemmed from its own stated commitment to scientific objectivity. Ever the taxonomist, Kinsey approached human sexuality much as he approached gall wasps—with charts, graphs, and statistics presented as neutral empirical facts free from the bias of arbitrary moral judgment. This conceit of neutrality would prove to be Kinsey's most enduring contribution to the discourse of sexuality in the second half of the twentieth century. That the new "high priest of sexual liberation"[6] should emerge from the biological sciences in part reflects the new positivist spirit that came to dominate professional academic social science following World War II. More significantly, it reveals the deep continuities between postwar sexual modernists and the Victorian moralists against whom they claimed to be in revolt.

Kinsey himself was the product of an all-too-typical late-Victorian WASP upbringing. Born on June 23, 1894, he spent his early years in Hoboken, New Jersey. Like many northern Protestants of the time, his family fled the dirty, cramped, working-class ethnic city for the cleaner, safer environs of suburbia. An independent, freethinking soul from the start, Kinsey suffered from the twin oppressions of conservative evangelical Methodism and authoritarian child rearing. Like so many reformers of his generation, Kinsey was a sickly child and longed to prove his manhood through vigorous physical activity. He read *Tarzan,* worshiped Theodore Roosevelt, and joined the Boy Scouts, an organization with deep intellectual roots in the Victorian quest for the strenuous life (as well as in a parallel reform movement to stop boyhood masturbation).[7]

The love of nature that Kinsey developed in the Boy Scouts eventually provided the impetus for his dramatic break with the oppressive authority of his father. Against his father's wishes, Kinsey dropped out of the engineering program at Stevens Institute (Frederick Winslow Taylor's alma mater) to pursue the study of biology at Bowdoin College. Cut off from the financial support of his father, Kinsey secured the patronage of a wealthy widow and immersed himself in the secular evangelical ethos of Bowdoin life, a classically progressive blend of moral reformism and technocratic scientism. Pursuing graduate study at Harvard, Kinsey moved from liberal Protestantism to atheism: he came to believe that objective scientists, not moral reformers, should have the authority to direct public policy on matters ranging from industrial development to eugenics. In 1920, Kinsey began his academic career at Indiana University—a modern mega-university that was a product of the same progressive ethos that had so powerfully shaped Kinsey himself. At Indiana, Kinsey pursued teaching and research in zoology, specializing in the taxonomy of the gall wasp.

Kinsey struggled to live up to the expectations of conventional midwestern family life but found himself uncontrollably attracted to his male students. He organized zoological field trips deliberately to provide opportunities for seduction and began to indulge in blatant voyeurism and exhibitionism. The modern research university proved the ideal setting for Kinsey to channel his personal desires into his professional work. Kinsey justified sex research on the general grounds of the scientific imperative to explore every aspect of the natural world.

Much of the sex research at the time had been done under the cover of the scientific study of marriage, so Kinsey designed a marriage course as the teaching component of his new research specialty. The practice of using students as research subjects eventually got Kinsey into trouble with the administration. By 1940, he had resigned from the marriage course but continued his sex research, which included weekend explorations of the gay underground in Chicago. Through the 1940s, Kinsey sought funding for a full-blown research center devoted to the study of human sexuality. In 1947, with the generous support of the Rockefeller Foundation, Kinsey established the Institute for Sex Research at Indiana University.

Recent revelations concerning Kinsey's private struggles have obscured the historical significance of his public victory in establishing his Institute.[8] Kinsey clearly wrestled with many personal demons, and he clearly faced much opposition from conservative administrators and foundation officers. Still, the idea of an institute for sex research is perfectly consistent with the scientific ideal of objectivity that shaped the research university in the late nineteenth century. Kinsey may have attacked the dominant "Victorian" conception of morality, but he did so in the name of an equally Victorian conception of science, as much as the relatively more modern ethic of tolerance. Long before Kinsey, nineteenth-century "sexologists" such as Havelock Ellis, Richard von Krafft-Ebing—and of course Sigmund Freud—had succeeded in legitimating the application of scientific procedures to the study of sex.[9] The officers at the Rockefeller Foundation may have been uneasy with some of Kinsey's conclusions, but they had no doubt that sex was a suitable subject for Baconian inductive inquiry.

A vast literature of historical works published over the last twenty years has called into question the clichéd opposition of Victorianism and modernism. From the dark musings of Michel Foucault to the Enlightenment optimism of Peter Gay's celebration of the "bourgeois experience," historical scholarship has refused the simplistic equation of Victorianism with repression.[10] This discredited equation nonetheless remains available for selective invocation by historians still concerned to fight the very *Victorian* battle *against* repression. Thus, even as the most recent biography of Kinsey draws a convincing portrait of the man as a classic Victorian anal obsessive neurotic consumed by a rage for "order and control" in every aspect of his life, it presents his inclusion of sex within this regimen of self-discipline as a distinctively, and heroically, modern advance.[11] I do not deny that Kinsey's work provoked controversy and opened to public discussion issues previously confined to private life or the medical profession. I do, however, insist that the general acceptance of Kinsey's challenge to "traditional" morality suggests that historians can no longer rely on *Ozzie and Harriet* as a shorthand for the culture of the 1950s. Historians have for quite some time been uncovering the "hidden" 1950s of private sexual and cultural experimentation, only to read it as an anticipation of the public liberation of the 1960s. Such a read of Kinsey tells us more about the enduring appeal of the straw man of Victorian repression than it does about the sexual culture of the 1950s.

Sexual Behavior in the Human Male reflects this culture less in its content than in its form. In presenting the full range of possible sexual behavior, Kinsey clearly transgressed the norms of public discourse for his day; in speaking the unspeakable in the language of objective science, he reinforced the most deeply held prejudices of his day. Kinsey devotes the first third of his book to an explication of his statistical sampling methods. Having established his scientific credentials, he proceeds in the final two sections to address the general social factors affecting sexual "outlet" and the specific sources of these outlets, namely, masturbation, nocturnal emissions, petting, heterosexual intercourse, homosexual contacts, and animal contacts. He concludes on a statistical note, with a chapter on clinical tables and an appendix on his sampling techniques.

For all its methodological preoccupations, the book explicitly links science to social reform. In the preface, Alan Gregg of the Medical Sciences division of the Rockefeller Foundation praises Kinsey for approaching sex "as a biologist would examine biological phenomena . . . without moral bias or prejudice derived from current taboos." Gregg then places Kinsey's achievement in a broader historical context:

> The history of medicine proves that in so far as man seeks to know himself and face his whole nature, he has become free from bewildered fear, despondent shame, or arrant hypocrisy. As long as sex is dealt with in the current confusion of ignorance and sophistication, denial and indulgence, suppression and stimulation, punishment and exploitation, secrecy and display, it will be associated with a duplicity and indecency that lead neither to intellectual honesty nor human dignity.[12]

No mere triumph over moral bias, the claims to objectivity in Kinsey's book stand as confirmation of this broader historical narrative of human liberation. More than Gregg, Kinsey tends to confine his narrative of progress to the more modest claims of methodological advance, but he still happily reports that his empirical studies confirm the existence of a popular "faith . . . in the scientific method" and a widespread belief that "the whole of the social organization will ultimately benefit from the accumulation of scientifically established data."[13] As the initial *New York Times* review suggests, the 700-plus pages of raw, positivist sex data did not obscure the guiding presence of this humanist story.

The *Times* review set the tone for the book's initial reception. Soon leading public intellectuals of the day, such as Reinhold Niebuhr, Margaret Mead, and Lionel Trilling, chimed in with a more critical appraisal. Much of the highbrow commentary focused on Kinsey's methods. Critics objected not merely to the accuracy of specific findings but to Kinsey's general reduction of sex to quantitatively measurable, morally neutral behavior. Trilling's review, the most balanced and insightful of these critiques, follows the *Times* in praising the book's "good impulse toward acceptance and liberation." Still, Trilling fears that the report's reductive empiricism renders it "ill at ease with any idea that is in the least complex." Kinsey's pose of neutrality masks a bias against "the idea that sexual behavior is involved with the whole of the individual's character." Speaking for a whole generation of Freudian humanists, Trilling decries Kinsey's silence on the existential agon of sex.[14]

Trilling traces the limitations of the report less to Kinsey than to American culture. According to Trilling, the "symptomatic significance lies in the fact that the Report was felt to be needed at all, that the community of sexuality requires now to be established in explicit quantitative terms." The production of the book suggests that "now science seems to be the only one of our institutions which has the authority to speak decisively" on sex, or on any matter previously felt to require serious moral reflection. The popular reception of the book, in turn, raises serious questions about the place of science in a democratic society. On this issue, Trilling expresses particular concern for Kinsey's pose of objectivity. The social sciences can "no longer pretend that they . . . merely describe what people do." Through its service to the capitalist corporation and the totalitarian state, "sociology has shown its instrumental nature." Fearing its continued power "to manipulate and adjust," Trilling attacks social-scientific enlightenment as itself "an act of control." The unsuspecting masses have proven themselves capable of "yielding to understanding as never to coercion," and the Kinsey Report threatens to "do harm by encouraging people in their commitment to mechanical attitudes toward life."[15]

For all of its insights, Trilling's critique ultimately remains as symptomatic as the Kinsey Report itself. Like Mead before and Marcuse after, Trilling raises the haunting specter of manipulative social science only to invoke the saving angel of democratic social science. For all of his elitist fears concerning "the book's indiscriminate circulation," Trilling insists that "there is something good about the manner of publication, something honest and right." Beyond its conclusions concerning sexual behavior, the Kinsey Report raises awareness of the need for the mass cultivation of a sociological sensibility appropriate to the sociological nature of modern American culture: "If, then, we are to live under the aspect of sociology, let us at least all be sociologists together—let us broadcast what every sociologist knows, and let us all have a share in observing one another, including the sociologists."[16]

Trilling's dissatisfaction with Kinsey's narrowly quantitative observations does not lead him to question the basic rightness of the empirical, scientific process of observing and documenting human sexual behavior. Ultimately, Trilling's critique demands no more than that the positivist pursuit of fact be balanced by the humanist reflection on value, with maximum participation in both processes by all citizens. Coming from a figure generally regarded as at the conservative extreme of the liberal consensus, this assessment shows the extent to which, by the 1950s, social science had progressed from a tool for analyzing culture to itself an integral feature of the whole way of life of the American people.

In the decade and a half following the release of the Kinsey Report, sex maintained its high profile in the observation industry of the sociological society. By early 1964, *Time* magazine could publish a cover story proclaiming the years since the Kinsey Report a "second sexual revolution." According to *Time*, the 1950s saw a revolt against "traditional rules" regulating sexual behavior, accompanied by an "almost frantic attempt by sociologists and psychologists to give people something to hold on to without falling back on" the codes of the past. The *Time* article occasioned the publication of *Sex in America,* a collection of essays by leading doctors, psychiatrists, historians, and journalists exploring what the advertising copy called "the sexual crisis of our time." Deliberately diverse, ranging "from popular magazine . . . to psychological analyses, from imaginative philosophical speculation to rather stiff sociological reports," the book represents something like the collective sexual wisdom of middlebrow American culture in the 1950s. Edited by Henry Anatole Grunwald, a future editor in chief of *Time* who had worked on the magazine's original Kinsey story, *Sex in America* reveals the general acceptance of a moderate new sexual ethic, "permissiveness with affection," that confounds historical clichés concerning the "repressive" 1950s.[17]

The collection opens with the reprinted *Time* article, "The Second Sexual Revolution: A Survey." Declaring a sexual end of ideology, the article expresses not shock or alarm but amusement that people could be shocked or alarmed about sex at this late date in modern history. Some forty years since the first revolution of the Jazz Age, Freud appears himself a relic of the Victorian era, and the sexual radicalism of his more politically minded disciples has been assimilated and domesticated into the cultural mainstream. Even the Kinsey studies appear hopelessly dated, as suggested by a quote from Kinsey's successor at the Institute for Sex Research, Dr. Paul Gebbard: "What do you do after you show it all? I've talked to some of the publishers, and they are a little worried." Mainline religious leaders appear unwilling to offer any resistance to this "orgy of open-mindedness." Ministers who used to say, "Stop, you're wrong," now simply ask, "Is it meaningful?" With even the churches on board, there is very little sexual orthodoxy to revolt against. Would-be sexual radical Norman Mailer appears as a pathetic, comical figure whose desire to shock reflects little more than nostalgia for a Victorianism capable of being shocked. In sex as in politics, postwar America has witnessed an exhaustion of new ideas.[18]

Much like the Trilling review, the *Time* article expresses regret less for the passing of traditional standards than for the failure of Americans to live up to the responsibilities of their new freedom. The second sexual revolution has democratized a sexual ethic previously restricted to a bohemian elite, but the quantitative expansion of this freedom has brought with it a vulgarly measured understanding of the nature of sexual expression. The defense of quality against quantity serves as the consistent humanist ethic of the essays of *Sex in America*. The contributors repeatedly bemoan what the psychoanalyst Rollo May labels the New Puritanism: "Our modern sexual attitudes have a new content, namely, full sexual expression, but in the same old Puritan form—alienation from the body and feeling, and exploitation of the body as though it were a machine." For May, Mailer's sexual scalp hunting is merely the literary reflection of a broader social climate in which the "great new sin . . . is no longer giving in to desire . . . but not giving in to it fully or successfully enough." Young people are so pressured into having sex that "they feel guilty about feeling guilty" because "everyone is telling them that sex is healthy." Essays by Margaret Mead and Bruno Bettelheim see this pressure as especially harmful to young women—*not* out of any concern for female chastity per se but from an understanding that preoccupation with sex, and the unplanned pregnancies that often result from promiscuity, inhibit the educational and professional advancement of women.[19]

In this new sexual climate, young people "are likely to be driven to an early sexual sophistication beyond their emotional means." The *Time* article attacks the promotion of sex at the expense of love. Sex pursued for the wrong reasons, be they basely physical or impossibly spiritual, "becomes elusive, impersonal, ultimately disappointing." Critical of current trends, the article nonetheless refuses to return to past certainties:

> To describe the situation is not to plead for censorship. It remains for each man and woman to walk through this sexual bombardment and determine for himself what seems tasteless or objectionable, liberal or licentious, entertaining or merely dull. A healthy society must assume a certain degree of immunity on the part of its people.[20]

Time assumes what the more optimistic intellectuals of the 1950s went to such great lengths to argue: the persistence of autonomy despite the pressures to conform in mass society. A procedural norm, "immunity" implies no substantive restrictions on sexual behavior, merely a proper matching of physical acts with "emotional means" available to the individuals engaging in such acts. Accepting the reduction of sex to personal choice, *Time* asks no more than that Americans act as educated sexual consumers.

Sex in America enlists the leading public intellectuals of the day to invest this consumerism with world-historical moral seriousness. David Riesman departs from the temporizing tone of *The Lonely Crowd* to deliver a more direct attack on permissiveness as a new type of sexual conformity. Riesman offers his jeremiad in defense of a subtle, nuanced understanding of the ironies of historical progress, not traditional morality. In his essay "The New College Atmosphere" he declares that "permissiveness, liberating in its earlier installments, creates unanticipated problems as it spreads." Peer pressure toward premarital sex actually allows young "boys and girls . . . less permission than they once did to proceed in their relations to each other and to themselves at idiosyncratic rates." Permissiveness, "like any movement of liberation," produces new forms of unpermissiveness. This sexual dialectic reflects the broader historical dialectic of modernity: "industrialization has accompanied the liberation . . . from traditional and conventional bondages—but only at the cost, as we now realize, of subordinating both sexes to the authority of state and society." Riesman sees in modern culture an "authoritarian dialectic" vacillating between the stigmatization of differences based on "outer profiles" and "visibilities," and what he calls the "liberal reaction-formation" of denying previously stigmatizing differences such as race and sex in the name of an abstract ideal of equality.[21] By failing to acknowledge distinctions based on potentially stigmatizing characteristics, simple tolerance actually undermines the fostering of diversity.

Riesman concludes his essay with a plea for what amounts to the sexual equivalent of Ruth Benedict's world made safe for differences:

> Our goal is a world in which we rely neither on the authoritarian visual syndrome of seeing only culturally provided outlines nor the reaction-formation against this, but a more inclusive, holistic, Gestaltist way of feeling and reacting to ourselves and to others and to things . . . in which any of us may freely choose what country he "belongs" to, what class, what occupation, what subculture—and since biology makes it hard to choose one's sex, what quota of "masculine" and "feminine" qualities we will employ to pay taxes, modest taxes, to our constitutional and physiological inheritance. And among all these groups, taxes should be levied, not for mutual aggression and in-group pride, but for . . . mutual interest and discovery.[22]

Here Riesman extends the problem of sexual conduct to embrace broader issues of gender identity. For both sex and gender, he offers a mixed economy appropriate to the welfare state ideal of consensus political theorists. Individuals must pay their "taxes" to the authority of state and society, but state and society must provide conditions that allow for the maximum possible sexual freedom and diversity. This sexual regulatory ideal appears in several of the essays in *Sex in America* under the rubric of "permissiveness with affection."

True to its stated value of autonomy, *Sex in America* ironically questions the very ethic it offers as the best successor to tradition. Ira L. Reiss, the sociologist who coined the term "permissiveness with affection," proclaims it a revolutionary new "person-centered" sexuality, the moral equivalent of the efforts at school desegregation in the South. *Time*, somewhat less enthusiastically, defines the ethic as follows: "(1) morals are a private affair; (2) being in love justifies pre-marital sex, and by implication perhaps extramarital sex; (3) nothing really is wrong as long as nobody else 'gets hurt.'" Grunwald contributes even further ed-itorial skepticism: "As for a code based on 'permissiveness with affection,' the most serious difficulty, of course, is that affection springs up easily and is subject to all kinds of changing definitions." Grunwald consistently dismisses concepts such as "relationship ethics" and "interpersonal morality" as vacuous tautologies guided only by fleeting emotions. He endorses the centrality of sex to what Max Lerner calls "a healthy expressive life" but appears somewhat hesitant to accept Lerner's assessment of the "quest for new standards" as "itself a sign of cultural strength."[23] At the conservative end of the consensus on sexual freedom, Grun-wald nonetheless refuses any return to traditional morality. As selected and arranged by Grunwald, the essays in *Sex in America* affirm a general, post-Kinsey, humanist insistence on the need to move from quantity to quality in the frank and open discussion of sexual freedom. Grunwald's conservatism, like Trilling's, lies merely in his heightened sensitivity to the problem of determining quality in a world without God or tradition.[24]

Denis de Rougemont's "The Rising Tide of Eros" concludes the collection on just such a note of irony. De Rougemont follows the argument of his influential *Love in the Western World* by relativizing eroticism only to essentialize historical change. According to de Rougemont, the simultaneous suspicion of the flesh and insistence on bodily resurrection produced in Western Christianity a tension be-tween the body and the spirit unknown in the cultures of Asia and Africa. The or-thodox condemnation of gnosticism forced gnostic heretics to develop a secret, coded language to communicate their extreme rejection of the material world. The gnostic Catharist heresy proved influential among late medieval troubadours, whose cryptic love poetry ironically established the sensual as itself a spiritual category. Unlike sex, which is instinctual and procreative, this resulting eroticism linked bodily pleasure to spiritual truth.

This fatal conflation continues unabated in "modern lyricism and the novel, which speak of virtually nothing but a 'profane' love, without any longer know-ing its origin or its goal." De Rougemont locates the significance of the contem-porary sexual revolution not in "the degree of this century's immorality . . . but rather the (unconsciously religious) attitudes which justify that immorality." Cen-turies past have known lust, but in the twentieth century

what is liberated is expression, the way of talking about the subjects of love, of spec-ulating about them or of showing them on the screen. Hence it is not sex but eroti-cism, not sensuality but its public avowal, its projection before our eyes, that sud-denly provokes us to an awareness too long postponed.[25]

In retrospect, permissiveness with affection appears merely a slightly domesticated, social-scientific expression of the older erotic-Romantic effort to link sex to truth. Grunwald privileges de Rougemont with the final word in the collection but never directly addresses the relation of *Sex in America* to this erotic tradition.

The vapid insistence that sex be "meaningful" itself signals a troubling move toward sexual "depth" alien to most of the traditional cultures of the world. Tradition, however, must give way to history. As fact, history refuses to judge. De Rougemont approaches eroticism with the same positivist neutrality with which Kinsey approached sexual behavior in the human male: "To deplore the phenomenon is futile. The point is to understand its causes and above all its significance." As value, history affirms the progress of the modern West:

> I understand why contemporary literature scorns the puritanical and identifies it with madness, stigmatizing it as both ridiculous and dangerous. But I am not forgetting that without the sexual discipline which the so-called puritanical tendencies have imposed upon us since Europe first existed, there could be nothing more in our civilization than in those nations known as underdeveloped, and no doubt less: there would be neither work, organized effort, nor the technology which has created the present-day world. There would also not be the problem of eroticism! The erotic authors forget this fact quite naively.[26]

Literary erudition aside, de Rougemont offers another ironic reflection on the dialectic of repression and liberation within the iron cage of modernity. Grunwald endorses this narrative in his prefatory editorial comments. More significantly, he grants de Rougemont the final words of the volume, without editorial comment:

> The discoveries of depth analysis, the relaxation of sexual taboos, the increase of comfort and leisure, birth control, mass media—all function in the same irreversible direction . . . we can emerge from the inevitable chaos caused by so rapid a development only by advancing, not by turning back to the disciplines of earlier periods.[27]

This commitment to ceaseless change against the assurances of fixed norms links the diverse essays of *Sex in America* to each other, and it links the collection as a whole to the broader "consensus" culture of the 1950s.

The supposed sexual revolution of the 1960s appears in retrospect less a change in attitudes than in techniques. The image of naked hippies frolicking in the mud at Woodstock should not obscure the solidly technological infrastructure of counterculture sexuality. Most of the essays in *Sex in America* were written before, or very soon after, the Food and Drug Administration approved the sale of a female oral contraceptive—"the pill"—in 1960. The volume's most enthusiastic prophet of a new "sexual utopia" conceded that the fight against "ancient ideas about sex freedom for children and teenagers" would require "contraceptive skill much beyond our present attainment." He hastened to add, "but that is on the way." The pill inaugurated the contraceptive revolution necessary to make the second sexual revolution of the 1950s a way of life for most Americans in the 1960s. Newspapers and popular magazines heartily endorsed the spread of contraception. In *Griswold v. Connecticut* (1965), the Supreme Court declared unconstitutional laws restricting access to contraceptives by married couples; a few years later, it struck down similar restrictions on unmarried couples. By the late 1960s, the federal government began to integrate birth control into its War on Poverty, hoping that increased access to contraceptives would curb the birth rate among the poor, who appeared unwilling to follow their middle-class betters in the move away from the baby boom to smaller families.[28] At the dawn of the counterculture, sexual "freedom" was already firmly within the mainstream of American culture. Birth control, not sex, separated the flower children of the Woodstock generation from their middle-class parents.

The liberal–radical consensus on heterosexual promiscuity necessitated the creation of a bold new frontier in sex relations. Those in the vanguard of the third sexual revolution of the late 1960s turned to homosexuality. Kate Millett made Jean Genet the critical conscience of *Sexual Politics* precisely because the homosexual remained the "nigger" of love even within radical New Left circles. Firmly within the erotic tradition of "profane love," Millett writes, "its clandestine and forbidden character alone tends to grant homosexual love the glamour waning in literary accounts of heterosexuality."[29] To Millett's chagrin, heterosexual promiscuity maintained enough glamour to sustain the enthusiasm of postadolescent middle-class male radicals eager to implement the revolutionary praxis of Miller, Mailer, and Lawrence; the men who dismissed feminist concerns had even less interest in incorporating homosexuality into New Left politics. Feminists who accepted Millett's critique of patriarchy nonetheless proved hesitant to accept her bisexuality; lesbianism remained a divisive issue within feminist organizations throughout the 1970s.

Only with the public health crisis of AIDS did homosexuality enter the political mainstream. The high profile that the epidemic brought to homosexuals elicited a hostile, at times violent response from "straight" America, yet it also created a new category of prejudice—homophobia—and gave homosexuals an unprecedented moral and social legitimacy as noble, suffering victims. This real social change should not be confused with substantial cultural transformation. Long before AIDS, Kinsey had established the moral neutrality of homosexuality in the popular imagination. By the time *Sex in America* was published, homosexuality had already achieved a more broadly humanistic moral legitimacy within middlebrow American culture.

Grunwald devotes the penultimate section of *Sex in America* to what was then known as "the invert's problem." He addresses this problem through excerpts from the psychologist R. E. L. Masters's 1962 work, *The Homosexual Revolution.* Masters shares *Time*'s weary impatience with postwar America's obsession with sex. Americans who once "pretended that sex did not exist" now "scream its existence to the rooftops." Even "'the homosexual problem' has become a topic for conversation on almost all levels of our society." In light of Kinsey's research, homosexuality "can no longer be justly regarded as the unnatural vice of a few degenerates." Changes in awareness and perception of homosexual behavior suggest that

> we are undergoing presently what I have called a homosexual revolution. To date it has been a rather quiet revolution, though a very busy and far-reaching one. It is too soon to say whether the revolt of the homosexuals will become a truly dramatic uprising— like, say, the revolt of the American Negroes. That may be a matter of what is necessary, and of course the invert leaders would prefer a swift bloodless *coup d'état* to long and open warfare. Up to now homosexuals have won a succession of victories without any general recognition by the public that there is even an uprising in progress.[30]

Legal rulings decriminalizing homosexual acts between consenting adults, as well as an increasing openness to homosexual themes in popular entertainment, suggest a "profound and sweeping change in American attitudes." Masters notes how even the popular advice columnist Ann Landers feels "able to deal sympathetically with a letter from a homosexual reader."[31]

These relatively modest social gains belie a dynamic ideological ferment that had exhausted its full range of possibilities even before entering the mainstream sensibility of *Time* magazine. Masters's brief history of homosexual activism shows how, by the time of the Montgomery bus boycott, the homosexual revolution had already traveled the full trajectory of what would later be seen as the necessary advance from integration to separatism, from homosexual rights to homosexual power. According to Masters, the "homophile movement" began with the modest "desire to improve the lot of the invert in society." In 1950 homophile activists established the Mattachine Society, the first institution devoted to the advocacy of homosexual rights; in 1951, Donald Webster Cory's *The Homosexual in America* provided the movement with its "first real and effective manifesto."

The Mattachine Society took its name from the medieval Mattachines, court jesters or fools who were often homosexuals. Despite this provocative title, the group conducted itself with solid middle-class propriety and discouraged the extravagant mannerisms popularly associated with homosexuals. Preaching evolution rather revolution, it focused its efforts on combating civil rights violations. The Mattachine Society espoused high moral standards geared toward integrating homosexuals into the heterosexual mainstream and vehemently disavowed sadomasochism and pedophilia. Strongly patriotic, it made special efforts to refute the popular notion that homosexuality was a communist plot to subvert American democracy. The Mattachines suffered some police harassment early on, but their general low profile and social conservatism earned them a fair degree of tolerance. Dissatisfied with this conservatism, radical elements within the society soon broke off to form a rival organization, One, Inc. Established in 1952, One, Inc. quickly became "the largest, most powerful, and most militant of the homophile groups" in America. One, Inc. officially demanded legalization of homosexual marriage and adoption, while its magazine, *One,* provided a forum for more extreme elements advocating promiscuity and the genetic superiority of homosexuals.[32]

Masters's assessment of the homosexual revolution follows the general humanist editorial line of *Sex in America*. Masters sympathizes with the Mattachine Society's "attempt to wrest from heterosexual society the rights and privileges withheld from inverts by that society." To the degree that homosexuals are good citizens and do not force their behavior on others, he accepts the legitimacy of their "revolution." Predictably, he is more skeptical of the agenda behind One, Inc. "No sooner does [the homosexual] begin to enlist some friendly interest in his cause than he attempts to alienate that sympathy by making demands that our society is at least decades away from being willing to grant." Masters proved correct in his timing, and his objections to One, Inc. are as much practical as principled. He appears less concerned with the substance of issues such as homosexual marriage than with extremism in any form; he reserves his sharpest criticism for the "sordid, merely animal eroticism" of the general heterosexual revolution. This righteous indignation is, moreover, medical and not moral: "Hopefully this too will pass—and health will replace sickness once and for all." In his editorial comments, Grunwald voices more skepticism on the possibility of a healthy homosexuality; still, he praises Masters's "tolerance and understanding" and accepts his medical standard of judgment. The place of "The Homosexual Revolution" in *Sex in America* indicates the secure, if still evolving, place of homosexuality in the postwar regime of tolerance.[33]

The rhetoric of revolution nevertheless proved resilient. By the late 1970s, the movement for gay liberation had been canonized as "the last wave emanating from the seismic disturbances of the sixties."[34] Frances Fitzgerald's *New Yorker* series on the gay Castro district of San Francisco, perhaps the most popular account of the emergence of a homosexual subculture during the 1970s, reveals the limitation of this framework for understanding gay liberation. Reissued as the first chapter of her *Cities on a Hill*, Fitzgerald's journalistic anthropology of four post-1960s alternative communities, "The Castro" does indeed mark the movement of homosexuality from a narrowly sexual to a broadly social phenomenon

within popular intellectual discourse. Still, Fitzgerald's own somewhat contradictory evaluation of the Castro shows this move to be spatial rather than temporal, a reshuffling of the cultural deck rather than a substantive development in cultural ideology. Fitzgerald insists that the Castro "was something new under the
sun" but, as old as John Winthrop's vision of a City on a Hill, a light to all the nations. She wants to tell the story of the shift from the "homogeneous" society of
the 1950s to the "multicultural and pluralistic" society of the 1960s, yet she also
wants to tell a neo-consensus story of the enduring American tradition of self-
creation and cultural reinvention, a secularized evangelicalism "characterized by
an emphasis on direct experience rather than knowledge of doctrine or ritual practice, and, as a consequence, by anti-intellectualism, ahistoricism, and a pragmatic
experimentalism."[35] The foundational social-scientific story of the shift from tradition to modernity enables her to tell both stories. Integrated into this metanar-
rative of modernization, homosexuality, like heterosexuality before it, progresses
from prohibition to promiscuity to a mature, responsible ethic of permissiveness
with affection.

   Fitzgerald explicitly places *Cities on a Hill* in the tradition of *Middletown* and
The Lonely Crowd. She approaches these "cities" as "single organisms or personalities," each with its own "kinship systems, customs, and rituals," much like
the Dobu, Zuni, and Kwakiutl tribes of Ruth Benedict's *Patterns of Culture*. Integration, which "primitive" cultures achieve by maintaining a distance from
modernity, is somehow established by these cities through their passage into
modernity. Thus, in Fitzgerald's account of the birth of the gay Castro district, the
San Francisco of the 1960s appears much like the Middletown of the 1890s:
"Until 1965 San Francisco was much as it had been since the turn of the century:
a manufacturing city, a port, and a collection of ethnic villages." The Castro district primarily housed working-class Irish Catholics who attended Most Holy Re-
deemer parish, and a "big-city Democrat of the old school" still served as the
city's mayor. Investing urban industrialism with *Gemeinschaft* status, Fitzgerald
presents the San Francisco of the early 1960s as a "provincial" city.[36]

   White ethnics fled as the city's manufacturing base eroded. The consequent decline in property values made the district a haven for the overflow of bohemians
and hippies who descended on the Haight-Ashbury district to experience the bur-
geoning counterculture. More than the political New Left, the counterculture was
accepting of homosexuality. Gays gradually made the district their own, restoring
old homes to their previous glory and establishing a high-end consumer lifestyle
through various shops, boutiques, and restaurants. To this conventional story of
middle-class gentrification, the Castro added a sexual free-for-all, institutionalized through a network of bars, bathhouses, and sex clubs, that privileged anonymous sex as the distinctive feature of an authentically gay culture.[37]

Under the leadership of Harvey Milk, gays became a political force in the city. With this new public presence, gays made San Francisco the gay capital of America, if not the world. Gays continued to make political gains even after Milk's assassination, though more extreme forms of gay culture, such as sadomasochism, continued to cause tension with "straight" liberal allies such as Diane Feinstein. These tensions exploded into open warfare with the emergence of AIDS as a world health crisis in the early 1980s. Gays at first closed ranks and treated any practical measures proposed by liberals to curb the spread of the disease, such as the closing of the bathhouses, as a threat to their whole way of life. After much contentious denial, gay leaders gradually acknowledged the potentially deadly consequences of sexual promiscuity. AIDS thus brought the end of an era. Beginning her story with the libidinal anarchy of the 1978 Gay Freedom Day parade, Fitzgerald ends with the Castro in 1985, still "a gay neighborhood" but now "stable and domesticated." On a final note of irony, Fitzgerald concludes with a vignette of a sincere young gay man, searching for a committed relationship, asking another man out on a date.[38]

This anecdote functions less as evidence of assimilation to a heterosexual norm than as a critique of an established homosexual norm. Fitzgerald praises gay liberation for moving beyond the civil rights agenda of the homophile movement but sees in its questioning of all established sexual norms the establishment of new norms that proved equally oppressive. She looks back on the homosexual revolution of the 1970s and finds what David Riesman found in the heterosexual revolution of the 1950s: a potentially emancipatory movement that degenerated into a new conformity. Amid the variety of styles—cowboy, preppie, body builder, and the "clone" look of short hair, clipped mustache, bomber jacket, and blue jeans—the tyranny of fashion ruled. Prior to her concluding anecdote, Fitzgerald quotes a Castro resident to precisely this effect:

> During the seventies the gay movement here created an almost totalitarian society in the name of promoting sexual freedom. It evolved without any conscious decision, but there was so much peer pressure to conform that it allowed no self-criticism or self-examination. At some point there would have to be less sexual, political, and visual conformity. People grow up and change. But AIDS forced a reexamination in the way that few issues do. What we're seeing now is a revolution. We're seeing a reevaluation of life and relationships and what being gay is all about. We haven't got the answers yet but at least the questions have been posed.[39]

Indeed, the autonomous have always been questioners. Gay liberation expanded the range of acceptable questioning, but in doing so merely reinforced the dominant understanding of sex as a question to be asked. The homosexual revolution thus followed the heterosexual revolution in linking sex to knowledge and in reducing sex to choice.

The integration of homosexuality into the discourse of conformity finds its purest expression in the lesbian writer Adrienne Rich's concept of "compulsory heterosexuality." In 1978, at the height of the gay male liberation movement, Rich wrote "Compulsory Heterosexuality and Lesbian Existence" in protest against "the pressures to conform in a society increasingly conservative in mood." Rich attacks both male homosexuals and straight female feminists for refusing to acknowledge "lesbian existence as a reality and a source of knowledge." She directs most of her critical fire toward feminists who have done little more than tolerate lesbianism as an "alternative lifestyle." Offering yet another critique of repressive tolerance, Rich charges that surface tolerance of homosexuality masks a deep, coercive, heterosexual orthodoxy:

> The assumption that "most women are innately heterosexual" stands as a theoretical and political stumbling block for feminism. It remains a tenable assumption partly because lesbian existence has been written out of history or catalogued under disease, partly because it has been treated as exceptional rather than intrinsic, partly because to acknowledge that for women heterosexuality may not be a "preference" at all but something that has had to be imposed, managed, organized, propagandized, and maintained by force is an immense step to take if you consider yourself freely and "innately" heterosexual.[40]

Compulsory heterosexuality denies women true sexual "choice." Against this pressure to conform, lesbians must unite politically to assert "collective power to determine the meaning and place of sexuality in their lives." As process rather than substance, lesbian existence entails the "continuing creation of the meaning of that existence" by autonomous lesbian subjects. Shattering the "great silence" on lesbian existence will in turn bring about a broader social transformation, "a freeing up of thinking, the exploring of new paths . . . [and] new clarity in personal relationships."[41] By unmasking the coercive heterosexual orthodoxy, Rich relativizes procreation only to essentialize self-creation.

Rich's theory and the Castro's practice follow from certain intellectual assumptions regarding sex that were established as intellectual orthodoxy in the 1950s. In his essay on the Kinsey Report, Trilling at least acknowledged the intellectual problem with the desire to establish "a democratic pluralism of sexuality." With particular reference to Kinsey's desire to promote tolerance for homosexuality, Trilling observed,

> how very characteristically *American* a document the Report is. In speaking of its motives, I have in mind chiefly its impulse toward acceptance and liberation, its

broad and generous desire for others that they be not harshly judged. . . . That this generosity of mind is much to be admired goes without saying. But when we have given it all the credit it deserves as a sign of something good and enlarging in American life, we cannot help observing that it is often associated with an almost intentional intellectual weakness. It goes with a nearly conscious aversion from making intellectual distinctions, almost as if out of the belief that an intellectual distinction must inevitably lead to a social discrimination or exclusion. We might say that those who most explicitly assert and wish to practice the democratic virtues have taken it as their assumption that all social facts—with the exception of exclusion and economic hardship—must be *accepted,* not merely in the scientific sense but also in the social sense, in the sense, that is, that no judgment must be passed on them, that any conclusion drawn from them which perceives values and consequences will turn out to be "undemocratic."[42]

This intellectual weakness links Kinsey to Trilling, whose humanism could never transcend ironic reflection on its own limitations. It links the heterosexual revolution to the homosexual revolution, which together invested the rising tide of eros with the "objective" logic of historical inevitability. Finally, it links America to the modern West, which has declared that "it is forbidden to forbid."

Conclusion

Liberation, conceived as the instrumental control of nature in service of man, remains the faith of contemporary American intellectual life. In this conclusion, I sketch an outline of a genuinely alternative faith rooted in what may be called a Catholic mode of social thought. In direct contrast to the lingering Protestant ethos that Frances Fitzgerald has labeled the "evangelical mode," the Catholic mode emphasizes doctrine, ritual, historical continuity, respect for intellectual authority, and a suspicion of pragmatic experimentalism.[1] A cultural orientation rather than a set of specific beliefs, this Catholic mode requires no more confessional commitment than the evangelical mode that has for so long shaped the contours of American cultural and intellectual life.

This Catholic mode has in recent years spoken to a broad, ecumenical audience as at no time since the natural law revival of the 1940s. Despite the continued suspicions of militant secularists such as David Hollinger, Catholic philosophers such as Alasdair MacIntyre and Charles Taylor command unprecedented attention and respect from contemporary intellectuals across disciplinary and confessional lines. The most exciting development in contemporary Protestant thought, the "radical orthodoxy" of theologians such as John Milbank and Catherine Pickstock, is, despite persistent confessional divides, clearly within this Catholic mode. Long the chief secular alternative to Catholic organicism, the communitarian movement in sociology has likewise found in Catholicism social and intellectual resources lacking in the secular social sciences. The Episcopalian sociologist Robert Bellah, one of the few thinkers to address the religious dimension of contemporary multiculturalism, has recently pointed to Catholic sacramentalism as an antidote to the radical, antinomian individualism he rightly sees at the heart of so much contemporary talk of supposedly *cultural* diversity.[2]

Still, past developments suggest the inherent difficulties and dangers that await any rapprochement between Catholicism and mainstream American intellectual discourse. The midcentury career of the natural law philosopher Jacques Maritain provides the clearest cautionary tale for those who would seek to wed Catholicism and Americanism. In his 1946 work, *The Person and the Common Good,* Maritain developed a genuinely theological conception of the human person as the best hope for reconciling tradition and modernity, the sacred and the secular. By the time of his 1958 work, *Reflections on America,* he had come to accept the social world of secular American pluralism as the ideal environment for the flourishing of this sacred person. A brief examination of these two works shows that Maritain's social theory ultimately undermines his theology, reducing religion to mere "inspiration," a sacred means to the secular end of social order.

A neo-Thomist philosopher who helped revive the natural law tradition, Maritain was also a French émigré who experienced firsthand the rise of fascist regimes in Europe. Even as he turned to traditional Catholic philosophy as an antidote to modern nihilism, he also worked to secure an unprecedented respect for the dignity of the individual within Catholic social thought. Drawing in part on the new Catholic philosophy of "personalism," Maritain invoked the concept of the "human person" as a middle ground between the medieval organism of traditional Catholic social thought and the anarchic individualism at the root of modern social theory. This Catholic effort to temper traditional organicism with the concept of the human person paralleled secular efforts to temper modern individualism with the concept of culture. This common search for a *via media* has often obscured substantial philosophical differences. For Catholic thinkers, the concept of the human person called attention to the integrity of the individual *within* an organic social order, whereas for secular thinkers, the concept of a "new individualism" affirmed the integrity of the individual *in relation to* the objective processes of culture and society.[3] Maritain and secular liberals such as John Dewey agreed on the need to develop some intellectual justification for economic and social planning short of totalitarian state regimentation; they disagreed on the role of religion within this general social ideal. The persistent anti-Catholicism of postwar intellectual life points to the inherent tension between the Catholic and the liberal *via media.*

Maritain begins his 1946 work, *The Person and the Common Good,* very much in the mode of the liberal *via media* of postwar consensus thought. He presents his personalism as a set of aspirations rather than a rigid dogma, and he insists that it is "opposed to both the idea of the totalitarian state and that of the sovereignty of the individual." With a chapter titled "Individuality and Personality," Maritain appears set to offer yet another new individualism; however, writing from a Thomistic theological perspective, he presents the opposition of individuality and personality as a "metaphysical distinction" between the material and the spiritual aspects of the human soul. Maritain associates personality with a "generosity or expansiveness in being" and "communication with *other* and *the others*"—tropes consistent with the secular new individualism—but he refuses to set personality against a vulgar material individuality. Individuality represents the principle of separation "in as much as matter requires the occupation in space of a position distinct from every other position." Still, human souls exist as individuals "not . . . by reason of their own entity but by reason of their transcendental relation to matter understood as implying position in space." Separation implies relation, between both matter and matter and matter and spirit. Secular individualism affirms an instrumental relation between mind and matter, whereas Maritain's conception of the human soul sees the material and the spiritual as united by a teleological orientation toward an "absolute ultimate end."[4] The acceptance of a normative order outside of the self, be it rooted in divinity or nature, has been at the heart of the secular suspicion of Catholic social theory.

Instrumental and teleological philosophical orientations imply competing social visions. Secular individualism figures every social institution as a laboratory for developing and transforming nature and culture. Maritain's personalism, in contrast, demands that "everything . . . the whole universe and every social institution—must ultimately minister to . . . must foster and strengthen and protect the conversation of the soul, every soul, with God" (*PCG,* 16). Consequently, the main *social* activity of a personalist society is, of all things, contemplation. Maritain insists on the priority of the speculative over the practical in social life:

> And if a man be called to abandon his contemplation to come to the aid of his brothers or to serve the good of the community, the reason for this call is not at all because the good of the practical order is of itself superior to his solitary contemplation. He must accept it only because the order of charity can require that an urgent necessity of a less elevated good, in the circumstances, be given priority. (*PCG,* 27)

Nothing could be further from secular American social theory, which has never shed its residual Protestant contempt for contemplation as sloth, or at best a fugitive and cloistered virtue. The social centrality of contemplation assumes a society oriented toward permanence rather than change, an orientation anathema to secular instrumental individualism.

Maritain makes no attempt to establish an elaborate chain of causality connecting the speculative to the practical life. He in no way argues that contemplation makes contemplatives more responsible or more productive citizens; rather, contemplation serves the political order by sustaining nonpolitical ends. Maritain writes that

> the common good of the city or of civilization . . . does not preserve its true nature unless it respects that which surpasses it, unless it is subordinated, not as a pure means, but as an infravalent end, to the order of eternal goods and the supra-temporal values from which human life is suspended. (*PCG,* 62)

Contemplation serves the common good because "the common good is not only a system of advantages and utilities but also a rectitude of life, an end, good in itself or, as the ancients expressed it, a *bonum honestum" (PCG,* 53).

The secular instrumental tradition has no place for contemplation because it sees the good in utilitarian terms. Secular individualisms of the kind that triumphed in postwar America reduce ethics to a dialog of desire between the individual and an instrumental social whole. In this tradition, the "personal is political" because the political affects the personal, that is, it may restrict or expand individual freedom conceived in terms of libertarian choice. Secular individualisms have tended to view the relation between the personal and the political in terms of causality. Social-scientific awareness of interdependence, in turn, has "progressed" to the point where everything can be seen as causally related: thus everything is personal, and everything is political.

Against this logic, Maritain's personalism establishes a theological relation between the personal and the political. Maritain writes:

> The human person is engaged in its entirety as a part of political society, but not by reason of everything that is in it and everything that belongs to it. By reason of other things which are in the person, it is also in its entirety above political society. For in the person there are some things—and they are the most important and sacred ones— which transcend political society and draw man in his entirety above political society—the very same whole man who by reason of another category of things, is a part of political society. By reason of certain relations to the common life which concern our whole being, we are a part of the state; but by reason of other relations (likewise of interest to our whole being) to things more important than the common life, there are goods and values in us which are neither by nor for the state, which are outside of the state. (*PCG,* 72–73)

Maritain conceives of the relation between the person and the common good "in terms of reciprocal subordination and mutual implication" (*PCG,* 65). This means first of all that the person is "superior to every value of mere social utility" (PCG, 67). "The human person, as a spiritual totality referred to the transcendent whole, *surpasses* and is superior to all temporal societies" (*PCG,* 61). Maritain declares "with respect to the eternal destiny of the soul, society exists for each person and is subordinated to it" (*PCG*, 61).

Still, Maritain insists on the mutuality and reciprocity of subordination. Superior to mere utility, nevertheless,

> a human life is less precious than the moral good and the duty of assuring the salvation of the community, is less precious than the human and moral patrimony of which the community is the repository, and is less precious also than the human and moral work which the community carries on from one century to the next. (*PCG*, 67)

I know of no clearer statement of the Catholic understanding of the place of the human person in society. I know of no clearer challenge to the secular evangelical ethos that has dominated American public discourse in the twentieth century. In a sense, David Hollinger is correct when he writes of Catholicism as a formidable enemy to the liberal consensus. At midcentury, Catholicism—not race, class, gender, ethnicity, or sexuality—stood as the only serious alternative to secular cosmopolitanism.

Ironically, Maritain eventually came to see American religious pluralism as the best approximation of his Catholic vision. In his *Reflections on America,* published in 1958, he writes that "if a new Christian civilization, a new Christendom, is ever to come about in human history, it is on American soil that it will find its starting point."[5] In language reminiscent of *The Person and the Common Good,* Maritain declares America to be beyond individualism and totalitarianism, "personalist and community-minded at the same time" (*RA*, 179). However, his personalism quickly slides into the language of secular liberal individualism. Maritain praises American democracy not for sustaining "the order of eternal goods" but for fostering "a continuous process of self-creation" (*RA*, 168). He assesses American democracy in the following manner:

> Existing in history, and being a human thing . . . it must be perpetually defended and improved, it must be a new conquest and creation for each generation. It permits of no inertia, no passivity, no rest. It must be unceasingly regenerated by the life-breath of a free people and so it is one with this very life-breath. (*RA*, 169–70)

Maritain sees a similar flux and fluidity in American intellectual life, yet he cites the popularity of the writings of the Trappist monk Thomas Merton as evidence of America's respect for the contemplative life. Even more disturbingly, he cites the prominence of none other than John Dewey, the arch instrumentalist, as evidence of American respect for the life of the mind.

Neo-Thomism and pragmatism could not be more opposed as philosophical orientations, but Maritain's whole reading of the dynamics of American society appears disturbingly indebted to Dewey. In classic Deweyan fashion, Maritain sees American life in terms of the conflict between "the people" and the "structure or ritual of civilization" (*RA*, 21). The spirit of a freedom-loving people is gradually overcoming the oppressive structure of industrial capitalism in America, thus opening up the possibility of the realization of the American promise of perpetual change and diversity. Maritain sees an "organic multiplicity" in the American federal system, "a kind of puzzling diversity which resembles a medieval feature (I am thinking, for instance, of the diversity from state to state in the laws regarding daylight savings time)"[!] *(RA,* 162). Maritain sees this diversity held together by "a deep-rooted, sometimes hidden, sometimes unconscious, but actual and alive religious inspiration . . . embodied in the temporal, secular, lay life of this country" (*RA*, 183). Maritain concludes, "thanks to the spirit of fellowship and mutual toleration . . . this inspiration is compatible with the multiplicity of religious denominations which can be seen" in America (*RA*, 185).

Maritain's reading of religious pluralism in *Reflections on America* contrasts sharply with his understanding of the social nature of religion in *The Person and the Common Good.* In *Reflections on America,* Maritain capitulates to the classic bourgeois view of religion by divorcing religion from the institutional structure of society and reducing it to "inspiration." I have no convincing causal explanation for the contrast between Maritain's theology and his social theory. I present it rather as a cold war era symptom of what John Milbank, in his *Theology and Social Theory,* has identified as the persistent failure of modern theologians to develop a social philosophy that escapes the conventions of secular social theory.[6] As long as believers concede a place, in matters of faith, for what Maritain refers to as "helpful and necessary systematic surveys and scientific analyses," faith will remain marginal to society, at best an intense, private "experience" (*RA*, 16). As long as believers concede a place, in matters of morals, for "an extensive study written by a team of experts, especially a psychologist, an anthropologist, a sociologist, and a philosopher-all of them guided, one would hope, by a genuinely philosophical inspiration," morality will remain marginal to society, at best a technical matter of hygiene and the harm principle (*RA*, 59).

By the early 1960s, Maritain achieved acceptance among liberals as a "safe" Catholic thinker. Critics praised Maritain's ability to draw on Catholic traditions without succumbing to a "nostalgia for the body politic of the Middle Ages."[7] A comparison of *The Person and the Common Good* and *Reflections on America* suggests that Maritain avoided a conventionally Catholic nostalgia for the Middle Ages only to embrace a conventionally American nostalgia for the nineteenth century. The Tocqueville revival of the 1950s, as well as the periodic revivals since then, point to the enduring appeal of the American tradition of denominationalism as a reasonable middle course between the traditional religious establishment and modern secularism. The understanding of religion that shapes this American tradition has its roots in John Locke's "Letter Concerning Toleration." Locke's vaunted tolerance implies a very particular conception of religion as private inspiration and voluntary association (a conception of religion very close to the conception of culture in modern secular pluralist thought). In the debate over the character of the postwar religious revival, few questioned this basic consensus on the nature and social character of religion. For one brief moment in *Protestant, Catholic, Jew,* Will Herberg dared to pose the problem of religion in substantively social terms: "It is this secularism of a religious people, this religiousness in a secularist framework, that constitutes the problem posed by the contemporary religious situation in America."[8] Herberg never pursued this line of questioning, and his existential opposition between vital and conformist religion evaded the confrontation with a thickly communal conception of religion.

Herberg's passing observation is the consuming question of the Catholic intellectual confrontation with social modernity. Through the middle of the twentieth century, Catholicism countered the dominant antinomianism of American culture with a theological insistence on the priority of external sacramental forms to inner spiritual experience, and a practical social realization that we are communal before we are individual. Catholic resistance to American models of church–state relations stemmed from an understanding of the inescapably social nature of Catholic religious life; to accept the American institutional model would be to submit to the American theological model. The subsequent history of liberal Catholicism in America bears out these fears. In the wake of fascism, Catholic thinkers such as Maritain struggled to reconcile traditional Catholic teaching on religious establishment with a new acceptance of the principle of religious toleration, yet efforts to articulate a distinctly Catholic understanding of tolerance fell all too easily into the conventional American language of denominationalism.

For Catholicism, secularism is a matter of form, not content. The religious crisis of modern society lies not primarily in a crisis of belief but in what the Anglo-Catholic T. S. Eliot described as "our implication in a network of institutions from which we cannot dissociate ourselves: institutions the operation of which appears no longer neutral, but non-Christian." In his 1940 work *The Idea of a Christian Society,* Eliot wrote of how secular society places Christians under the "compulsion to live in such a way that Christian behaviour is only possible in a restricted number of situations." Even in the few remaining "Christian" situations, secular society forces the believer "to be conscious, without remission, of a Christian and a non-Christian alternative at moments of choice."[9] This general Catholic suspicion of personal choice as corrosive to the integrity of religion has fueled secular suspicion of Catholicism as creeping fascism. At the same time, the history of the free market of religion in America has confirmed all the Catholic fears of the consequences of official state neutrality, namely, the dilution of doctrine and ritual, the reduction of religion to the personal, evangelical mode identified by Fitzgerald and Bellah.

In arguing against the nineteenth century, I am not arguing for the Middle Ages. *Reflections on America* shows the dangers of civil religion to traditional Catholicism, yet the strongly Catholic vision of *The Person and the Common Good* clearly poses a danger to non-Catholics. To the degree that it restricts the free expression of traditional, thickly social forms of religious belief, the U.S. Constitution represents a new form of coercion; to the degree that it prevents the imposition of religious belief on unwilling citizens, it marks a positive advance in human freedom. Faced with these opposing tendencies, I cannot present Catholicism as an alternative *for* America; I wish merely to argue for the establishment of conditions under which Catholicism could thrive as an alternative *within* America.

Apart from consideration of the truth claims of Catholicism, this goal should find support among the secular pluralists if only on the grounds of supporting cultural diversity. Despite my criticisms of cultural instrumentalism, I do believe that the secular notion of culture as a whole way of life shares much with the Catholic insistence that, in Eliot's words, "religious and social life should form . . . a natural whole."[10] Constructive dialog on these matters will, however, require secular engagement with the Catholic insistence that cultural integrity requires a large degree of isolation. Through the middle decades of the twentieth century, the Catholic Church supported an immense network of parallel institutions that sustained a distinct subculture. The enthusiastic patriotism that accompanied this separatism proved to be the downfall of the subculture, but the institution building of the Church offers the best model for cultural diversity in the future. The path to meaningful diversity lies not in the refinement of abstract, neutral, universal principles that affirm the dignity of all faiths and value systems, but in the fostering of alternative, local institutions rooted in very particular faiths and value systems.

Education offers the most obvious starting point for such an institutional reorientation. The public school movement of the nineteenth century marked the first significant institutional effort to establish, and inculcate, a set of abstract, universal, social principles to reinforce the abstract, universal, political principles of the U.S. Constitution. The fiercest opposition to the public schools came from Catholic priests who saw them for what they were: machines for making Unitarians. Without the benefit of the concept of cultural hegemony, these priests realized that education is never neutral. They asked only that Catholics be free to send their children to Catholic schools without bearing the additional tax burden of supporting public schools—a tithe, in effect, to promote Protestantism and later secularism. Today, the public school system remains in the vanguard of promoting false universalisms. Advocates of new multicultural curricula who are quick to point out the biases of even earlier secular liberal curricula should by now be willing to acknowledge the unavoidable bias of any possible multicultural curriculum. The public control of education is not a constitutional necessity. If the government is to be true to its stated value of promoting diversity in education, it must be willing to support a variety of particular, "biased" curricula or must surrender education completely to the private sphere.

The private corporation offers the most necessary locus for such an institutional reorientation. The growth of industrial capitalism and the expansion of national and international markets disrupted those local "island communities" that sustained more thickly social forms of religious life. Even in a generally deritualized Protestant America, preindustrial work habits allowed for seasonal religious festivals that sustained older public understandings of religion, despite official disestablishment.[11] Long before the explosion of the culture industry provided the technical means of disseminating alternative secular values, the imposition of standardized industrial discipline fostered the increasing privatization of religion; much like the family, religion came to be seen as a haven from the heartless world of capitalist social relations. The *Trustees of Dartmouth College v. Woodward* (1819) decision, which established the legal precedent for the legitimacy of the private corporation, has bequeathed a daunting tradition of legal interpretation that continues to promote the flourishing of corporate capitalism, but the private corporation is not a constitutional necessity. The concentration of such power free from public accountability would have struck the founders, and many nineteenth-century "liberals," as nothing short of tyranny. As currently exercised by the private corporation, the constitutional rights of property and free speech work to restrict the equally constitutional right to the free exercise of religion. The secular/capitalist insistence on the sufficient freedom of private religion amounts to nothing less than a return of the repressed "separate but equal" tradition long since abandoned as a principle for race and gender relations. The time has come to see the *Dartmouth College* decision as we now see *Plessy v. Ferguson.*

This being said, I have no illusions about the desire of Americans to entertain such constitutional comparisons. America may have the soul of a church, but it has the body of a factory. Most Americans, including Catholics, generally accept this factory, provided it runs smoothly and delivers the goods. The "moral economy" has long since given way to the procedural norms of distributive justice, and public religion has long since traded ritual for moralism. These facts cannot be denied.

Still, other facts remain. A substantial majority of Americans—Protestant, Catholic, Orthodox, Jewish, and Muslim—still take as authoritative certain premodern texts, and a substantial minority of this group still order at least part of their lives according to certain premodern rituals. The best hope for an alternative to the cultural instrumentalism of secular pluralism lies in expanding the scope of activities that receive the sanction of these texts and rituals. This expansion out from the narrowly private confines currently allowed religion would entail a reclamation of those spheres of activity usurped by the state and the private corporation—in particular education, welfare, and the promotion of the arts. It would not entail using politics to impose a single set of truths on an unwilling citizenry. Maritain's insistence that "every social institution . . . must foster and strengthen and protect the conversation of the soul, every soul, with God" violates the constitutional protection of religious freedom only if everyone belongs to the same social institutions. The alternative to the current segregation of religion is not integration but separatism. Such separatism marks a retreat only from the Enlightenment ideology of liberal universalism, not from participation in the political institutions that are, admittedly, the legacy of this ideology. A strongly separatist understanding of religious freedom shares much with the quasi-nationalist strains of contemporary multiculturalism and the democratic localism of some secular forms of communitarianism. Despite (or perhaps because of) substantial differences in worldview among these groups, a separatist political coalition would have the greatest potential to articulate a real alternative to the empty "diversity" of liberal pluralism. The fostering of local institutions, rooted in distinct, particular traditions, promises the most meaningful alternative to both the religious intolerance of the past and the secular intolerance of the present.

Notes

INTRODUCTION

1. Ruth Benedict, *The Chrysanthemum and the Sword: Patterns of Japanese Culture* (1946; reprint, Boston: Houghton Mifflin, 1989), 14–15.

2. Herbert Marcuse, "Repressive Tolerance," in *A Critique of Pure Tolerance*, ed. Herbert Marcuse, Barrington Moore Jr., and Robert Wolff (Boston: Beacon, 1969), 84, 115.

3. For a review of one representative debate that reveals the continuation of this liberal ideal even within the multiculturalist attack on liberalism, see Christopher Shannon, "A World Made Safe for Differences: Ruth Benedict's *The Chrysanthemum and the Sword*," *American Quarterly* 47, no. 4 (1995): 676–79.

4. Erik H. Erikson, *Identity: Youth and Crisis* (New York: Norton, 1968), 15.

5. Erik H. Erikson, *Childhood and Society* (1950; reprint, New York: Norton, 1963), 268.

6. For Erikson's critique of manipulative social science, see Erikson, *Childhood*, 417, 422.

7. For a brief treatment of this problem in the historiography of the culture concept, see Shannon, "World," 661–62.

8. Erikson, *Childhood*, 286.

9. Erikson, *Childhood*, 286.

10. Erikson, *Childhood*, 279, 406–7, 412–13.

11. Erikson, *Childhood*, 416.

12. Christopher Shannon, *Conspicuous Criticism: Tradition, the Individual, and Culture in American Social Thought, from Veblen to Mills* (Baltimore: Johns Hopkins University Press, 1996).

13. Erikson, *Childhood*, 419, 420, 421, 422, 423.

14. Erikson, *Childhood*, 421, 424.

15. For my understanding of the place of Catholicism in midcentury intellectual debates, I am deeply indebted to Edward A. Purcell Jr., *The Crisis of Democratic Theory:*

Scientific Naturalism and the Problem of Value (Lexington: University of Kentucky Press, 1973).

16. See Purcell, especially 164–71.

17. Philip Gleason, "The Study of American Culture," 192; and "Hansen, Herberg, and American Religion," 243; both in his *Speaking of Diversity: Language and Ethnicity in Twentieth—Century America* (Baltimore: Johns Hopkins University Press, 1992), 192, 243.

18. Hook quoted in John T. McGreevy, "Thinking on One's Own: Catholicism in the American Intellectual Imagination, 1928–1960," *Journal of American History* 84 (June 1997): 127; Sidney Hook, "The New Failure of Nerve," *Partisan Review* 10 (January—February 1943): 17, 19, 20.

19. Hook, "New Failure," 6, 7, 8, 9, 10, 15.

20. McGreevy, "Thinking," 97, 127–128.

21. David Hollinger, "Science as a Weapon in *Kulturkampf* in the United States During and After World War II"; and "Jewish Intellectuals and the De-Christianization of American Public Culture in the Twentieth Century," in *Science, Jews, and Secular Culture: Studies in Mid-Twentieth-Century American Intellectual History* (Princeton: Princeton University Press, 1996), 33, 159. Nearly every essay in this collection contains some grave reference to T. S. Eliot's infamous remark about "free-thinking Jews" in *After Strange Gods*. Hook's repeated anti-Catholic utterances receive no such moral scrutiny.

22. Howard Brick, *Daniel Bell and the Decline of Intellectual Radicalism: Social Theory and Political Reconciliation in the 1940s* (Madison: University of Wisconsin Press, 1986).

23. Dwight Macdonald, "The Responsibility of Peoples," in *Memoirs of a Revolutionist: Essays in Political Criticism* (New York: Farrar, Straus & Cudahy, 1957), 39.

24. Max Horkheimer and Theodor W. Adorno, *Dialectic of Enlightenment* (1944; reprint, New York: Seabury, 1972), xiv, xvi, 9, 24.

CHAPTER 1: INTEGRATING THE WORLD

1. On Boas, see George W. Stocking Jr., "Franz Boas and the Culture Concept in Historical Perspective," in *Race, Culture, and Evolution: Essays in the History of Anthropology* (New York: Free Press, 1968).

2. See, in general, Ruth Benedict, *Patterns of Culture* (Boston: Houghton Mifflin, 1934).

3. Margaret Mead, *Ruth Benedict* (New York: Columbia University Press, 1974), 57; Margaret M. Caffrey, *Ruth Benedict: Stranger in This Land* (Austin: University of Texas Press, 1989), 315–16.

4. Judith Schachter Modell, *Ruth Benedict: Patterns of a Life* (Philadelphia: University of Pennsylvania Press, 1983), 268–70; Caffrey, *Ruth Benedict*, 321.

5. Mead addresses the colonial context of anthropology and its future role in preserving the "dignity of man" in *And Keep Your Powder Dry: An Anthropologist Looks at America*

(New York: Morrow, 1942), 8–9, 241, 247. John W. Dower characterized the culture-and-personality approach of Mead and Benedict as an example of "humanistic science" in his *War without Mercy: Race and Power in the Pacific War* (New York: Pantheon, 1986), 119.

6. On these stereotypes of the "other," see Dower, *War,* chap. 5, "Primitives, Children, Madmen."

7. Ruth Benedict, *The Chrysanthemum and the Sword: Patterns of Japanese Culture* (1946; reprint, Boston: Houghton Mifflin, 1989), 13. All future following references to this work are cited parenthetically in the text as *CAS.*

8. Mead contrasts America and Europe in this fashion in *And Keep Your Powder Dry.*

9. Dower, *War,* 19, 128, 304.

10. On cosmopolitanism, see David Hollinger, "Ethnic Diversity, Cosmopolitanism, and the Emergence of the American Liberal Intelligentsia," in *In the American Province: Studies in the History and Historiography of Ideas* (Bloomington: Indiana University Press, 1985), 56–73. Though he does not explicitly examine the language of "responsibility," Christopher Lasch has provided the best account of the political ethic of liberal intellectuals in his *True and Only Heaven: Progress and Its Critics* (New York: Norton, 1991), especially chap. 10, "The Politics of the Civilized Minority."

11. Arthur M. Schlesinger Jr., *The Vital Center: The Politics of Freedom* (1949; reprint, Boston: Houghton Mifflin, 1989), xvi, 30, 51, 253.

12. Schlesinger, *Vital Center*, 51, 171, 232–33, 253–54.

13. On these developments, see in general Andrew J. Rotter, *The Path to Vietnam: Origins of the American Commitment to Southeast Asia* (Ithaca: Cornell University Press, 1987).

14. For information on Lansdale, I am indebted to an unpublished paper by Jonathan Nashel, "Edward Lansdale's Cold War Vision." See also Richard Drinnon, *Facing West: The Metaphysics of Indian-Hating and Empire Building* (Minneapolis: University of Minnesota Press, 1980).

15. William J. Lederer and Eugene Burdick, *The Ugly American* (1958; reprint, New York: Norton, 1965), 12, 94, 107, 267. The following references to this work are cited parenthetically in the text as *UA.*

16. Frances Fitzgerald, *Fire in the Lake: The Vietnamese and the Americans in Vietnam* (1972; reprint, New York: Random House, 1989), 16. The following references to this work are cited parenthetically in the text as *FL.*

CHAPTER 2: CULTURE AND COUNTERCULTURE

1. Daniel Bell, "The End of Ideology in the West," in *The End of Ideology: On the Exhaustion of Political Ideas in the Fifties* (1960; reprint, Boston: Free Press, 1962), 402, 403, 405.

2. Bell, "End of Ideology," 403, 402.

3. Bell, "End of Ideology," 400, 402–3, 405.

4. Bell, "End of Ideology," 403.

5. Bell, "End of Ideology," 400.

6. Wilfred M. McClay, *The Masterless: Self and Society in Modern America* (Chapel Hill: University of North Carolina Press, 1994), 237–40.

7. David Riesman, with Nathan Glazer and Reuel Denney, *The Lonely Crowd: A Study of the Changing American Character* (1950; reprint, New Haven: Yale University Press, 1961), xi. The following references to this work are cited parenthetically in the text as *LC*.

8. Wilfred McClay has correctly placed *The Lonely Crowd* firmly within the jeremiad tradition. Unlike most historians, McClay understands the book more as a symbol than an argument: "Perhaps a suitably symbolic way of reading *The Lonely Crowd* would dwell less on its internal inconsistencies than on its cultural consistencies, the way in which its internal tensions were perhaps even more meaningful than its explicit argument, as a window onto the actual cultural task a book is performing" (267).

9. This self-negating preface owes much to the introductory material in the Middletown books of Robert and Helen Lynd. See chapter 2 and chapter 5 of Shannon, *Conspicuous Criticism: Tradition, the Individual, and Culture in American Social Thought, from Veblen to Mills* (Baltimore: Johns Hopkins University Press, 1996).

10. Years later, in a less confident time, Daniel Bell would cite similar musings by Michel Foucault as symptomatic of the decline of civilization. See Daniel Bell, *The Cultural Contradictions of Capitalism* (New York: Basic, 1978), 52.

11. McClay, *Masterless*, 240.

12. C. Wright Mills, *White Collar: The American Middle Classes* (New York: Oxford University Press, 1951); Mills, *The Power Elite* (New York: Oxford University Press, 1956).

13. C. Wright Mills, "The Problem of Industrial Development," in *Power, Politics, and People: The Collected Essays of C. Wright Mills*, ed. Irving Louis Horowitz (New York: Oxford University Press, 1963), 150.

14. Students for a Democratic Society, "Port Huron Statement," in *The New Left: A Documentary History*, ed. Massimo Teodori (New York: Bobbs-Merrill, 1969), 166–67.

15. For an entertaining account of Kesey and the Merry Pranksters, see Tom Wolfe, *The Electric Kool Aid Acid Test* (New York: Bantam, 1968).

16. Theodore Roszak, *The Making of a Counter Culture: Reflections on the Technocratic Society and Its Youthful Opposition* (Garden City, N.Y.: Doubleday, 1969). The following references to this work are cited parenthetically in the text as *MCC*.

17. Marcuse, "Repressive Tolerance," 84, 115.

18. For the best recent account of the rationalization of religion during the Reformation, see Eamon Duffy, *The Stripping of the Altars: Traditional Religion in England, 1400–1580* (New Haven: Yale University Press, 1992). The Reformation cannot, of course, be reduced to rationalization. Still, even the most sympathetic accounts of the persistence of the older, sacramental, enchanted worldview among reformed groups confirm the basic outlines of Weber's oft dismissed, but still not refuted, thesis on the Protestant ethic and the spirit of capitalism. See, for example, Leigh Eric Schmidt, *Holy Fairs: Scottish Communions and the American Revivals in the Early Modern Period* (Princeton: Princeton University Press, 1989), especially chap. 1, "From Reformation to Revival."

19. Paul Goodman, *Growing Up Absurd: Problems of Youth in the Organized System* (New York: Random House, 1960), 15–16.

20. Riesman, *Lonely Crowd,* 297.

CHAPTER 3: THE NEGRO DILEMMA

1. Ralph Ellison, *"An American Dilemma*: A Review," in *Shadow and Act* (1964; reprint, New York: Random House, 1972), 308.

2. On Robert Park, see Barbara Ballis Lal, *The Romance of Culture in an Urban Civilization: Robert E. Park on Race and Ethnic Relations in Cities* (New York : Routledge, 1990); and Fred H. Matthews, *Quest for an American Sociology: Robert E. Park and the Chicago School* (Montreal : McGill–Queen's University Press, 1977).

3. Ellison, *"American Dilemma,"* 316, 315–16.

4. Ellison, *"American Dilemma,"* 313, 315–16, 304.

5. Ellison, *"American Dilemma,"* 313–14, 316.

6. Alain LeRoy Locke, "The New Negro," in *The New Negro: An Interpretation* (1925; reprint, New York: Arno, 1968), 3, 4, 6, 8, 9.

7. Locke, "New Negro," 4–5.

8. Warren I. Susman, "The Culture of the Thirties," in *Culture as History: The Transformation of American Society in the Twentieth Century* (New York: Pantheon, 1984), 150–85.

9. Richard Wright, "Blueprint for Negro Writing," in *Richard Wright Reader,* ed. Ellen Wright and Michel Fabre (New York: Harper & Row, 1978), 43–44, 49.

10. Ellison, quoted in Jerry Gafio Watts, *Heroism and the Black Intellectual: Ralph Ellison, Politics, and Afro-American Intellectual Life* (Chapel Hill: University of North Carolina Press, 1994), 46.

11. John S. Wright, "To the Battle Royal: Ralph Ellison and the Quest for Black Leadership in Postwar America," in *Recasting America: Culture and Politics in the Age of Cold War,* ed. Lary May (Chicago: University of Chicago Press, 1989), 258.

12. Ralph Ellison, "Change the Joke and Slip the Yoke," in *Shadow and Act,* 56.

13. Ralph Ellison, introduction to *Invisible Man* (1952; reprint, New York: Random House, 1989), xiv. The following references to this work are cited parenthetically in the text as *IM.*

14. Ralph Ellison, "Richard Wright's Blues," in *Shadow and Act,* 87.

15. Ralph Ellison, "Harlem Is Nowhere," in *Shadow and Act,* 296.

16. Ralph Ellison, "Some Questions and Some Answers," in *Shadow and Act,* 265.

17. Ellison, "Some Questions," 265, 269–70; "Change the Joke," 48.

18. Ellison, "That Same Pain, That Same Pleasure: An Interview," in *Shadow and Act,* 22.

19. Ellison, "Some Questions," 269; "Harlem," 300; "Remembering Jimmy," in *Shadow and Act,* 244.

20. See Shannon, *Conspicuous Criticism,* especially chap. 2, *"Middletown* as Transition?"

21. Ralph Ellison, "On Bird, Bird-Watching, and Jazz," in *Shadow and Act,* 221–32; "Change the Joke," 58

22. Ellison, "Richard Wright's," 78–79, 94.

23. LeRoi Jones, *Blues People: The Negro Experience in White America and the Music That Developed from It* (New York: Morrow, 1963), 201–2.

24. Quoted in George Brown Tindall with David E. Shi, *America: A Narrative History* (New York: Norton, 1992), 2:1356.

25. Kwame Ture and Charles V. Hamilton, *Black Power: The Politics of Liberation* (1967; reprint, New York: Random House, 1992), 37.

26. Anonymous brief review, *New Yorker* 43, no. 50 (1968): 112.

27. Harold Cruse, *The Crisis of the Negro Intellectual* (New York: Morrow, 1967), 546. The following references to this work are cited parenthetically in the text as *CNI,* 28. H. Rap Brown, quoted in Tindall and Shi, *America,* 1356.

CHAPTER 4: BEYOND THE UNMELTABLE ETHNICS

1. Nathan Glazer and Daniel Patrick Moynihan, *Beyond the Melting Pot: The Negroes, Puerto Ricans, Jews, Italians, and Irish of New York City* (1963; reprint, Cambridge: MIT Press, 1967), 155. The following references to this work are cited parenthetically in the text as *BMP.* Will Herberg, *Protestant, Catholic, Jew: An Essay in American Religious Sociology* (1955; reprint, Garden City, N.Y.: Anchor, 1960), 10.

2. Oscar Handlin, *The Uprooted: The Epic Story of the Great Migrations That Made the American People* (New York: Grosset & Dunlap, 1951), 3, 259, 303, 306, 307.

3. Herberg, *Protestant,* 254.

4. Quoted in Christopher Lasch, *The True and Only Heaven: Progress and Its Critics* (New York: Norton, 1991), 445.

5. See in general Sacvan Bercovitch, *The American Jeremiad* (Madison: University of Wisconsin Press, 1978).

6. Kevin P. Phillips, *The Emerging Republican Majority* (Garden City, N.Y.: Anchor, 1969), 166, 469–470, 471.

7. Phillips, *Emerging,* 469–70.

8. Phillips, *Emerging,* 166, 471.

9. Michael Novak, *The Rise of the Unmeltable Ethnics: Politics and Culture in the Seventies* (New York: Macmillan, 1972), xii. All future references to this work are cited parenthetically in the text as *RUE.*

CHAPTER 5: THE FEMINIST MYSTIQUE

1. Alice Echols, *Daring to Be Bad: Radical Feminism in America, 1967–1975* (Minneapolis: University of Minnesota Press, 1989), 15–16. With a foreword by Ellen Willis.

2. Betty Friedan, *The Feminine Mystique* (1963; reprint, New York: Dell, 1983), xii, 403. The following references to this work are cited parenthetically in the text as *FM.*

3. Benjamin Spock, *The Common Sense Book of Baby and Child Care* (1946; reprint, New York: Pocket Books, 1976), xv, 1, 6, 7, 17, 35.

4. Kenneth C. Davis, *Two–Bit Culture: The Paperbacking of America* (Boston: Houghton Mifflin, 1984), 7.

5. Spock, *Baby,* 17.

6. Susan M. Hartman, *From Margin to Mainstream: American Women and Politics since 1960* (New York: Knopf, 1989), 52, 59.

7. Hartman, *Margin,* 59.

8. See Echols, *Daring,* 44.

9. Echols, *Daring,* 15.

10. Echols, *Daring,* 16, 87, 199, 212.

11. Echols, *Daring,* 267.

12. Kate Millett, *Sexual Politics* (New York: Avon, 1970), 93. The following references to this work are cited parenthetically in the text as *SP.*

13. For an example of this critique, see Echols, *Daring,* 293.

CHAPTER 6: COMPULSORY SEXUALITY

1. John D'Emilio and Estelle B. Freedman, *Intimate Matters: A History of Sexuality in America* (New York: Harper & Row, 1988), 317–19.

2. Frances Fitzgerald, *Cities on a Hill: A Journey through Contemporary American Cultures* (New York: Simon & Schuster, 1986), 83.

3. My understanding of the concept of sexuality draws heavily on the work of Michel Foucault, though I come to very different conclusions about its place in modern culture. See Michel Foucault, *The History of Sexuality* (New York: Vintage, 1980). Translated from the French by Robert Hurley.

4. On film censorship during this period, see Gregory D. Black, *The Catholic Crusade against the Movies, 1940–1975* (New York: Cambridge University Press, 1997); Leonard J. Leff and Jerold L. Simmons, *The Dame in the Kimono: Hollywood, Censorship, and the Production Code from the 1920s to the 1960s* (New York: Weidenfeld and Nicolson, 1990); and Frank Walsh, *Sin and Censorship: The Catholic Church and the Motion Picture Industry* (New Haven: Yale University Press, 1996).

5. James H. Jones, *Alfred C. Kinsey: A Public/Private Life* (New York: Norton, 1997), 564; D'Emilio and Freedman, *Intimate Matters,* 285.

6. Jones, *Kinsey,* xi.

7. For this biographical sketch, I draw generally from Jones's book.

8. Jones's book is particularly deficient in this respect. Jones treats Kinsey primarily as a victim of social intolerance. Confirming every cliché of historical interpretation, Jones shares Kinsey's sadness that his "pleas for sex education went largely unheeded" and accepts Kinsey's own assessment that despite his own best efforts, "the sexual attitudes that had so filled him with guilt as a boy still stalked Americans." See especially Jones, *Kinsey,* 4, 127, 706.

9. Jones, *Kinsey,* 294–296.

10. See Foucault, *History of Sexuality*; and Peter Gay, *The Education of the Senses* (New York: Oxford University Press, 1984).

11. Jones, *Kinsey,* 230.

12. Alfred C. Kinsey, Wardell B. Pomeroy, and Clyde E. Martin, *Sexual Behavior in the Human Male* (Philadelphia: Saunders, 1949), v.

13. Kinsey, *Sexual Behavior,* 4.

14. Lionel Trilling, "The Kinsey Report," in *The Liberal Imagination: Essays on Literature and Society* (Garden City, N.Y.: Doubleday, 1950), 234, 227, 230–31.

15. Trilling, "Kinsey Report," 216–17, 219.

16. Trilling, "Kinsey Report," 219–20.

17. "The Second Sexual Revolution: A Survey," in *Sex in America*, ed. Henry Anatole Grunwald (New York: Bantam, 1964), 7–8; preface to *Sex in America*, vii. Unless otherwise noted, the following articles cited all come from this collection. Despite his involvement in *Time's* sex coverage, Grunwald, like most members of his generation, looks back on the 1950s as a new Victorian era. See his memoir, Henry A. Grunwald, *One Man's America: A Journalist's Search for the Heart of His Country* (New York: Doubleday, 1997), 230, 231, 338.

18. "Second Sexual Revolution," 3, 8, 14.

19. Rollo May, "The New Puritanism," 162; "Second Sexual Revolution," 10, 14; Margaret Mead, "The Social Shotgun," 110; Bruno Bettelheim, "Sex and Equality," 203.

20. Graham B. Blaine, "Sex on the Campus," 28; "Second Sexual Revolution," 4.

21. David Riesman, "The New College Atmosphere," 33, 35, 37, 38.

22. Riesman, "New College," 38.

23. "Ira L. Reiss, "The Four Sexual Standards," 93, 95; "Second Sexual Revolution," 7; Grunwald, comments following Reiss, "Four Sexual," 107; Lester A. Kirkendall, "'Interpersonal' Morality," 115, 124–25; Max Lerner, "The Moral Interregnum," 78, 81, 88–89.

24. See, for example, his comments following Mary Steichen Calderone, "The Case for Chastity," 151.

25. Denis de Rougemont, "The Rising Tide of Eros," 291, 304, 305, 323.

26. De Rougemont, "Rising Tide," 303, 310–11.

27. De Rougemont, "Rising Tide," 210–11.

28. "Walter R. Stokes, "Sexual Utopia," 155. D'Emilio and Freedman, *Intimate Matters*, 250–51. Donald T. Critchlow, *Intended Consequences: Birth Control, Abortion, and the Federal Government in Modern America* (New York: Oxford University Press, 1999), 59, and chap. 3, "Implementing the Policy Revolution under Johnson and Nixon."

29. Millett, *Sexual Politics,* 440, 441.

30. R. E. L. Masters, "The Homosexual Revolution," 250, 256, 257.

31. Masters, "Homosexual Revolution," 260, 261.

32. Masters, "Homosexual Revolution," 259, 262, 267, 272.

33. Masters, "Homosexual Revolution," 257, 272, 281, 282.

34. Fitzgerald, *Cities,* 83.

35. Fitzgerald, *Cities,* 15, 23, 24, 388.

36. Fitzgerald, *Cities,* 16, 19, 44–45, 49, 67, 100.

37. Fitzgerald, *Cities,* 49, 67, 100.
38. Fitzgerald, *Cities,* 119.
39. Fitzgerald, *Cities,* 47, 62, 116–17.
40. Adrienne Rich, "Compulsory Heterosexuality and Lesbian Existence," in *Blood, Bread, and Poetry: Selected Prose, 1979–1985* (New York: Norton, 1986), 24, 27, 28, 50.
41. Rich, "Compulsory Heterosexuality," 51, 67.
42. Trilling, "Kinsey Report," 234.

CONCLUSION

1. I here play off the Catholic mode against the specific characterization of the evangelical mode given in Fitzgerald, *Cities on a Hill,* 388. See also, in general, her final chapter, "Starting Over."

2. For a representative sampling of this thought, see Alasdair MacIntyre, *After Virtue: A Study in Moral Theory* (Notre Dame: University of Notre Dame Press, 1981); MacIntyre, *Three Rival Versions of Moral Enquiry: Encyclopedia, Genealogy, and Tradition* (Notre Dame: University of Notre Dame Press, 1990); and MacIntyre, *Whose Justice? Which Rationality?* (Notre Dame: University of Notre Dame Press, 1988); Charles Taylor, *Sources of the Self: The Making of Modern Identity* (Cambridge: Harvard University Press, 1989); John Milbank, *Theology and Social Theory: Beyond Secular Reason* (Oxford: Blackwell, 1990); John Milbank, Catherine Pickstock, and Graham Ward, eds., *Radical Orthodoxy: A New Theology* (London: Routledge, 1999); and Catherine Pickstock, *After Writing: On the Liturgical Consummation of Philosophy* (Oxford: Blackwell, 1998). For Bellah's account of the relation of Protestantism and Catholicism to contemporary multiculturalism, see Robert N. Bellah, "Is There a Common American Culture?" *Journal of the American Academy of Religion* 66, no. 3 (1998): 622, 623; and Bellah, "Religion and the Shape of National Culture," *America* 181, no. 3 (1999).

3. See Shannon, *Conspicuous Criticism,* chap. 3, "A New Individualism."

4. Jacques Maritain, *The Person and the Common Good* (Notre Dame: University of Notre Dame Press, 1946), 12, 13, 15, 35, 37, 41–42. The following references to this work are cited parenthetically in the text as *PCG.*

5. Jacques Maritain, *Reflections on America* (New York: Scribner's, 1958), 188. The following references to this work are cited parenthetically in the text as *RA.*

6. See Milbank, *Theology and Social Theory.*

7. Joseph W. Evans, "Jacques Maritain and the Problem of Pluralism in Political Life," in *Jacques Maritain: The Man and His Achievement,* edited with an introductuion by Joseph W. Evans (New York: Sheed & Ward, 1963), 218.

8. Herberg, *Protestant,* 3.

9. T. S. Eliot, *The Idea of a Christian Society,* in *Christianity and Culture* (1940; reprint, New York: Harcourt Brace Jovanovich, 1968), 17, 23, 24.

10. Eliot, *Idea,* 47.

11. See Schmidt, *Holy Fairs.*

Index

abortion, 106, 108
Acquired Immune Deficiency
Syndrome (AIDS), 120, 124
ADA. *See* Americans for Democratic
Action
adolescence, 34
AIDS. *See* Acquired Immune
Deficiency Syndrome
Adorno, Theodor W.: *The
Authoritarian Personality*, 67;
Dialectic of Enlightenment, xxi
Age of Jackson, The. See Schlesinger,
Arthur, Jr.
American Capitalism. See Galbraith,
John Kenneth
American Dilemma, An, 47–49; 56.
See also Myrdal, Gunnar.
*American Catholics and Intellectual
Life. See* Ellis, John Tracy
*American Freedom and Catholic
Power. See* Blanshard, Paul
American Humor. See Rourke,
Constance
Americans for Democratic Action
(ADA), 13
Anthony, Susan B., 92
anthropology, 1–5, 8, 20, 30, 33, 45, 50
anti-intellectualism, 81

antinominianism, 127
Armstrong, Louis, 53, 56, 57, 61
authority, xvii, xviii, 23, 45
autobiography, 10–12, 83–84
autonomy, 9, 27, 32, 33–35, 37, 39,
116, 124

Balcony, The, 40
Banfield, Edward C., 71. *See also
Moral Basis of a Backward
Society, The*
Bell, Daniel, 27–29, 36–37, 45, 66
Bellah, Robert, 127, 134
Benedict, Ruth, xi, xiii, 1–13, 19, 25,
30, 50, 94, 117, 123. *See also
Chrysanthemum and the Sword,
The*
Bettelheim, Bruno, 116
Beyond the Melting Pot, 65, 68–78.
See also Glazer, Nathan;
Moynihan, Daniel Patrick
birth control, 119–20
black power, 39, 47, 60–64; *Black
Power*, 60. *See also* Carmichael,
Stokely
Blanshard, Paul, xx
Blues People. See Jones, LeRoi
Boas, Franz, xiii, 2, 30, 48, 50

147

About the Author

Christopher Shannon was raised in Rochester, New York. He received his B.A. from the University of Rochester and his Ph.D. in American studies from Yale University. He has taught American history at the University of Iowa and currently serves as associate director of the Cushwa Center for the Study of American Catholicism at the University of Notre Dame. The author of *Conspicuous Criticism: Tradition, the Individual, and Culture in American Social Thought*, as well as many articles and reviews on various aspects of cultural and intellectual history, Dr. Shannon lives in South Bend, Indiana, with his wife, Karen.